NATIONAL GEOGRAPHIC

TRAVELER
St. Petersburg

D0108168

NATIONAL GEOGRAPHIC

TRAVELER
St. Petersburg

Jeremy Howard
Photography by Yuri Belinsky

National Geographic
Washington, D.C.

Contents

How to use this guide 6–7 About the author & photographer 8
The regions 51–238 Travelwise 239–265
Index 266–270 Credits 270–271

Page 1: Young sailors, Lt.
Schmidt Embankment
Pages 2–3: City skyline—
Peter & Paul Cathedral,
Hermitage, and
Admiralty
Left: Church of the
Savior on Spilled Blood

How to use this guide

See back flap for keys to text and map symbols

The *National Geographic Traveler* brings you the best of St. Petersburg and the nearby imperial palaces in text, pictures, and maps. Divided into three main sections, the guide begins with an overview of history and culture. Following are seven regional chapters with featured sites selected by the author for their particular interest and treated in depth. Each chapter opens with its own contents list for easy reference.

The regions, and sites within them, are arranged geographically. A map introduces each region, highlighting the featured sites. Walks, plotted on their own maps, suggest routes for discovering an area. Features and sidebars offer detail on history, culture, or contemporary life. A More Places to Visit page generally rounds off the regional chapters.

The final section, Travelwise, lists essential information for the traveler—pre-trip planning, getting around, communications, money matters, and emergencies—plus a selection of hotels, restaurants, shops, and entertainment.

To the best of our knowledge, site information is accurate as of the press date. However, it's always advisable to call ahead.

Color coding

Each region is color coded for easy reference. Find the region you want on the map on the front flap, and look for the color flash at the top of the pages of the relevant chapter. Information in **Travelwise** is also color coded to each region.

116

Summer Palace

www.rusmuseum.ru

🗺 53

✉ Kutuzov Naberezhnaya 2

☎ 314-0374

🕐 Closed Tues. & Jan.–April

💲 $$

🚇 Metro: Gostiny Dvor

Visitor information

for major sites is listed in the side columns (see key to symbols on back flap). The map reference gives the page where the site is mapped. Other details are the address, telephone number, days closed, entrance fee ranging from $ (under $5) to $$$$$ (over $25), and the nearest metro stop or transportation options. Visitor information for smaller sites is provided within the text. Admission fees are based on the prices foreigners pay.

TRAVELWISE

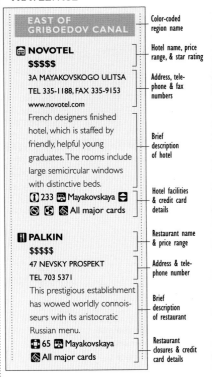

Color-coded region name

Hotel name, price range, & star rating

Address, telephone & fax numbers

Brief description of hotel

Hotel facilities & credit card details

Restaurant name & price range

Address & telephone number

Brief description of restaurant

Restaurant closures & credit card details

EAST OF GRIBOEDOV CANAL

🏨 **NOVOTEL**
$$$$$

3A MAYAKOVSKOGO ULITSA
TEL 335-1188, FAX 335-9153
www.novotel.com

French designers finished hotel, which is staffed by friendly, helpful young graduates. The rooms include large semicircular windows with distinctive beds.

🛏 233 🚇 Mayakovskaya 🔄 📶 🅿 ♿ All major cards

🍴 **PALKIN**
$$$$$

47 NEVSKY PROSPEKT
TEL 703 5371

This prestigious establishment has wowed worldly connoisseurs with its aristocratic Russian menu.

🍽 65 🚇 Mayakovskaya
♿ All major cards

Hotel and restaurant prices

An explanation of the price bands used in entries is given in the Hotels & restaurants section beginning on p. 248.

CITY MAPS

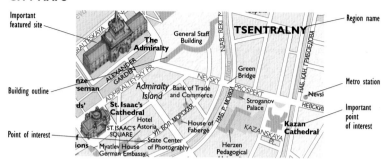

Important featured site

Building outline

Point of interest

Region name

Metro station

Important point of interest

- A locator map accompanies each regional map and shows the location of that region in the city.

WALKING TOURS

Featured site (in bold) on walk route

Point of interest not on walk route

Direction of route

Start point

Red numbered bullets link sites on map to descriptions in the text

Walk route

- An information box gives the starting and finishing points, time and length of walk, and places not to miss along the route.

EXCURSIONS

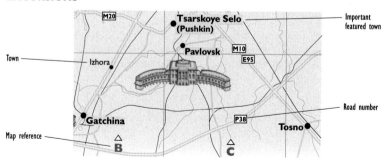

Town

Map reference

Important featured town

Road number

- Cities and sites described in the Excursions chapter are highlighted in yellow on the map. Other suggested places to visit are shown with a red diamond symbol.

NATIONAL GEOGRAPHIC

TRAVELER

St. Petersburg

About the author & photograher

Writer **Jeremy Howard,** born and bred in Amersham, England, first arrived in St. Petersburg in 1981, shortly after graduating from Lancaster University with a degree in religious studies and social anthropology. He was then on his way around the world for a third time, his itchy feet having taken him across Europe, Asia, and North America in 1978 and 1980. Of all the places he visited it was St. Petersburg, then Leningrad and part of the USSR, that left the most indelible mark.

Having made up his mind to study the art of St. Petersburg, Howard learned Russian, wrote about the city and his travel experiences for publications in the UK, and ended up doing a Ph.D. on the former Russian capital's most innovative group of artists from the early 20th century at the University of St. Andrews, Scotland. By the time his doctorate thesis was finished in 1990, he had visited St. Petersburg a score of times, lived there for a year and a half, and married there. Ever since, he has been teaching and researching the history of Russian and East European art from his base at St. Andrews while also residing as frequently as possible in St. Petersburg. Among his books are *Art Nouveau: International and National Styles in Europe* (1996) and *East European Art* 1650–1950 (2006).

A St. Petersburg/Leningrad native, photographer **Yuri Georgievich Belinsky**'s interest in cameras began in high school. As a senior, he interned with the Leningrad photo department of TASS. After working in documentary cinema, he was offered a job at TASS in 1967. Yuri Belinsky now serves as staff correspondent of ITAR–TASS Photo Agency in St. Petersburg specializing in pictures of Russia and its people. He has taken many prestigious photo prizes including second place in the World Press Photo competition's miscellaneous category for a photo captioned "Bosom friends: clown Karandash walking with his dogs" (1978).

Travelwise has been compiled and written by Madina Howard, with contributions by Albina Ozieva and Natasha Moroz.

History & culture

**Bronze Horseman,
monument to Peter I**

St. Petersburg today

ST. PETERSBURG CONSIDERS ITSELF THE "CAPITAL OF THE NORTH," THE "cultural capital," and the "maritime capital" of Russia. Traveling into the center from the airport, train station, or harbor there's no doubt that it is also the capital of Russia's tsarist heritage. Having been the actual capital of imperial Russia until 1917, the city has had time to work out its alternative status. It no longer seeks the hullabaloo of central government and presidential offices: With its palaces and parks, cathedrals and canals, monuments and museums, avenues and islands, it rises above all that.

The old rivalry with Moscow still exists, and always will, but there's a healthier feel to it than there was in the past. The 20th-century chip on St. Petersburg's shoulder is being knocked off by a 21st-century confidence, even hedonism. Not everything is rosy, however; the architecture, art, music, and summer White Nights are sublime, but there remains a lot of cleaning to do, sidewalks and roads to even out, quarters to improve. Money, resources, and morale are low in important parts of the public sector, notably health, education, and even heritage. Perhaps the discovery in 2006 that 221 masterpieces of Russian jewelry have gone missing from the Hermitage will get those proclaiming an economic boom to invest more effectively in their future and past.

At the last count, St. Petersburg's population numbered 4,700,000, not including the 300,000 legal *gastarbeiters*—guest workers—working in the construction and service industries. In theory, 5,000,000 people spread over a large, 231.7-square-mile (600 sq km) area shouldn't pose a density problem. But regardless of how many new housing blocks are going up (and there are plenty), the legacy of Soviet communal living still lingers. In the mid-20th century, hordes of families drafted from the countryside to turn Leningrad into an industrial base were squeezed into apartments made from existing houses. Behind the facade of grandeur there can still be squalor.

THE MOOD OF A CITY

Despite the behind-the-scenes hardships, Petersburgers have had a reputation for being snobbish. There's lots of neighborly friendliness but it's countered by a certain superiority. The effusive kissing, instant intimacy, or adulation of celebrity common in more typically Russian towns is muted here. Shows of fame and money are considered vulgar, contemptuous. Such fanfare was restricted to one street—Nevsky Prospekt. Or so it seemed until recently.

The manner in which the city developed has inevitably shaped the outlook of its citizens. The faces and architecture of St. Petersburg clearly testify to the fact that the city is Russia's most cosmopolitan realm. The cliché that the city was to be the country's window on Europe holds true, but St. Petersburg's appearance also owes a debt to Asia and North Africa. German and Italian architects, French and Scottish engineers, Caucasian and Chinese restaurateurs, Jewish scientists, not to mention a whole mix of peoples from within what is currently the Russian Federation and Commonwealth of Independent States (CIS) all have made contributions. So just as the metropolis was built on a series of bogs, Russian nationalism here finds itself weak and on suspect ground. For the building of both its culture and infrastructure has always been done by non-Russians, or those of mixed blood. Case in point: The lineage of Alexander Pushkin, the father of Russian literature, is Abyssinian. In part.

St. Petersburg today is a hybrid creature just as it always has been. Its international stage draws actors from far and wide. Nowhere is this seen more unequivocally than in its soccer team, Zenit FC. Recent trainers have been Czech and Dutch, the architect of its new stadium (to be) is

Nevsky Prospekt, the famous hub of the city, is St. Petersburg's busiest and most fashionable street.

Japanese, some players are Korean. The entire city, apart from those individuals repulsed by the show of "vulgar" sponsorship deals, supports the team.

Petersburg restraint runs deep. This is not a city for color. It has "white" nights in summer, "black" days in winter. And in a climate that is pretty severe, almost everything turns rapidly pale. There is no metropolis its size farther north. Occasional brilliant yellows, reds, and blues punctuate a skyline dominated by buildings painted white, off-white, creams, grays, and browns. This palette defines the city, giving it its authority and cool sense of sobriety. Still, the flashes exist, and not just as the firework displays that seem to happen daily, the town's set of new color-music fountains, or the recent craze for flickering neon casino signs. They survive because, first, for all the

Lutheran effacement that Tsar Peter introduced to Russia with St. Petersburg, he could not, nor would not, expunge his country's relish of the vivacious or spectral, residual traditions of Russian Orthodoxy. Second, some of Peter's successors relished pomp and splendor. The state of things is revealed by just a glance around a palace interior or two, a glimpse of the Church of the Savior on Spilled Blood, or a peek at the

Palace Square with the Alexander Column is the heart of St. Petersburg.

gilded sculptures, railings, and lampposts of a few bridges.

NEW AGE

To a certain extent the early 21st century has seen Petersburg become Putinburg. The new era began with local elections in March

1990. Anatoly Sobchak (1937–2000), a respected lawyer, university professor, and reformist politician was elected as Leningrad council leader and assumed the new title of mayor. His deputy was a 39-year-old named Vladimir Putin, who had been working for the state security services (KGB) since 1975. The following year the 69-year-old Union of Soviet Socialist Republics (USSR) disintegrated and a con-

troversial fresh start for its second city began. No longer could the city's older citizens proudly or sarcastically claim: "I was born in St. Petersburg, grew up in Petrograd, and will die in Leningrad." For on June 12, 1991, much to the chagrin of Moscow, 54 percent of voting Leningraders backed Sobchak's referendum to change the city's name back to that of its imperial past. On September 6, 1991, after a 77-year gap,

St. Petersburg was once more. (To those on intimate terms with it, the "Saint" is knocked off.)

There was a lot of work to be undone, more to be done. In 1996, Sobchak was ousted by voters disappointed with the nature and pace of his reforms, as well as with what seemed his personal extravagances. Simultaneously Putin went to Moscow where his rise in government cir-

Rimsky-Korsakov's opera *Tale of Tsar Saltan* staged at the Mariinsky Theater

cles was swift. By 2000 the Leningrader was president of Russia. Within a couple of years he had a soul mate—the confident, professional, and clean-as-a-whistle Valentina Matvienko—in charge in Petersburg, and a confirmed Petersburger himself. Budgets were sorted out, Soviet

hangovers were tackled, and the private sphere was embraced as energetically as it had been a hundred years before.

In 2003, St. Petersburg celebrated its tricentennial in style. The sprucing up was on an unprecedented scale, goods and foreigners poured in, banks lent, new hotels (always a problem) opened. Even some of the museums perked up. Trading on the past got into full swing. The city collectively awoke to the marketing of the tsars and their empire. The year was one long party that saw Petersburg retake its "rightful" place as Russia's cultural capital.

Pride of place went to the Konstantin Palace, 12 miles from the city, at Strelna, along the southern shore of the Gulf of Finland. Tsar Peter commissioned the creation of this imperial palace in 1708 with

the intention that it be a "second Versailles." Circumstances resulted in Peterhof becoming the tsar's principal country residence, and this palace being built later and named for Tsar Paul's son, Konstantin, who lived here until his death in 1831. In 2003, after a major reconstruction, it was turned into the magnificent seaside residence of the president of Russia, and jointly became the Palace of Congresses and also a museum.

Neva bridges are silhouetted during the White Nights.

The world's attention focused on the palace in 2006, when Russia hosted the G-8 Summit of world leaders on its grounds. No doubt George Bush, Tony Blair, and Jacques Chirac ate and drank from plates and cups made at the city's Imperial (now Lomonosov State) Porcelain Factory.

The State Hermitage is one of the richest and most visited museums in the world.

WHITE KNIGHTS/WHITE NIGHTS

Paralleling the thrust of the "Venice of the North" into the global political spotlight is its real push as a cultural force. Its white knights are the Hermitage Museum and Mariinsky Theater. The first, under the directorship of Mikhail Piotrovsky, is not content with being possibly the world's greatest museum and art collection, and just confined to St. Petersburg: It has opened satellites in London and Amsterdam, and has plans for more elsewhere. In addition, it has opened its front door (and courtyard); for the first time since 1917, visitors don't have to creep in the back as if engaged in some Bolshevik subterfuge.

Mariinsky Theater, the second ambassador, guided by conductor Valery Gergiev, has jumped to the top of the world's rankings for ballet and opera. The Mariinsky, known as the Kirov to Westerners, now tours almost continuously and partners the best of elsewhere. Back at home, both of these Petersburg figureheads are growing into little empires with new acquisitions, new

buildings, and new interests. A visit to each is a top priority for most visitors.

Equally attractive to visitors, and residents, is the chance to witness White Nights St. Petersburg, when it stays light for more than 20 hours, the bridges go up, the atmosphere is Bacchanalian, and the panoramas and silhouettes are second to none. To experience the White Nights of St. Petersburg is to partake of a unique city-nature relationship. During June and early July, the White Nights offer the city at its most ebullient.

Above all, the White Knights/Nights offer an inimitable and tempting range of cultural fare: the southern ring of beautiful and historic palace-park estates; the northern "pleasure" islands; a multitude of small and sometimes quirky museums, which convey so much about St. Petersburg's past and present state of things; and the different churches, the mosque, and Buddhist temple, many of which are newly restored. Visitors often are rewarded (time, season, and conditions permitting) with viewing the city's striking, landmark

Vladimir Putin, president of Russia, was born and bred in St. Petersburg when it was Leningrad.

monuments in ways that reveal unexpected beauties: Who could forget the Admiralty's spire in the summer dawn or the river embankments as seen from the middle of a frozen waterway in winter?

A PROMISING FUTURE

For all the good moves being made by the Hermitage, Mariinsky, and White Nights festivities, there have been some casualties. One is prices, another taste. For several years now the Mariinsky has priced itself out of reach of many people, though it, like many museums (the Hermitage included), still charges different rates for foreigners and Russians. As for taste—well, the city's old-fashioned sense of austerity and refinement has come under attack. This might not be a bad thing—it needs shaking out of its false sense of properness. But kitsch is kitsch, wherever it is, and in Petersburg it's on the move, but not yet the rampage: Four-wheel drives clog the streets; the beautiful people control the clubs; advertising banners and billboards hide buildings; heritage trails that illustrate the lives of Dostoyevsky, Rasputin, and Romanov wind through the city; idling buses serve as public toilets on Palace Square; a rash of bronze monuments of questionable artistic merit, and to even more questionable figures, proliferate in public squares; a welter of so-called chocolate and waxwork "museums" have opened; and lots of venues stage high-kicking folk dancing for tourists.

But Petersburg has always been a place of calculated proportions, of measure. It's a town that by design should simmer not bubble. Such, however, is its inherent contradiction and great magnetism. In this place of control and polite society, where scale is inhuman, the spirit cries out. Questions of freedom, dignity, and self-expression won't go away in this cosmopolis that is the vision of a man who was simultaneously the epitome of intuitive consideration and ruthless despotism. It's not by chance that the city's two unofficial names are the imperious "Petropolis" and the charming "Piter." Welcome to Petersburg. ∎

Food & drink

THE FOREIGN STEREOTYPES OF RUSSIAN FARE TWO OR THREE DECADES AGO were black (rye) bread, cucumber, meat and potatoes, porridges and soups, caviar, tea served from samovars, and vodka. There was more truth in these being the staples than of beef stroganoff or chicken Kiev, which were always more popular outside of Russia. The stereotypes survive but the reality of Russian cuisine, from restaurant to domestic dinner table and gourmet to fast food, has significantly changed—and for the better.

During the Soviet era, the cuisine was somewhat lackluster, but party tables were typically laden with food, chocolates, and alcohol. A variety of *zakuski* (cold dishes), primarily salads and pickles, formed the basis of the fare, the quantity often doing away with the need for main courses, especially as they were accompanied by multiple toasts with spirits and wines. To an extent this fare remains, but Petersburgers have rediscovered traditional Russian cuisine; the markets are awash with a variety of foods and eating establishments abound.

DISHES

Many meals begin with a traditional hors d'oeuvre, a small fish dish made of herring, sturgeon, or salmon and fringed with a very light salad. Red and black caviar is also favored, but its expense limits its use. Fillets of fish also may be added to the small salads that serve as appetizers; these often feature plenty of mayonnaise, mushrooms, cabbage, beets, carrots, and occasionally walnuts. Petersburgers love their *pirozhki* (pasties) and *bliny* (pancakes). While the former have always been available from street sellers, the

latter are making a real comeback at fast-food outlets. Both dishes can be stuffed with a variety of fillings (savory or sweet); meat, mushroom, cheese, or egg and green onion are standard fillings when the pirozhki or bliny serves as an appetizer. Traditionally bliny were made with buckwheat or rye flour, but white flour is more common nowadays. Russians eat bliny at the start of spring to celebrate Fat Tuesday.

Soups are very popular appetizers and are often eaten in conjunction with zakuski. The perennial favorite, *borshch*—red beet and cabbage soup—is, like most Russian soups, usually served with fresh herbs and sour cream *(smetana)*. Russians believe red beets have special healing qualities. *Shchi,* a cabbage soup made with fresh cabbage in summer and sauerkraut in winter, often

Caviar (above) is a favorite, but luxury appetizer. Street cafés (right) have proliferated across the city since the 1990s.

counts pork as an ingredient. *Solyanka* is a really hearty, salty soup made with meat and gherkins. A summer option, not to everyone's taste, is *okroshka*, a cold soup based on *kvass*, a drink made from lightly fermented rye bread.

Main meals are either meat or fish based. Petersburgers love fish, especially freshwater fish. Regardless of its preparation, fish traditionally comes served with a dill sauce and a side dish of potatoes or flavorsome buckwheat. The latter may also double as a morning porridge *(kasha)* or, when mixed with forest mushrooms and sour cream, be served with beef stroganoff. Meat dishes often take the form of meat pies *(kotlet)*, kebabs *(shashlik)*, or small ravioli-like dumplings *(pelmeny)*. The last, of Siberian origin, may be downed with a glass of vodka; beer is the usual quaff with sausages *(kolbasa)*.

DESSERTS

Petersburgers enjoy their sweets. The variety of desserts is astonishing, with all kinds of cakes, pastries, and cookies. Favorites include *vatrushki* (which resemble Danish pastries), *pryaniki* (gingerbreads), *syrniki* (sweet cheese pancakes), and the ubiquitous *morozhenoe* (ice cream). Wrapped chocolates are very popular; St. Petersburg has at least two major and decent chocolate factories (Krupskaya and Krasny Oktyabr).

DRINKS

The ubiquitous tea is usually drunk black and taken with mouthfuls of *varenye* (jams) spooned from a glass side dish. It's a whole ritual. The jams tend to be made from forest fruits, with black currant a particular favorite. Unfortunately samovars seem to be a thing of the past.

The fruit-based soft drinks *kissel* and *mors*, and the slightly beer-tasting kvass, are surviving the onslaught of mass-marketed carbonated drinks well.

Vodka reigns supreme over a range of alcoholic tipples. It is the Russian national drink and St. Petersburg shows no sign of being an exception to the rule. But beer is widespread, with competing local breweries—Baltika and Nevskoe among them—producing a variety of brews. Wine is growing in popularity, with Russian champagne, produced in the south of the country and available at a reasonable price, particularly flourishing. It's a heady choice that rounds off the day nicely for those who prefer to forgo the vodka. ■

History of St. Petersburg

IT SEEMS TO MAKE PERFECT SENSE: A CITY WHERE ONE OF EUROPE'S GREATEST short rivers from the continent's largest lake reaches the sea. Flat land, plentiful fresh water, maritime potential. The city's founder, Tsar Peter I (commonly known as Peter the Great) of the Romanov dynasty, described it as "Paradise" and envisaged it as the "New Jerusalem." It was to be a city of symbols. This wasn't just Tsar Peter's city but the "rock" upon which would be built a new Russia (and with it a changed Russian church), watched over by the Apostle Peter, the tsar's heavenly protector and the gatekeeper of heaven. The city's name alone was the signal of a most grand design.

EARLY HISTORY

Although St. Petersburg is a modern city that dates to 1703, the romantic myth that it was founded in an empty wilderness persists. That myth has been woven into history by the first verse of the epic poem, which for generations has captured the essential vision and plight of St. Petersburg: Alexander Pushkin's 1833 "The Bronze Horseman."

> Upon a shore of desolate waves
> Stood He, with lofty musings grave,
> And gazed afar. Before him spreading
> Rolled the broad river, empty save
> For one lone skiff stream-downward
> heading.
> Strewn on the marshy, moss-grown bank,
> Rare huts, the Finn's poor shelter, shrank,
> Black smudges from the fog protruding;
> Beyond, dark forest ramparts drank
> The shrouded sun's rays and stood brooding
> And murmuring all about.
> He thought;
> "Here, Swede, beware—soon by our labor
> Here a new city shall be wrought,
> Defiance to the haughty neighbor.
> Here we at Nature's own behest
> Shall break a window to the West,
> Stand planted on the ocean level;
> Here flags of foreign nations all
> By waters new to them will call,
> And unencumbered we shall revel."
> —translation by Walter W. Arndt

Unfortunately, the river's name, Neva, is Finnish for "open bog." The islands and shores of the Neva Delta formed part of the territories of a province called Izhora (and Ingria/Ingermanland) and before that Vod.

Several different nations—the indigenous Izhorians and Votes and the invading Finns, Karelians, Russians, and Swedes—took turns settling the land. By the ninth century, the Vikings had established their most important eastward-heading trade route through here, and by around the 11th century much of the surrounding territory was controlled by the principality of Novgorod (founded by Rurik the Viking in 864). In 1240, just 10 miles (16 km) upstream from today's city center, the Novgorodian prince Alexander Yaroslavich defeated the colonizing Swedes, driving them back to the Baltic. After his much heralded triumph, he became known as Alexander of the Neva (Alexander Nevsky) and was posthumously named a saint. His actions and status would play much in Tsar Peter's mind as he developed his city.

Warring factions continued to clash for control of the Neva Delta until 1478, when Novgorod became part of a unified Russian state, Izhora, that was administrated from Moscow. The Neva remained under Russian dominion until 1609. Then, during the so-called Troubled Times, when Russia suffered a power vacuum after the disastrous end to Ivan IV's (the Terrible) reign, the Scandinavians moved in.

Neva Town

In 1611 the Swedes established Nyenshants (Neva Redoubt), a fortress on the east bank of the Neva opposite where today the

The portrait of Peter the Great as a knight (State Hermitage), reputedly by Jean-Marc Nattier, was commissioned in Paris in 1717.

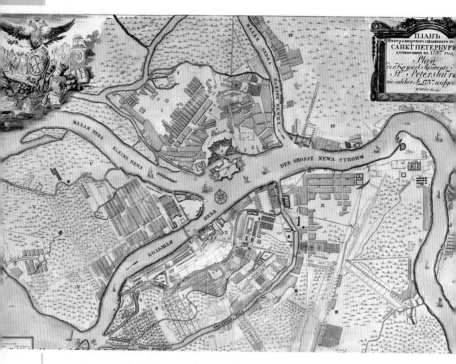

A 1737 map of St. Petersburg shows the spread of the city across the archipelago in the Neva Delta, with development centering around the SS Peter and Paul Fortress.

Smolny Institute stands. This trading post graduated to town status, becoming Nyen Staad, by 1632. Seventeenth-century Swedish maps show that the town consisted of the walled "King's estate," with a large two-story mansion, an inn, a hundred houses, a brick factory, kitchen gardens, a hospital, and Swedish and German (Lutheran) churches; suburbs; a bridge across the Okhta River; and, on the other side of the Neva (where the Smolny is) a Russian Orthodox community and sizable Saviors' church. Villages, hamlets, farmsteads, and fishermen's dwellings lined the banks of the Neva in both directions. The population was small and consisted primarily of Finns, some Izhorians and Russians, and a new influx of Swedish landlords. The Swedes also took control of the former Russian fortress of Oreshek at the source of the Neva, renaming it Nöteborg. It would prove to be Peter's key to the founding of St. Petersburg.

PETER THE GREAT

For all the early history of settlement in the area, in the 17th century the chances of a Russian city being founded in the Neva Delta were extremely slim; that it further would become the Russian capital within a decade of its founding was simply unimaginable: The first two Romanov tsars, Peter's grandfather and father, suffered crippling losses to Sweden. But then Peter arrived on the scene and reversed Russia's fortunes. He successfully expelled the Swedes and boldly envisioned the creation of a northern capital as intrinsic to his modernizing, imperial mission.

(A note about dates: The Julian calendar had been in use up until the 1917 revolution. Dates according to the current Gregorian calendar are given in parentheses.)

Peter was born in Moscow on June 9 (May 30), 1672, to the second wife of Tsar Alexey, who already had five sons and eight daughters from his first wife. It looked unlikely that Peter would inherit the throne (only males could inherit); however, three of the sons had already died, Feodor had fragile health, and Ivan was mentally and physically infirm. Alexey died young, when Peter was just four, and Peter's eldest half brother, 14-year-old Feodor, naturally succeeded, but he died of scurvy six years later without an heir. As a result, Peter's half sister Sophia became Regent in 1682 to both Peter and Ivan, ensuring that her side of the family, not Peter's, held the reins of power.

A fractious relationship between the two sides persisted until 1689, when Peter suppressed a rebellion of the elite Moscow guards, the Streltsy, that had been encouraged by Sophia, and banished her to a convent. That same year, his mother forced him into marriage; his son Alexey was born the following year. His mother, who had exercised power after Sophia's banishment, died in 1694, and Ivan in 1696. At the age of 24, Peter truly began to reign.

Tsar Peter's grand idea

As a fatherless youth, Peter had a childhood characterized by a remarkable freedom. Often living on the Transfiguration estate north of Moscow, he grew interested in model military maneuvers and mechanical crafts. He developed a passion for sailing and dreamed of creating a navy for a Russian empire blessed with ports on several coasts. In 1697, after becoming sole ruler of Russia and expanding his empire to the Black Sea, Peter left on a 16-month tour of Europe. A 6-foot-8-inch-tall giant, he nonetheless traveled incognito as part of a 250-person Grand Embassy sent by himself from Moscow. He spent most of his time learning shipbuilding (and getting acquainted with other crafts and modes of life) in Holland. In addition, he spent several weeks apiece in the German states, England, and Austria.

On his travels Peter met Augustus II, the elector of Saxony and king of Poland, with whom (and Christian V, king of Denmark) in 1699 he signed an anti-Swedish coalition. The following year the Great Northern War began, initially between Sweden and Denmark but Russia, Poland,

and Saxony soon involved themselves. Peter, having introduced decrees on military conscription, Western-style changes in dress, and the shaving of beards, signed a 30-year truce with the Turks and turned his attention to the Swedes. Defeated at the Battle of Narva in late 1700, and faced by

The spire of the Peter and Paul cathedral glows as one of the city's chief landmarks.

the "boy king" Charles XII of Sweden, Peter was determined to turn things around. In October 1702, his Russian forces took Nöteborg by the source of the Neva. Peter renamed it Schlüsselburg (Key Castle). With Charles principally engaged in fighting Poland, Peter advanced on Nyenshants, capturing it on May 12 (May 1), 1703. Two weeks later, he established a Russian fort 2 miles (3.2 km) downstream on Hare Island—it was named St. Petersburg on July 9 (June 29), 1703.

The founding of St. Petersburg

Like Amsterdam and Venice, with which it is often compared, the inhospitable site of St. Petersburg required artificial foundations consisting of huge piles driven into swampy

Peter established the Alexander Nevsky Monastery as the spiritual guardian of his new capital.

ground. But unlike them, St. Petersburg was the creation of a single will, conceived as a whole, and built through a demonstration of absolute power. Workers were conscripted, taxes raised, foreign specialists recruited. Spring floods, frozen winters, and fetid bogs had to be mastered. And the Swedes still had to be kept at bay.

The immediate task in 1703 was to secure the new fort on Hare Island. Thousands of tree fellers and 20,000 sappers raised ramparts and bastions on the island and on Birch Island (now Petrograd Side) to its north. The next year saw further protection built in the form of another bulwarked fort, Kronstadt on Kotlin Island, 18 miles west in the Gulf of Finland, and the Admiralty Wharf, a fortified shipyard on the south bank of the Neva.

Ten days after founding the Hare Island fort, the city's first house, Peter's wooden cottage, was completed on Birch Island. The stage was set for the development of the New Jerusalem. But no significant progress occurred until after Peter scored a decisive victory over the Swedes in the 1709 Battle of Poltava—which would precipitate the advantageous 1721 Treaty of Nystad by which Russia kept all of Sweden's eastern Baltic empire except Finland—and Charles XII's exile in Ottoman lands: Peter captured the Swedish fortresses on the east Baltic (including Riga, Vyborg, and Reval) in 1710 and the mass migration of workforce, court, government institutions, and army from Moscow and across Russia began in earnest. Construction accelerated and Peter officially declared St. Petersburg the Russian capital in 1712.

In 1710 the permanent population of St. Petersburg numbered about 8,000. By the time of Peter's death in 1725, it had boomed to 40,000. In addition, the number of construction workers had jumped from around 10,000 to 30,000; there were thousands of nonpermanent foreigners—military officers, civil servants, diplomats, merchants, technicians, skilled laborers, artists, Swedish prisoners of war. Headed by the Italian-Swiss architect Domenico Trezzini, the Office of Defense and Construction controlled the city's physical development. It alone employed thousands of craftsmen and laborers and produced more than ten million bricks and three million tiles annually. And this was not enough.

After renaming Birch Island into St. Petersburg Island and its fort into the Peter and Paul Fortress, city planners decided to shift the center of the city west to the largest island of the Neva archipelago, Elk Island. Trezzini drew up a gridiron plan and the island became known as Basil's (Vasilevsky). It became the realm of the Izhorian governor, Peter's right-hand man, Prince Alexander Menshikov. Unfortunately, it proved prone to flooding.

In 1721 the center was moved again, this time south and definitively to the Admiralty Side. Plans dating from this time show arterial roads radiating out from the Admiralty; however, the construction of canals and embankments and the draining of the land took priority. Significant buildings of the era include the SS Peter and Paul Cathedral in the fortress, Menshikov Palace, Peter's Summer and Winter Palaces, the Alexander Nevsky Monastery, and the first palaces at Peterhof, Oranienbaum, and Katrintal (the last now known as Kadriorg, in Tallinn, Estonia).

While St. Petersburg grew, so did Peter's family. Peter's first marriage ended in 1699, when he forced his wife Eudoxia to take the veil. Later, about the time he founded St. Petersburg, he started an affair with a Livonian peasant girl, Martha Skavronska, whom he married in 1712; she became Empress Catherine in 1721, when Peter took the title of emperor. They had two daughters who survived, Anna and Elizabeth. Having arranged the marriage of his meek 21-year-old son Alexey to a German princess in 1711, Peter then fell out with Alexey, accused him of opposition to his reforms, and interrogated (i.e., tortured) him in the Peter and Paul Fortress, where he died in 1718, a few days after receiving a death sentence. In the interim, Martha gave birth to two sons (both of whom died in early childhood) and Peter went on another major tour of western Europe for 18 months. In 1722, he passed a law allowing the ruling monarch to appoint "whom he wishes to the succession." He named his wife his successor.

PETER'S SUCCESSOR'S

In 1730, following the rapid deaths of Peter's wife and grandson, his niece Anne (the daughter of his infirm brother Ivan) succeeded to the throne. She arrived in St. Petersburg from Courland (part of present-day Latvia) with her lover Ernst-Johann Bühren (Biron to the Russians) who was to be recognized as the "first man of the empire." Biron set up the Secret Chancellery, an inquisitorial office, and began a ten-year reign of terror and self-indulgence.

Another terror, fire, devastated the Admiralty quarter in 1737; however, this adversity was turned to advantage when the architect Pyotr Yeropkin regularized the urban plan to the integrated, rational, and harmonious layout that characterizes the heart of 21st-century St. Petersburg. Quarters and amenities were coordinated; canals and ring roads were linked to the strengthened and straightened three-prong radial avenues leading out of the Admiralty; wooden buildings between the Neva and Moika Rivers were banned; and the embankments were standardized. This planning allowed for integrated (and absolutist) future urban development on a scale hitherto unknown in Russia and beyond.

The reign of Elizabeth, Peter's daughter (R. 1741–1761), marks the next major epoch for St. Petersburg. Although often decried for her ignorance and love of frivolous and cruel excess, Elizabeth actually oversaw the completion of several of her father's projects that had stalled in the years since his death. As such she endowed the city with its high baroque palaces and churches; advanced Peter's ideas for Academies of Science and Art through setting down their statutes (1747 and 1757 respectively) and encouraged Mikhail Lomonosov in his opening of Russia's first chemical laboratory, colored glassworks, and mosaic workshops; founded one of Europe's first porcelain factories (1744); and opened many banks and bridges. She oriented St. Petersburg taste toward that of Paris. In addition, Russia

gained more territory from Sweden and scored victories over Prussia in the Seven Years' War; a professional Russian theater was created; literary journalism took off; Russia's first university was founded (in Moscow); and the elite military school Corps of Pages was established. Elizabeth died before her envisaged retirement to the convent she created at Smolny.

CATHERINE THE GREAT'S RULE

From its very inception, St. Petersburg's historical growth has closely identified with the character of the reigning Russian ruler. It fell to a princess from a small north German principality to leave the next profound mark on the metropolis whose population had topped 100,000 by the mid-18th century: Sophia of Anhalt-Zerbst (1729–1796), who subsequently became Empress Catherine II (the Great).

Elizabeth died childless, so the throne passed to her weak nephew Peter (1728–1762). He had been brought up a Lutheran in the north German duchy of Holstein before becoming Elizabeth's charge in 1742. Elizabeth arranged his marriage to Sophia in 1745 and then nurtured Sophia in the ways of the Russian court while Peter remained obsessed with Prussia and its king, Frederick II. His time as Russian emperor amounted to less than six months before he was deposed in a coup backed by his wife; he mysteriously died a week later.

Catherine the Great usurped not only her husband but also her eight-year-old son Paul, who she claimed had not been fathered by Peter and whom she disowned. Ironically, she grabbed the reins of power on the grounds that Russia needed freeing from foreign influence. During her 17 years as Peter's wife she had converted to Russian Orthodoxy, imbibed the works of the Enlightenment, and entertained herself with a series of lovers. By the time she came to the throne as a 33-year-old widow, her approach to governance and life was well set. She worked and played hard, turning the Russian Empire into an ordered machine that operated according to enlightened absolutist rules. She considered herself the true follower of Peter the Great and the one whom fate had decreed to realize his vision. The emblem of her reign may be said to be the Bronze Horseman monument to Peter in Decembrist's Square.

For all her despotism and debauchery, Catherine introduced many essential changes to Russian society in general and St. Petersburg in particular. Hers was the epoch of a strict new classical order, of burgeoning civil rights, of free schooling, and of great architectural and urban-planning projects for the capital and the provinces. Under the guidance of the French philoso-phers François Marie Voltaire and Denis Diderot she amassed great art collections and with them established the Hermitage. She built and opened great institutions such as the Imperial Academy of Arts, Smolny Institute, Assignation Bank, post office, and library. Undoubtedly it was Catherine, and her favorite advisor, Grigory Potemkin, who turned Russia into a major European power, not least through her ultimately unrealized Greek Project, which envisaged the restoration of Constantinople into an Orthodox realm. As part of this plan, Russia

Detail of Swedish artist Alexander Roslin's portrait of Catherine II (1777)

acquired major new territories in southeastern Europe (including the Crimea). Her defeat of the Ottomans found numerous symbolic reflections in St. Petersburg and the palatial estates of its environs. In addition, feeling threatened by the far-reaching potential of the 1789 French Revolution, she acted in unison with two other fearful central European monarchies, Prussia and Austria, to partition Poland.

as mad, paranoid, and ugly, before he became tsar, Paul had been popular and happily married to Sophia-Dorothea, duchess of Württemburg (in Russia known as Maria Feodorovna), with whom he produced four sons and six daughters.

Paul's most conspicuous contribution to the streets of St. Petersburg was scores of striped sentry boxes and barriers, erected as part of an extremely wide range of tight-

Ten giant granite Atlantes support the portico of Nicholas I's New Hermitage (1842–1851).

NAPOLEONIC SHADOWS

The one thing Catherine and her successor shared in common was hostility toward republican France. By the time her son Paul (1754–1801) became tsar of the world's most extensive monarchy in 1796, the population of St. Petersburg had grown to around 250,000. Scorned by his mother and brought up by his grandmother Elizabeth, Paul held a grudge against Catherine and sought to overturn all of her policies. He turned her palaces into barracks and stables, reintroduced his father's pro-Prussianism, built himself a castle with moat, and pronounced himself grand master of the Knights Hospitaller, or Order of St. John, a faternal society. Although regarded by many

ened security measures undertaken due to Paul's manic fears for his life. Ultimately, and perhaps not surprisingly, his antiliberal and pro-Prussian measures led to his murder in his castle bedroom in 1801. His son and heir Alexander, who had been brought up by Catherine, knew of the plot.

Tsar Alexander I (1777–1825) attempted to return to and advance from the enlightened absolutist values of his grandmother. He founded ministries and the Council of State; reduced the court's pomp and ceremony; set up the stock exchange; established the Russian town-planning service; and began something of an industrial revolution. (The most visible sign of the latter in central St. Petersburg was the construction of numerous new iron bridges.) For all his pragmatism, Alexander appeared uncertain on how to handle the European strides being made by Napoleon and his Grand Army. Leo Tolstoy's historical novel *War and Peace* captures the spirit of St. Petersburg during these times.

Napoleon's invasion of Russia in 1812 devastated the country and counted considerable losses on both sides. Alexander, facing his previous lack of decisive leadership, rallied his troops and pursued the retreating French and successfully entered Paris in 1814, unequivocally raising St. Petersburg's standing in Europe. In the aftermath of victory, a new decisiveness marked the last decade of Alexander's reign. This wholesale repressiveness in internal matters coincided with the construction of a new wave of state institutions in the Russian capital. This era vaunted the imposing empire style of architecture, whose regulating order began to dominate the city and its inhabitants.

Opposition grew to this stifling of the earlier reformist spirit. Many, including the young poet Alexander Pushkin, were sent into internal exile for championing anti-establishment causes. With a growing intelligentsia (St. Petersburg University opened in 1819) and fueled by republicanist ideals as well as calls for a constitutional monarchy, an uprising against Alexander was planned for 1826 by groups of officers and nobles. However, Alexander, who talked of abdicating, died under suspicious circumstances, and without a male heir, on the Black Sea coast in November 1825. So on December 14, the day that the Senate and Holy Synod were to pledge allegiance to the next tsar, Alexander's brother Nicholas, the Decembrists (as they came to be known) sought to halt events and demand the introduction of new democratic rights through the establishment of a National Assembly. Ill-organized, they were outwitted and then violently routed.

TSARIST WAYS

The reign (1825–1855) of Tsar Nicholas I began inauspiciously and did not improve. He ruled with an iron fist, militarizing St. Petersburg as never before and personally intervening in all kinds of matters. The city,

endowed with colossal, controlling, architectural ensembles, became even more imperial and more like a massive barracks. Soldiers, secret police, spies and informers were posted everywhere. Serfdom, "the ownership of souls," was reinforced. Potential subversives and revolutionaries, and anyone deemed having dubious connections with them (like the writer Fyodor Dostoyevsky), were dealt with summarily and frequently sent to Siberian labor camps or worse. The 1830 Polish uprising against Nicholas's regime led to a wave of repression.

Oddly enough, this time coincided with the age of Romanticism, of dreams of love, spirituality, and escape, to which Nicholas, despite his icy severity and lack of imagination, paradoxically also subscribed (he loved the Gothic Revival style and Walter Scott's novels). The tsar opened Russia's first public museum, the New Hermitage. Riding the coattails of Romanticism, and in spite of the heavy hand of censorship, came criticism, cynicism, parody, and satire. Pushkin's "Bronze Horseman" appeared, as did Nikolay Gogol's "Nose" and *The Government Inspector.*

Perhaps it was also part and parcel of Russian romance to entertain ideas of the empire reaching the Bosphorus and Constantinople. Nicholas certainly did, and those aspirations ultimately led to his abysmal failure in the Crimean War (1853–56) with Britain, France, and the Ottoman Empire. He died, after catching a cold inspecting his palace guard in St. Petersburg, just as his army lost the main town of the Crimea, Sebastopol.

In 1855, Nicholas's son, Alexander (1818–1881), became Tsar Alexander II and immediately set about ending the war in the south. He released many of his father's political prisoners, issued the decree of the Emancipation of the Serfs, set up elective district councils, abolished corporal punishment, gave Finland more control over its own affairs, and reformed the legal system. But, like his father before him, he brutally crushed a Polish insurrection (1863) and went to war against the Ottomans (1877), though in his case he was successful in freeing much of the Balkans from Turkish control. He also greatly extended the Russian Empire into Central Asia.

Known as the "tsar liberator," Alexander II was the first tsar to encourage capitalism, to build permanent bridges over the Neva, to introduce (horse-drawn) trams, and to build a network of railway stations in St. Petersburg, thereby creating new, fast links between the city and other parts of the Russian Empire and Europe.

Unfortunately for him he opened a Pandora's box. The peasants still languished economically and the councils were a sham. The numbers of beggars, tramps, and street crimes multiplied. As the power of money increased, corruption reached unprecedented levels. Opposition became radicalized with young nihilists denying established authority, populists seeking a peasant and proletarian uprising, and Slavophiles calling for pan-Slav unification. Restrictions were placed on educational curricula in an attempt to halt the spread of independence of thought. There were mass protests and mass arrests. An age of political propaganda began, concurrent with a wave of political shootings and bombings. Ultimately, on March 1, 1881, the People's Will group assassinated the tsar on the embankment of the Catherine (Griboedov) Canal as he rode back to the Winter Palace from an inspection of the guards.

Alexander III (1845–1894) assumed the throne following his father's death. Fearing

A family portrait of the last of the Russian tsars, Nicholas II

for his life, he spent most of it away from St. Petersburg at the royal palace at Gatchina. Politically more conservative than his father, he sought to reinforce autocracy, enacted a series of reactionary measures and stimulated notions of Russian national uniqueness. His embrace of Orthodoxy and "Russia for the Russians" set in motion processes of Russification of the empire's ethnic minorities and a heightened wave of anti-Semitism. The fact that most of his own blood was German and that he was married to a Danish princess did not matter. He limited access to higher and secondary education, restricted the franchise, and introduced more national forms of dress to the military and court. Simultaneously the government of Alexander III accelerated industrialization; the exploitation of oil, coal, and iron resources took off.

But Alexander's agenda of counterreform provoked severe reactions in the guise of student campaigns, organized workers' movements, socialism, Marxism, and a new pitch of nationalism among the non-Russian peoples of the empire. Dmitry Mendeleyev, the brilliant chemist and deviser of the Periodic Table of Elements, was stripped of his professorship at St. Petersburg University and denied the status of academician for supporting student campaigns and for being a materialist (he was also ethnically a Kalmyk).

Alexander III's reign also saw the population of St. Petersburg top one million for the first time, the use of electrical power in the city, and Vladimir Lenin's elder brother, Alexander Ulyanov, a member of the People's Will group, hanged in Shlisselburg fortress for his part in a plot to assassinate the tsar.

THE LAST TSAR

When 26-year-old Nicholas II succeeded his father in 1894, he complained to his family that he was not ready to rule: He could only attempt to follow his father's lead. So he adhered to Alexander's prejudices, tyrannies, and worldly detachment. Still, he opened the Russian Museum and the Trans-Siberian Railway, and during his reign St. Petersburg gained a wealth of stylish hotels, apartment blocks, banks, shops, villas, and recreational facilities. This was the silver age of Russian culture with the arts and social scenes of the capital flourishing like never before. All was not well, however. Nicholas spent most of his time living quietly with his young family at Tsarskoye Selo—he had married Princess Alice of Hesse, granddaughter of Queen Victoria of Great Britain, who became Empress Alexandra—instead of engaging fully with matters of state. Imperial Russia drifted toward disaster.

Revolutionary movements were organizing, workers were striking, assassinations were occurring. Russia fought an absurd, disastrous, and demoralizing war with Japan (1904) and then, on January 9, 1905, Bloody Sunday occurred. Some 140,000 factory workers marched on Palace Square in St. Petersburg to present a petition calling for workers' rights, not the least of which was an eight-hour day. Grand Duke Vladimir called out the army and police to dispel the march, resulting in the death and wounding of 2,000 to 4,000 people.

The situation further deteriorated. Sailors mutinied, there was a general strike, pogroms took place, the electricity supply was cut. As a concession an elected parliament, the Duma, was initiated, but with a tsar ever distrustful of representative politics, it was rapidly dissolved. Under the leadership of Leon Trotsky (1879–1940), workers' councils known as soviets were formed to push the proletarian cause. Founded in 1898, the Russian Social Democratic Labor Party now divided into two sections: the conspiratorial Bolsheviks, led by Vladimir Ilyich Lenin (real name Ulyanov, 1870–1924), and the more open Mensheviks. Lenin was forced into emigration in 1907. Fearful for the survival of her hemophiliac son Alexey, Empress Alexandra fell under the spell of Grigory Rasputin, a Siberian, reputedly a holy man and healer. She was convinced he could not only cure the pains of her son but also the pains of the Romanov empire.

Rasputin advised against entering the Balkan War in 1913, and Russia didn't. At first. But the Minister of War announced, "We are ready!" as the war evolved into World War I. The giant Teutonic sculptures were thrown off the top of the new German Embassy, the city changed its name from the Germanic St. Petersburg to the more Russian Petrograd, and troops marched off to spectacular defeats, with almost four million Russian casualties by late 1915 and double that a year later. With a religious fervor and contempt for the organs of state, Rasputin and Alexandra held the reins in St. Petersburg as the country spiraled out of control. On December 17, 1916, Prince Felix Yusupov—one of Russia's wealthiest citizens—had the "Holy Beast," Rasputin, murdered in his palace on the Moika Embankment.

Lenin (left) and Stalin made the imperial capital into Petrograd and then Leningrad.

A new order

No food. No fuel. Freezing cold. The bitter winter of early 1917 brought the February Revolution: Workers' lockouts, women's demonstrations, strikes, mutinies. The Duma refused Nicholas's order to dissolve and formed its own Provisional Government. Nicholas abdicated on March 2 and on the next day the Romanov dynasty, begun by the grandfather of Peter the Great, came to an end.

The Provisional Government, under the moderating leadership of the lawyer Alexander Kerensky, relocated from the Tauride Palace to the Winter Palace. A power struggle between left and right, and factions of both, erupted. Earlier, the Petrograd soviet had reorganized, with its base in the Smolny Institute, and Lenin had returned from his exile to lead the Bolsheviks. Now, on October 24, 1917, with a Bolshevik majority in the soviet, Lenin called for an end to the war, the seizure of land by the peasantry, and the seat of power given to the Bolsheviks. The following day the almost bloodless coup was enacted with the arrest of the government ministers in the Winter Palace.

Immediately a Council of People's Commissars was set up, headed by Lenin. Felix Dzerzhinsky organized the Cheka (the Extraordinary Commission for Struggle against Counter-Revolution, Speculation, and Sabotage), the new secret police. The utopian campaign for a fair, classless, materialist, and supranational society run by workers commenced with the replacement of the old Julian calendar with the more accurate, modern, and widespread Gregorian one and the nationalization of private concerns. The Plan for Monumental Propaganda—Lenin's plan for mass communication of socialist ideals—was also set in motion.

On March 3, 1918, Commissar of Foreign Affairs Trotsky signed the Treaty of Brest-Litovsk, handing almost all of the Russian Empire's western borderlands to the Germans. For Petrograd, tainted by its identification with tsarist autocracy, this signaled the end of its status as capital. Power was transferred to Moscow and, whipped up by foreign intervention, a devastating, essentially Reds (Bolshevik Communists) against Whites (anti-Bolsheviks), civil war ensued. It would last through to late 1920. In faraway Yekaterinburg, on July 16, 1918, the tsar and his family were executed by the Bolsheviks, who feared attempts to free and restore them.

THE USSR

By 1920, the toll of tragic events had reduced Petrograd's pre–World War I population of 2,000,000 to 720,000. At the end of the civil war, the city was as deprived of food and fuel as it had been four years earlier. The difference now, however, was that it was also deprived of many of its brighter spirits and, lacking its former status, it began turning provincial. The workers struck, the Kronstadt sailors rebelled, and martial law was declared. Lenin, driven by the need to rebuild the country, simultaneously introduced the New Economic Policy, which allowed small business economic freedoms in agriculture, industry, and trade, and stifled political and religious opposition. The Politburo, the head council of the Communist Party's Central Committee, ran the government. In December 1922, it

the pooling of peasant holdings into vast farms, and the most intensive industrialization possible. Leningrad would have faded in importance were it not for being the Soviet Union's most important port and one of its most vital industrial centers. The building of workers' quarters began on its fringes in the late 1920s, the first signs of a certain renewal.

Twin curses: Stalinism & Nazism

Just as Leningrad's culture began to reveal signs of promise, Stalin's mass purges and

The Nazis destroyed and looted St. Petersburg's imperial heritage, including Peterhof.

established the Union of Soviet Socialist Republics (USSR) across much of the old tsarist empire.

After suffering three strokes in 1922 to 1923, Lenin died on January 21, 1924. Three months later Petrograd was renamed Leningrad. Against Lenin's and Trotsky's wishes, the powerful tactician behind the renaming, Georgian Communist Joseph Stalin (real name Dzhugashvili, 1879–1953) was appointed general secretary of the party. Determined to build socialism in one state at whatever cost, Stalin introduced his Five Year Plans for economic development: the forced collectivization of agriculture,

show trials began. Churches were blown up, the Academy of Science was transferred to Moscow, and on December 1, 1934, the Leningrad party secretary, Sergey Kirov, was murdered (conveniently for the increasingly paranoid Stalin) in the Smolny. Thus began four years of terror, with tens of thousands of Leningraders arrested, sent to "corrective" labor camps (the Gulag), and executed. In the late 1930s, finally concerned by the rise of Hitler and Nazism, Stalin sought to buffer his country: He annexed its Baltic neighbors, fought a war with Finland, and signed treaties with various European states and a nonaggression pact with Germany.

Hitler did not honor the pact: On June 22, 1941, Germany invaded the Soviet Union on three fronts, including the Baltic. Hitler called for Leningrad to be wiped off the face of the Earth. By September, German forces had taken the Shlisselburg fortress and had surrounded Leningrad. A 900-day siege (the Leningrad Blockade) followed, during which the city was bombed from the air and the ground. The devastation surpassed that known by any other modern city at the time: The Road of Life across the frozen Lake Ladoga at the end of 1941 allowed some 1.2 million people to evacuate, but around 700,000 citizens died over the course of the siege; another 700,000 lost their homes. Fifteen million square feet of housing were destroyed, along with 526 schools and children's institutions, 21 scientific institutions, 101 museums and other civic buildings, the Pulkovo Observatory, the Botanical and Zoological Institutes, much of the university, 187 of the 300 18th- and 19th-century historical buildings, 840 factories, 71 bridges, and 300,000 square feet of rooms and 60,000 square feet of glass in the Hermitage.

There was no water, no electricity, no heat, and no bread, and all this during two of the coldest winters on record. Still Leningraders held out and defended their city as best they could. The Soviet Army finally expelled the German forces from the environs of Leningrad on January 27, 1944. By way of a parting shot, the invaders looted the palaces and turned them to ruins.

Following the siege, 1.5 million people received a Defense of Leningrad medal, 486 Leningraders were made Heroes of the Soviet Union, and on May 1, 1945, a week after Soviet troops had entered Berlin, Leningrad itself became a "hero city." Some triumphalist architecture was erected above and below ground, the latter in the form of the new network of metro stations.

Plans and hopes for a renaissance were short-lived. In 1948 the Leningrad Affair commenced, along with a new wave of purges. People regarded as Western sympathizers disappeared: heads of the university, industry, the Leningrad party, and army divisions. Even the new Museum of the

Defense of Leningrad was closed, its director sent to Siberia. The Leningrad party organization, under Secretary Petr Popkov, was accused of treason—of plotting Soviet participation in the war and of, under cover of the Council for the Defense of Leningrad, intending to hand the city to Hitler, establish a non-Communist regime, and make Leningrad the capital once more. The Kremlin erased the heroic memory of the siege by returning the city to prewar conditions. Thousands lost their lives in a mad reign of terror that lasted until Stalin's death on March 5, 1953.

Stalin's successor, Nikita Khrushchev, allowed Leningrad some relief. The mid-1950s to mid-1960s saw a rehabilitation of the city; optimism and a sense of stylish fashion flourished. New residential regions

Relaxation time in Kronstadt, Tsar Peter's home to the Baltic fleet on Kotlin Island

were built. By the '70s, the underground counterculture was well established, with unofficial art groups, informal music venues, bohemian cafés, and "self-publishing" of banned books and articles. Unfortunately, the city saw a return to more repression, corruption, and decay after Leonid Brezhnev (1906–1982) was appointed general secretary of the Communist Party in 1964. Only when the comparatively young Mikhail Gorbachev (b. 1931) became general secretary in 1985 did conditions improve. He introduced policies of glasnost (openness) and perestroika (restructuring) that shook up the bureaucracy and offered new hope to the strait-jacketed society. Once unleashed, the voice of opposition could not be restrained. It gathered pace and overtook Gorbachev.

A NEW ERA

Local elections in March 1990 installed reformist law professor Anatoly Sobchak, candidate of a new Democratic Platform, as the city's first mayor. The Baltic states and other Soviet republics declared independence from the USSR, as did the new parliamentary leader (and future Russian president) in Moscow, Boris Yeltsin. In June 1991 a local referendum changed the city's name back to St. Petersburg; the following year, the red flag of the Soviet Union flying over the Smolny—the local seat of government—was lowered and replaced by the Russian tricolor. The new era of post-Communist "Piter" continues today. ∎

The arts

THE ARTS PLAY AN INSTRUCTIVE AND IMPROVING ROLE IN ST. PETERSBURG, and have since the city's founding in 1703. The tsars, and later the Soviet government, encouraged the arts, using them as both tools for pleasure and for furthering understanding, particularly of their own agendas, to the masses. Questions of politics and what constitutes beauty have scythed through the whole development of St. Petersburg's art. The results have been both radical and reactionary.

The arts in St. Petersburg have always been subject to state control except for two short periods, which saw an outpouring of new wave art and design. The first, from 1870 to 1918, elevated Russia to new heights in terms of its contribution to world visual and musical culture. The second, ongoing since 1989, has been defined by a rapid assimilation of contemporary global trends, especially Western ones. During the two much longer, government-controlled eras, the city emerged as a world leader in classical academic and literary trends (1703–1870) and as a prime producer of socialist art (1918–1989); art as political propaganda largely defined these times. The rich legacy of each period is evident in the wealth of buildings, art collections, literature, and music whose renown has transcended all national boundaries.

ARCHITECTURE

That there is any architecture, let alone one of Europe's largest cities, in the Neva Delta is madness. This once marshland floods and freezes. Roads cave in, sidewalks break up. It is an area best suited for bugs, frogs, fish, birch trees, the occasional fisherman, and people en route elsewhere. A permanent settlement would seem impossible, yet they've been building here for more than 300 years, the lavish scale of which impresses one as a mighty display of strength in a battle against nature.

Baroque St. Petersburg

Although little survives of the city created by Tsar Peter as the Russian capital, his ghost lies behind its development right

into the 21st century. His network of streets, canals, and quarters, and the location of the city core, with its principal institutions around the broadest stretch

St. Petersburg's harsh winter climate makes maintaining the magnificent palaces all the more difficult.

of the Neva River, remain. Peter envisioned a military town that would also be a bastion of cultural progress based on enlightened European values. The rationale of Peter's vision is best experienced in the Peter and Paul Fortress (started 1703), Vasilevsky Island (construction here began 1725), his Summer Palace (started 1710), and his country estate at Peterhof (started 1714). Peter hired the Italian-Swiss architect Domenico Trezzini to oversee the artistic direction of the city and favored Dutch, Italian, French, and German architectural styles. This sea change marked a radical break with the Russo-Byzantine forms of medieval Russian cities such as Moscow and Novgorod.

Russia suddenly had long spires and curving gables—the SS Peter and Paul Cathedral shines as the prime example—and interiors, notably that of the relatively grand Menshikov Palace (1714), were transformed by the introduction of Dutch tiles, baroque and Oriental-style decorative art, furniture made with German techniques from foreign wood and leather, and English clocks. Gardens became landscaped works of art and erudition. Fountains were

installed, with the best ones erected in the Summer Garden and the Peterhof park; only the latter survive.

Peter's legacy stretches incalculably; however, his daughter Elizabeth is the one who realized the city's baroque magnificence. During her reign (1741–1761), St. Petersburg and its environs acquired their most extravagant faces. She lacked her father's vision but she knew how to spend money on palaces and artisans. Elizabeth favored Francesco Bartolomeo Rastrelli, an Italian born in Paris who arrived in Russia at age 16 after his father signed on to become a sculptor for Peter.

Rastrelli built the Winter Palace (1754–1762), the Peterhof Grand Palace (1745–1755), and the Catherine Palace (1752) at Tsarskoye Selo. Russia had never seen anything on their scale before. They rivaled Europe's greatest palaces, fulfilling Peter's absolutist desires. He had been greatly impressed by Versailles during his visit to the court of Louis XV in 1717 and had sought to match its grandeur in St. Petersburg.

The vast visual feast served up by Rastrelli, with a wealth of dynamic, colorful decoration and forms, was also felt in the Stroganov Palace (1752–54) and Smolny Monastery (1748–1764). As commissioned by Elizabeth, the latter's baroque fancy was tempered by a centralized cross plan and five cupolas, two elements that represent a return to old Russian sources. The Smolny Monastery's look proved pivotal in the continuation of such traditions in the northern capital. Amazingly, despite their subsequent torrid histories, Rastrelli's buildings still grace the city and act as key architectural landmarks.

Classicism

When Catherine II took the Russian throne in 1762, she ushered in a very long and distinct era of neoclassicism (called just classicism in Russia). It lasted through to the second half of the 19th century. This period saw the regularization of the city and its citizens. Plans were drawn up, Nevsky Prospekt formed, embankments made out of granite, bridges built, and institutions established and given permanent homes. The use of classical orders, which borrowed forms from ancient Greece and Rome, strict geometry, and a new dignified serenity expressed the idea of an enlightened and rationally organized imperial authority, resulting in the grand Academy of Arts (1764), the Hermitage, and Latin-style churches.

The architecture program of the Academy of Arts drew a mix of foreigners and Russians, who would largely be responsible for the grand pedimented porticoes, extended colonnades, great domes, and triumphal arches that characterize the main architectural ensembles in and around the heart of the city. Ten men in particular left their stamp on the city: Charles Cameron, Giacomo Quarenghi, Ivan Starov, Nikolay Lvov, Jean-François Thomas de Thomon, Carlo Rossi, Vasily Stasov, August Montferrand, Andrey Voronikhin, and Andreyan Zakharov. The Admiralty (1823), Smolny Institute (1808), Stock Exchange (1810), Kazan (1811) and St. Isaac's (1858) Cathedrals, the main squares in the city center, and the palatial estates in the vicinity owe their appearance to these men.

The eclectic 19th century

As the court's stranglehold on taste and appearance began to loosen in the 19th century, new architectural styles began to pepper St. Petersburg. The first signs of change were a couple of neo-Gothic churches (of the Nativity of St. John, 1777–1780) and the Alexandria estates at Peterhof (1826–29) and Tsarskoye Selo (1792–96) built during the classicist period.

The real spurt of adventurous new architecture, which mixed elements of past styles, occurred from the mid-19th century on. Andrey Stackenschneider's and Alexander Bryullov's new interiors for the Winter Palace paved the way. The nouveaux riche—industrialists, merchants, and bankers—embraced the eclecticism with much pomp and circumstance. Hence the wonderland of Baron Stieglitz's museum (1879), the financial "city" around the junction of Bolshaya Morskaya Street and Nevsky Prospekt, and, more pragmatically, the redbrick factories in the suburbs. Simultaneously, with trouble brewing, the tsarist regime sought to touch people's hearts and hark back to their roots by building in a neo-Byzantine style. The multicolored and multidomed intricate jigsaw of the super-picturesque Church of the Savior on Spilled Blood (1883–1907), dedicated to the memory of the assassinated "tsar liberator" Alexander II, set the wave of change in motion, clearing the way for art nouveau architecture.

Known in Russia at the time as "new style," or now as simply "modern," art nouveau was more a period than a single style. It lasted from around 1895 to 1916 and spread like wildfire across St. Petersburg. It had a new zip, offered new hope and potential, cleaned out the old, the cluttered, the jumbled, the national. Often it jumped from the ground in a lively play of sensual line and color. Sometimes, using granite, it could feel quite heavy, rooted, and northern. Or it combined iron, glass, and concrete to become a sleek form of modern classicism. Swedish architect Fredrik Lidvall popularized both trends.

The monarchy used art nouveau in palace interiors (e.g., Alexander Palace at Tsarskoye Selo), landlords employed it for their new apartment blocks, nouveaux riche loved it for their mansions and villas (Kseshinskaya Mansion, 1906), commerce relished it for its attention-grabbing qualities (Yeliseev's delicatessan and the Singer Sewing Machine headquarters on Nevsky, both early 1900s), transport systems used it to beautify the experience of travel (Vitebsk Railway Station, 1904), and health institutions enhanced patient stays with it (Orthopedic Institute in Alexander Park). Even the St. Petersburg Buddhist Temple (1914) embraced art nouveau.

Socialist times & beyond

The 20th century brought change again. Wars, revolutions, and the changing of the guard ushered in a sober style. As St. Petersburg became Petrograd and then Leningrad, architectural adventures wound down. At first, in the 1920s, there was optimism, with some experimental living projects, particu-

The Admiralty was built as the focal point of the city in the early 19th century.

larly in the western Kirov region, and some new stadiums, clubs, and factories. International Style—interwar sleek modern design—communities were built around the Narva Gates, the architecture stripped down to its functionalist essentials. This came to an end with the rise of Stalinism in the 1930s, which for St. Petersburg/Leningrad essentially meant the rise of a few megaclassicist hulks along Moskovsky Prospekt and the first line of the subway.

Since the 1990s a good number of glass-fronted shopping centers, elite blocks of apartment buildings on the islands, hotels, and banks have gone up, the result of a new quasi art nouveau age. Major international architects such as Sir Norman Foster, Dominique Perreau, and

Bartolomeo Carlo Rastrelli's "Peter the Great" (1740)

Kisho Kurokawa have won unprecedented competitions to build on the ashes and ruins of New Holland, the Mariinsky Theater quarter, and the Kirov stadium. The last is set to cost 240 million dollars and has been dubbed the "flying saucer." There's a lot of beautification being done and to do around the city, but the phoenix seems to be rising.

PAINTING & SCULPTURE

The foundation of St. Petersburg on the Baltic coast marked a sea change for Russian painting and sculpture. Up until the end of the 17th century, Byzantine traditions had prevailed, which basically meant beautifully stylized icons and frescoes depicting saints, Christ, the Virgin Mother, and biblical scenes. A stiff kind of portraiture (of clerics and royals) later emerged, made by Moscow icon painters, just as Tsar Peter reached adulthood.

Peter then traveled extensively in Europe and became enamored of the art he saw. On his return, he wholeheartedly encouraged a full-blown Europeanized and partly secularized interpretation of baroque and rococo trends. He ordered allegorical and mythological sculptures with sensual forms from Italy for the Summer Garden and the park in Peterhof and carved reliefs for the triumphal gate to the Peter and Paul Fortress.

When Frenchman Louis Caravaque (1684–1754) arrived in St. Petersburg in 1717, painting also took a sensual turn. He painted Peter's two young daughters with a rococo sensibility, even exposing Anna's right nipple (the 1717 double portrait is in Michael's Castle). His 1718 panorama "Battle of Poltava," which depicts Peter's victory over the Swedes in 1709, launched Russian history painting. It was reproduced as one of the first tapestries made at the new Petersburg Tapestry Factory. A couple of years later he organized a school of painting that would be the first step toward the establishment of the imperial Academy of Arts in 1764.

And what Caravaque did for painting, the Florentine Bartolomeo Carlo Rastrelli (1675–1744) did for sculpture, particularly his influential equestrian monument of Peter (modeled in 1725, cast in the 1740s), which stands outside Michael's Castle.

The Imperial Academy of Arts

Founded in 1764, St. Petersburg's Imperial Academy of Arts, the world's largest, controlled the arts from the 1760s to the 1860s. It trained painters and sculptors of Russian birth in the classical manner. The artists produced image after image of the gods and heroes of antiquity, anatomically perfect nudes, idealized landscapes, and their

wealthy patrons as personifications of culti-
vated class and beauty. Catherine II was a
rabid art collector (her collection, together
with Peter the Great's, form the foundation
of the Hermitage collection); her habit fired
an explosion of activity.

The works of academy artists abound
in the museum of the academy, the Russian
Museum, and throughout the city in the
form of public monuments. Some of it is
good, some of it is slavish copying, and some
of it has a distinctive Russian twist. As it
turned out, two Ukrainian painters, Anton
Losenko (1737–1773) and Dmitry Levitsky
(1735–1822), led the way in giving Russian
art the latter. Levitsky's work can be sublime.

The art, the majority of which followed a
canon of cold, distant passion and refinement,
announced and reinforced tsarist autocracy
from the walls of memorial cathedrals such
as the Kazan and St. Isaac's, the Admiralty,
Senate and Holy Synod, General Staff building, and the center of squares. Citizens and
foreigners could not but be impressed by the
scale and order conveyed by these monumental works. And none was more impressive than Étienne-Maurice Falconet's 1782
Bronze Horseman monument, the image of
Peter and Russia galloping forth.

With the academy and court holding
sway, there wasn't much room for originality.
Still, two painters, Karl Bryullov (1799–1852)
and Alexander Ivanov (1806–1858) began to
break the mold, to paint their emotions, to
open their souls, to express their doubts.
Bryullov's epic "Last Day of Pompeii"
(1830–33) is a thinly veiled comment on
doomed contemporary Russian society,
while Ivanov's studies for "The Appearance
of the Messiah" (1837–1857), where, as he
began to question his faith, the figure of
Christ got ever smaller, show less bravura.

Art breaks free

The increasingly turbulent political scene
in the the mid-19th century eventually led to
end of the establishment stranglehold on the
arts in 1863, when a group of student
painters refused to take part in the annual
Academy of Art gold medal competition
because the subject was prescribed, remote,
and mythological. They organized them-

selves into a cooperative (the Artel) and by
1870 were officially allowed to exhibit and
sell as an independent society: the Wanderers
(Peredvizhniki). They elevated the modern,

**Variety abounds at the Imperial Porcelain
Factory Museum.**

relevant, and national as they saw fit. They
painted life as it was, warts and all. Art historians regard them as critical realists, but
status quo monarchists of the day considered them dangerous subversives who were
connected to terrorist revolutionary movements. In reality, they were not so politically
radical. The work of Ilya Repin (1844–1930)
stands out among the Wanderers; his "Volga
Bargehaulers" (1870–73) seems to capture
the whole straining Russian Empire.

At the turn of the 20th century, Russian
art waltzed onto the world stage in dramatic

fashion. The St. Petersburg group World of Art (Mir Iskusstva), run by the impresario Sergey Diaghilev (1872–1929), took new risks. Opposed to the heavyweight subjects and treatment offered both by the realists and academics, this group let imagination run wild.

The result took Russian art into uncharted territory—art for art's sake, the painting of mood, light and artifice; the painting of questions rather than answers; and the painting of taboo subjects such as inner demons, eroticism, male effeminacy, pre-Christian religiosity, the trivial, and the satirical. The best artists were only satellites to the World of Art group: Mikhail Vrubel (1856–1910), a painter of psychological torment, and Isaak Levitan (1860–1900), whose landscapes expressed his inner soul. Diaghilev forged alliances with international artists and led the group into stage and costume design, notably his world famous Ballets Russes seasons in Paris. The most outstanding painter for these was Lev (Leon) Bakst (1866–1924).

The March 1898 opening of the Russian Museum in the very prestigious Mikhailovsky Palace in the center of town signaled the maturation of Russian art: It now had its own, official institution to chart its history. A new sense of appreciation and openness to experiment resulted.

Futurism of the early 20th century

The first three decades of the 20th century witnessed the art of St. Petersburg at its peak. Artists investigated materials, broached new viewpoints, challenged restrictions in media (including breaking down the boundaries between sculpture and painting), and abstracted from the visual. Members of the radical group Union of Youth (Soyuz Molodeozhi) started to stylize and primitivize their art; they joined with futurist poets to produce a new artistic language unhinged from reliance on subjects and narrative. This leap away from the conventions of composition and attachment to mundane reality led simultaneously to assemblage and fragmentation. It was also a quest for a new, higher, world, and altered state of consciousness—to *Victory over the Sun*, as they called their futurist opera in 1913.

Leading figures in the Union of Youth became key players in the reorganized art scene after the 1917 revolution. They included Kazimir Malevich (1878–1935), the creator of the notorious "Black Square," Mikhail Matyushin (1861–1934), Pavel Filonov (1883–1941), and Vladimir Tatlin (1885–1953). With the Academy turned into a set of Free Art Studios and then the Higher Art-Technical Studios, these artists directed work, formed the core of the Russian avant-garde, and led Russian art to establish its world-renowned art-revolutionary movements, suprematism, and constructivism. Probably the most significant work was Tatlin's radical 1919–1920 model for the "Monument to the Third International" in Petrograd.

Sidelined

After St. Petersburg lost its position as capital in 1918 and Stalin not only stifled artistic expression but also provincialized Leningrad for 50 years (1930s–1980s), the city's art scene was held in check. The academy was reduced in status to an institute while Moscow got the new USSR Academy of Arts. All art production had to be official, styles and "messages" were sanctioned. Artists were state employees and members of the Union of Artists.

In this atmosphere, though Leningrad produced some significant socialist realist painting, monumental sculpture emerged as the strongest art, since it took political propaganda onto the street. Beginning with Sergey Yevseev's "Lenin" on Lenin Square in 1926, vast monuments were created to socialist heroes and the defenders of Leningrad during the World War II siege, notably Nikolay Tomsky's "Sergey Kirov" (1938) on Kirov Square. In the wake of terrible suffering during World War II, a whole pantheon of sculpted heroes was erected in the new Victory Park. The best sculptor to emerge was Mikhail Anikushin (1917–1997), who in the post-Stalin years produced not only the "Monument to the Heroic Defenders of Leningrad" (1957–1975) on Victory Square, but also the eloquent "Pushkin" (1957) on Arts Square.

During the dark days of Soviet rule,

Kazimir Malevich's—a leading member of the avant-garde artist group, the Union of Youth— portrait of his friend Ivan Kliun (1913)

many artists had split personalities: They turned out "official art" in order to keep their state-given studios and "real art" for themselves and their immediate circles. Modernist traditions were maintained in this quiet way. In the 1980s a punkish anarchic group of rebels called the Mitki emerged from the shadows and led the new revolution against socialist revolutionary art. Today the group has become an institu-tion and maintain their own, occasionally open, art center-gallery.

Since the end of the Soviet era, all kinds of exhibitions, festivals, installations, and performance and video art are happening at a new Peter-like pace, encouraged in part by the 1995 opening of a branch of the Ludwig Museum in the Marble Palace, replete with its international gang of pop, conceptual and hyperrealist artists. A

Cesar Pugni's 1843 ballet *Ondine* performed at the Mariinsky Theater

gigantic wave of post-Soviet monumental sculpture is swamping the streets, often dedicated to neglected heroes and equally often of mixed quality. The thoughtful works by Mikhail Shemyakin (e.g., "Peter I" in the Peter and Paul Fortress, 1991) are particularly noteworthy.

MUSIC

The energy put into music in St. Petersburg hums on all fronts. Not only is the city one of the world's homes of classical music, but it is also the birthplace of the Russian rave and club scenes, and for the last decade or so of the USSR it hosted some of the very best semi-underground Soviet jazz, rock, and experimental music. In addition, spiritual music pours from the churches, where church choirs sing Orthodox hymns and chants and the bells of the SS Peter and Paul Cathedral peal concerts. Several festivals make use of the summer White Nights to showcase musical talents of all genres.

Classical

The foremost worldwide ambassador for St. Petersburg is the Mariinsky Opera and Ballet Theater, founded in 1860. It hasn't always been—its standards, morale, and reputation dipped in the late Soviet period, when it also went by the name Kirov Opera and Ballet Theater—but under the leadership of Valery Gergiev since 1988 it, and especially its orchestra, has again risen in esteem. The city's tradition in ballet and opera goes back to the 18th century, but it really took off after the Mariinsky became the venue for many premieres of the composers coming out of the Imperial Conservatory (now St. Petersburg State Conservatory) that was established two years later.

But classical music in St. Petersburg really started with the Philharmonic Orchestra, which, after its founding in 1802, attracted maestros such as Beethoven, who requested in 1824 that his "Missa Solemnis" be first performed by the orchestra and the singers of the Imperial Choir of the Court Capella (now the Glinka Choir of the State Academic Capella). Composers who actually came to St. Petersburg to perform with the Philharmonic include Liszt, Berlioz, Schumann, and Wagner. Tchaikovsky conducted his last symphony (the sixth) with the Philharmonic just before he died in 1893. Since 1921, it has played in the Grand Hall, one of the city's best halls for acoustics, located in the former Assembly of the Nobles. Once at the forefront of new classical music, premiering, for instance, Shostakovich's "Leningrad" (Seventh) symphony in 1942, today the Philharmonic focuses on classic works; the quality, however, remains undiminished.

Besides these two giants, many other classical music institutions thrive in the city, including the State Academic Capella with its renowned Glinka Choir and the conservatory's own company. In addition, organ concerts are given in some of the 19th-century churches, most of the palaces hold classical concerts at various times of the year, and the adventurous St. Petersburg Cello Ensemble, under the direction of Olga Rudneva, deliberately plays unusual venues.

Modern

Among St. Petersburg's modern music movements, jazz takes top honors. Survivors of the underground Soviet scene include David Goloshchekin, who runs the White Nights Swing Festival and, since the late 1980s, the Jazz Philharmonic Hall, which features traditional, or conservative, jazz. Experimental, jamming, funk, and new jazz sizzle in clubs such as Jam Point, JFC Jazz, and Take Five. The ever popular JazzQ festival takes place in July.

While the jazz scene flourished in a quiet, laid-back way in the 1970s and '80s, the underground rock scene made more noise. It became a real alternative to the popular—and officially sanctioned—and still most widely popular romantic variety show-type music. At the vanguard of the rockers was Viktor Tsoy, lead singer of the band Kino; he was later immortalized after his death in a 1990 car crash. Boris Grebenshikov is probably the city's most internationally known rocker, rocketing to fame as the frontman for the group Aquarium. But the most brilliant of the generation was Sergey Kuryokin, who died tragically young in 1996 after having brought his Pop Mechanics collective to the forefront of Russian experimental music.

In Kuryokin's and Tsoy's wake have come the groups Tequilajazzz, Marksheyder Kunst, Zoopark, and Spitfire, along with a wide range of raves, techno, rap, hip-hop, and house music. Top international performers play venues ranging from the Platforma and Fish Fabrique clubs to the Ice Palace stadium.

Folk music—complete with twanging balalaikas, accordions, national costumes, and cossack dancing—reigns in a variety of tourist venues. It can be heard, and seen, in a variety of venues.

THEATER

Russia's oldest state dramatic theater, the monumental Alexandra (Aleksandrinsky) on Ostrovsky Square, celebrated its 250th

Words, words, words

An old adage says that actions speak louder than words, but in St. Petersburg the opposite may be truer. The actions of Peter, Catherine, the 1917 revolution, and the siege may have "shook the world" but words have formed and shaken the city. Ever since Alexander Pushkin, the power of the Petersburg word has been double-edged. It has been a hymn of unique, hypnotizing beauty and a dagger twisting in the city's heart. The twinning of luxurious comfort and inhumane struggle sparked the inner fire of a plethora of writers.

When the founding father of Russian literature, Alexander Pushkin, wrote in 1833 "Bronze Horseman," the poem that like no other captures the awful yet majestic fight between nature and man that is St. Petersburg, he set in motion a chain of literary outpourings. The poem appeared after Pushkin's death in a duel. It was written after years of internal exile for liberal thinking, and when Tsar Nicholas I was acting as his personal censor.

Some critics argue that several notable writers preceded Pushkin, not least Gavrila

Alexander Pushkin (1799–1837)

Nikolay Gogol (1809–1852)

The city's great writers either were exiled or fled from Petersburg, such has been their and its threat. The relationship is always somehow tragic. The best don't really write about the city as such but the human condition, using the city to probe questions of life and art. It is a cruel, charismatic master.

> I love thee, Peter's own creation,
> I love thy stern and comely face…
> Thrive, Peter's city, flaunt thy beauty,
> Stand like unshaken Russia fast,
> Till floods and storms from chafing duty
> May turn to peace with thee at last….
> —Alexander Pushkin,
> "Bronze Horseman," 1833

Derzhavin (1743–1816), the first poet to paint a nocturnal picture of Petersburg. But it's the writers in Pushkin's wake who truly stand out. Ukrainian by birth, Nikolay Gogol arrived in Petersburg in 1829 at age 20. His experiences in the civil service and of the falsities of society life poured from his pen in a series of penetrating satires and surrealist tales about Petersburg folly and phantasmagoria. Scarred, he toured central Europe, the Holy Land, and Moscow, where he died extremely disturbed.

Up stepped Fyodor Dostoyevsky, whose 1866 novel *Crime and Punishment* posed the question "Who here in Russia doesn't consider himself a Napoleon?" Educated as an engineer in St. Petersburg, the self-tortured genius spent years imprisoned in Siberia for his thoughts. He returned to St. Petersburg in 1859 to author his greatest novels.

> Svidrigailov: "Brother, I am going to foreign lands."
> "Foreign lands?"
> "To America."
> "To America?"
> Svidrigailov took out a revolver and cocked it....
> —Fyodor Dostoyevsky,
> Crime and Punishment, 1866

Fyodor Dostoyevsky (1821–1881)

Writing became fashionable, censorship fluctuated, subjects and styles multiplied. Around the end of the 19th century, Russia's silver age dawned. It produced a galaxy of Petersburg stars, whose expressive, moody, biting poems and tales get lost in translation. Andrey Bely (1880–1934) wrote a symbolist novel called Petersburg (1913–14) in which it's hard to discern the living city at all. And, after seeing almost all of her generation of writers extinguished in one way or another by the Stalinist terror, Anna Akhmatova (1889–1966), herself frequently banned and under surveillance, became the elegiac guardian of their memory. Now her own memory, together with theirs, and that of her young follower, Joseph Brodsky, is evocatively preserved in the Fountain House. Having partially turned to writing in English, Brodsky died in New York.

> Away with time and away with space,
> I described everything through the white night:
> The narcissus in crystal on your table,
> The blue smoke of a cigar,
> And that mirror, where, as in pure water,
> You might be a reflection right now.
> —Anna Akhmatova,
> "Poem without a Hero," 1940–1962

Joseph Brodsky (1940–1996)

Other 20th-century English language writers who've captured more than a little of St. Petersburg's soul include Harrison Salisbury, whose epic narrative 900 Days (1969) brings home the horror of the Siege of Leningrad, as does, in a much more romantic way, Paullina Simons in The Bronze Horseman (2001); J. M. Coetzee in his Dostoyevskian Master of Petersburg (1994); and Malcolm Bradbury in the culture-time traveling novel To the Hermitage (2000). Finally, there's Vladimir Nabokov (1899–1977), who fled St. Petersburg. Is there any St. Petersburg in Lolita (1955)? There surely is in the anti-utopian Invitation to a Beheading (1936). ∎

anniversary on August 30, 2006, with a gala reopening after a 16-month renovation. A lot of work is still needed to rebuild its reputation to its pre-Stalin levels, but the classical repertoire and traditional academic forms on offer are promising.

From the 1830s through to the early 1920s, St. Petersburg produced some great playwrights and some very inventive theater, ranging from Gogol's 1836 *Government Inspector* (performed at the Alexandra) to circa 1914 futurist performances in the Stray Dog and Comedians' Halt cabarets. One of Russia's greatest directors, Vsevolod Meyerhold

The newly renovated auditorium of the Alexandra (Alexandrinsky) Theater

(1874–1940), brought his talents to the stages of St. Petersburg in the early 20th century, revolutionizing performance and set design on the one hand and supporting tradition on the other. The city holds his memory dear.

Today, most theaters perform conventional material from the classics to the popular. The Tovstonogov Grand (Bolshoy) Dramatic Theater (BDT) on the Fontanka probably has the best reputation while the Komissarzhevskaya on Italianskaya chooses safe bets. The Puppet-Marionette Theater on Nevsky offers unique entertainment.

FILM

The first piece of cinema shown in Russia was the work of the Lumière brothers; it played in the Aquarium Theater on May 4, 1896. Two days later St. Petersburg had its first cinema house, on Nevsky, and just over two decades later its first film studio. The studio became Lenfilm in 1934, and still produces movies today. They've made more than 1,500 films, including some Soviet classics and cults like *Chapaev* (1934), *Hamlet* (1964), and *The Hound of the Baskervilles* (1981). The outstanding director Alexander Sokurov has worked with Lenfilm since the 1970s; the West knows him best for his one-take trip around the Hermitage, *The Russian Ark* (2003). More recently, Andrey Kravchuk's *The Italian* (2005) has garnered international plaudits.

The image of St. Petersburg in films tends to be colored by a famous black-and-white scene of revolutionaries storming the Winter Palace in Sergei Eisenstein's 1927 *October* (more popularly known outside Russia as *Ten Days That Shook the World*). It created a whole myth that still lingers today. At the other end of the 20th century, the James Bond action movie *Golden Eye* (1995) offered a different take on good versus evil, while Ralph Fiennes's *Onegin* (1999) penetrated romantically deeper into the soul of the city. Today, the summer film and performance festivals offer more insight into the state of the acting arts. ∎

Palace Embankment and the land beyond to the Moika River composes St. Petersburg's imperial center. Peter built his first palace here and 200 years later a revolution overthrew the Romanov dynasty here. For a small area, it packs in an astonishing amount of history, world art, and empty space.

South Bank Neva

Detail of "Victory, Peace, and Plenty," Pietro Baratta, 1725; Summer Garden

South Bank Neva

WHETHER SUMMER OR WINTER THE HUB OF ST. PETERSBURG LIES ON THE south (left) bank of the widest part of the Neva River between the Summer and Winter Palaces. This small strip of land constitutes the eastern half of Admiralty Island. Only a few people live here, on the relatively short Millionaires' Street, which has fewer than 40 houses, yet this landmark area acts as a magnet for millions: It is the focal point of the city and the 300-year-old center of the world's largest empire.

The light-filled Pavilion Hall of the Hermitage is a principal St. Petersburg attraction.

South Bank Neva is defined by the Palace Embankment (Dvortsovaya Naberezhnaya), which runs its length. St. Petersburg's prime royal palaces were built here. Despite the variety of architectural styles, stemming from a construction period that ranged from the 1710s to the 1870s, the embankment presents a harmonious ensemble (it's best seen from the north bank or the bridges). As you walk between the Summer and Winter Palaces the scale gradually changes. Ultimately, for all the embankment's unity, differences loom large between the two palaces.

The Summer Palace, and its surrounding garden, speaks of the vision of Tsar Peter I, the founder of the city. It was abandoned after his death. The Winter Palace is the creation of his daughter Elizabeth and remained the main royal residence in Russia

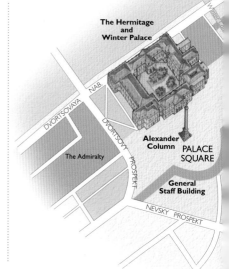

until the fall of the Romanovs in 1917. Each generation added their own imprint, within and beyond its walls.

It can be disappointing to discover that something as grand sounding as the Summer Palace of the Russian emperor is just a 14-room building that looks like a medium-size Dutch house. But this was just about the first brick building in the city and it accorded with both Peter's pragmatism and his desired Europeanization of Russia. The palace's surrounding garden served as his outdoor academy, where Russians would learn afresh about cultivation and civilization. The collection of allegorical statuary presaged the foundation of the world-famous art collections in the Winter Palace, housing the Hermitage museum, at the other end of the street. Peter's "modest" forays into art collecting paled

in comparison to Empress Catherine II; she amassed world art treasures on a hitherto unprecedented scale. The thousand halls of the baroque palace she inherited could not hold all her treasures, so she commissioned the Hermitage next door.

The other key feature of this area are the two open spaces that bookend the South Bank Neva. They both are very large (good for drilling the troops and crowd control) and very symbolic; both are fringed by post-Napoleonic empire-style great military buildings; and both are commemorative.

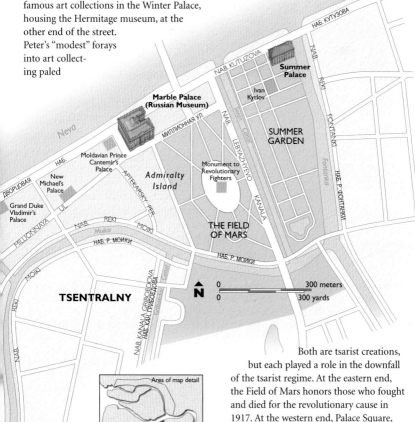

Both are tsarist creations, but each played a role in the downfall of the tsarist regime. At the eastern end, the Field of Mars honors those who fought and died for the revolutionary cause in 1917. At the western end, Palace Square, which memorializes the Russian victory over Napoleon, was the scene of the Russian revolution that brought about seven decades of Soviet rule. ■

Summer Garden

OCCUPYING A PRIME SITE ON THE SOUTH SIDE OF THE
Neva River, the Summer Garden was conceived by Peter the Great as
a principal place for amusement and education, where Russians
could gain acquaintance with contemporary European court values.
History has wrought many changes to its appearance, but it retains a
unique and charismatic atmosphere that is at once romantic and
regulatory. There are two entrance points, one in the north and one
in the south. If you enter through the southern one, Charlemagne's
gate, you'll sense gradual enrichment that builds to a crescendo.

Summer Garden
www.rusmuseum.ru

- Map p. 53
- 314-0374
- Metro: Nevsky
  Prospekt or
  Gostiny Dvor

Soon after Peter chose the site for
his Summer Palace (see pp. 56–
57) in 1704, he commissioned
several international landscape
designers and architects to turn
the small segment of marshy land
surrounding it into a formal
Dutch-style garden that would
serve as a playground for learning.
Jan Roosen, Gaspar Focht, Jean-
Baptiste Le Blond, and others
introduced a great range of trees
and shrubs from across Europe
and the Russian empire, arranging
them around a geometrical system

of avenues and paths. The flora
was complemented by sculptures,
60 fountains, a cascade, a pond, a
grotto, an amphitheater, greenhouses, and caged rare animals
and birds.

Disastrous events such as a
great flood in 1777 and the bomb-
ing and shelling during World
War II, together with the fashion
for English romantic gardens, dramatically altered the garden's original appearance. The fountains,
which gave the bordering Fontanka River its name, were the first

in Russia and were adorned with sculptures representing scenes from *Aesop's Fables.* They were destroyed in the 1777 flood and not replaced.

CHARLEMAGNE'S GATE TO FELTEN'S GATE

Relatively modest railings enclose the southern end of the garden; Louis-Henry Charlemagne designed them in the wake of the Napoleonic Wars and the 1825 Decembrist uprising. At the gate, Doric columns stand bedecked with Medusa head shields, crossed swords, spears, pikes, and eagles that symbolize the military prowess of the Russian capital. Entering the garden through Charlemagne's gates, one can appreciate how the Summer Garden is an oasis in the city. Nearby is the monumental pink porphyry vase that Charles XIV of Sweden gave to Nicholas I in 1839. It was made at the Älvdalen Porphyry Works in Dalarna and stands as an elegiac memorial to Swedish interests in the Neva Delta.

Immediately behind the Swedish vase is the **Carp Pond** in which swans often glide. Walking around the pond to its right, four avenues lead toward the Neva. The widest, **Main Avenue,** leads down the center of the garden. Lime and maple trees and marble statues commissioned by Peter from Italian (mainly Venetian) baroque sculptors line the path. Only about 90 of the more than 200 original statues survive; they form Russia's first collection of secular sculpture. Peter intended to use the statuary to acquaint his people with the art, mythology, and refined taste of antiquity.

Halfway down the path, near the Swan Canal on the left, you will see the expressive, late 17th-century **"Amor and Psyche."** A little farther along, on your right, is the monument memorializing Ivan Krylov, Russia's early 19th-century collector of fables. As if to replace the lost *Aesop's Fables* fountains, Krylov sits on a pedestal teeming with characters from his stories about human foibles. Baron Peter Clodt von Jurgensburg, St. Petersburg's leading sculptor of the age, finished the

work in 1855. Look for the monkey violinist and goat cellist.

At the northern end of the garden is Pietro Baratta's 1725 lion-trampling, torch-extinguishing sculptural group **"Victory, Peace, and Plenty."** It is an allegory for Russia's victory over Sweden in the Great Northern War and the favorable peace treaty of 1721. The tall and elegant railings designed by Yuri Felten (1773–1786) alongside the Neva rise just beyond, as does the garden's northern entrance.

The garden was much beloved by Russian poets, musicians, and artists and a few minutes of reflective pause to capture some of its nostalgic inspiration should be cherished. ∎

Artists young and old are drawn to, and inspired by, the tranquil setting of the Summer Garden.

Summer Palace

Summer Palace

www.rusmuseum.ru

🗺 Map p. 53

✉ Kutuzov Naberezh-
naya 2

☎ 314-0374

🕐 Closed Tues. &
Jan.–April

💲 $$

🚇 Metro: Nevsky
Prospekt or
Gostiny Dvor

FROM A DISTANCE, PETER THE GREAT'S BELOVED SUMMER Palace seems like a modest, straightforward, two-story Dutch house. While it definitely has something of these qualities, it's not so simple. First, its yellowish facade is covered with an ostentatious display of Russian maritime strength. Second, it served as a lifestyle laboratory, an experimental woodcraft workshop, and a meteorological station. Despite the fact that much of the original is missing—Peter's lathe and self-made furniture, the servants' quarters, the little harbor before the front door—the palace is still one of the most evocative monuments to the founder of St. Petersburg, and perhaps more than any other helps explain the man.

Peter's favorite family abode set new standards in taste and doubled as a workshop and meteorological station.

The Summer Palace was erected in the northeastern corner of the Summer Garden, conveniently close to the junction of the Fontanka and Neva Rivers. It was designed by Domenico Trezzini, a former military architect for the Danish king who was appointed head of Peter's Office of Defense and Construction in 1707. Built between 1710 and 1714, the palace was one of the first brick buildings in the city. Before you enter, take note of the **bas-reliefs** between the windows. They announce the arrival of Russia at the sea's edge and glorify the significance of this event. The reliefs culminate over the door in the enlarged, unframed image of a

highly militarized and regal
Minerva by the Berlin sculptor
and architect Andreas Schlüter.
As the goddess of war, state wisdom, science, and arts and crafts,
the image of Minerva was intended as an allegory for Peter's
endeavors. (She appears inside the
home as well.)

The interior of the Summer
Palace is divided between the
work-oriented ground-floor
apartments of Peter, and his family's residential rooms above. Each
floor has just seven main rooms.
While the staircase, the vestibule's
oak paneling, and Nicolas
Pinneau's carved wood relief of
Minerva (also in the vestibule)
are original, much of the early
18th-century furnishings on display are not; they do, however,
fairly faithfully represent the style
of the rooms during Peter's time.

PETER'S WORK SPACES
Peter's **study (and turnery)**
reveals his fascination with the
sea. An elaborate wind device (see
box) stretches from floor to ceiling on one wall and the decoration of the room has a nautical
theme, from the ships on the tiled
stove to those in the paintings on
the walls. The addition of Peter's
skipper uniform complements
the room.

Next door to Peter's study is
the **dining room;** the other
rooms on the ground floor are the
kitchen (with piped water, it was
the first example of plumbing in
St. Petersburg), two **reception
rooms** (note Georg Gsell's order-
bringing "Triumph of Minerva"
painted ceiling), the **secretary's
room,** and Peter's elaborately
decorated **bedroom.**

Visitors are led counterclockwise, starting with the first reception room. It was said that all and
sundry could come here with

Wind device

This ingenious instrument
was a key to safe passage
across and along St. Petersburg's
waterways. Peter ordered his
from Dresden. In keeping with
the period's style and instrument's use, a wealth of baroque
wooden bas-relief relating to
naval themes surrounds the
instrument's three large dials,
or faces.

The top face of the device is
a clock. The bottom two dials
show the strength and power
of the wind; this information is
gained through a mechanism
that fixes the device to the
bronzed weathercock on
the roof. Using the wind device,
the tsar, while working on
his studies or his lathe, could
be supplied with important
knowledge concerning the
best conditions for navigating
the Neva. ■

their requests or complaints.
Notice, however, the little door in
the wall; it used to have iron bars
and led to a lockup in the center
of the house in which offenders
would be locked (and freed) by
Peter himself.

THE UPSTAIRS ROOMS
After the first two audience rooms
for Peter's wife Catherine, you
pass into the family rooms, which
are slightly more intimate, femi-
nine, and domestic. They include
Catherine's bedroom, the
dance-exercise room, and the
nursery. The built-in glazed
cupboards in the delicately painted **Green Study** display Peter's
collection of gems, Chinese figurines, jade, porcelain, and ivory,
which he purchased in Holland. ■

Field of Mars

Field of Mars

 Map p. 53

ONE BEGINS TO GET A SENSE OF THE SCALE AND SCHEME OF things in St. Petersburg when walking around the unusual Field of Mars, a vast green space dotted with lilac bushes and dissected by broad gravel paths that lies right at the heart of the city.

Separated from the Summer Garden by the Swan Canal, the actual "field" was known as Tsaritsyn Meadow for much of the 18th and 19th centuries. Many things took place here, among them the parade and inspection of the Imperial Guard, popular fairs, and Peter's spectacular firework party in 1721 to celebrate his triumph in the Great Northern War and the conclusion of the Treaty of Nystad.

An Eternal Flame (above) was lit amid the graves of the Monument to Revolutionary Fighters (below) on the 40th anniversary of the February Revolution in 1957.

The field only received its present-day architectural borders after the Neva's granite embankments were built in the 1760s to 1770s.

In the 1780s, the northern boundary of Tsaritsyn Meadow was adorned with two large neoclassic mansions, the first for Count Ivan Betskoy, president of the Academy of Arts; the second, known as **Field Marshal Saltykov's House,** by the Italian architect Giacomo Quarenghi, for a merchant called Groten. The latter served as the British Embassy from 1863 until 1918, when a

shoot-out between the British naval attaché and the Bolshevik secret police (the Cheka) occurred here. Nearby stands the lonely bronze **monument to Alexander Suvorov** (by sculptor Mikhail Kozlovsky, 1801), the great general who, in the last years of the 18th century, led the Russian campaign in Poland and the Russian-Austrian strikes against Napoleon in north Italy. Suvorov is depicted as Mars, the Roman god of war. Facing the Neva, he stands aloft a round granite pedestal, bears a Russian imperial shield, and brandishes his sword protectively over two crowns and a tiara.

The former **Barracks of the Pavlovsky Regiment** (by Vasily Stasov, 1817–19), now home to the Lenenergo Company, dominate the western side of the field. This long building is notable for its three Doric porticoes crowned by militaristic sculptural reliefs. You can best appreciate the great expanse of the yellow-and-white edifice by walking parallel to it across the field.

In the middle of the field stands Lev Rudnev's low-lying granite **Monument to Revolutionary Fighters,** one of the first memorials created after the 1917 revolutions. It marks where 180 supporters of the February Revolution were buried, as well as many who lost died in the October Revolution and the ensuing civil war. During the Soviet years, the memorial became one of Leningrad's most sacred spots. ∎

Marble Palace

THE MARBLE PALACE COMPLETELY CONTRASTS WITH THE reflective space of the neighboring Field of Mars. It encapsulates the excesses of the tsarist regime against which those people buried in the field fought. When it was built (by Antonio Rinaldi, 1768–1785), on the site of St. Petersburg's first Post Court, it was the most expensive palace in St. Petersburg and was a present from Catherine the Great to her lover, the intriguing Count Grigory Orlov. It now houses some of the Russian Museum's more interesting exhibits.

Marble Palace
- Map p. 52
- Millionnaya Ulitsa 5
- 312-9196
  or 595-4248
- Closed Tues.
- $$
- Metro: Nevsky Prospekt

A masterpiece of early Russian neoclassic architecture, the palace originally had 32 varieties of marble and several sorts of granite, lazurite, and limestone adorning its walls. The handsome exterior comprises a rather subtle, harmonized combination of different marbles and granite. Inside, the Marble Hall and the main staircase, with their elegant virtuous bas-reliefs by Fedot Shubin and Mikhail Kozlovsky, Russia's leading sculptors of the late 18th century, offer the best glimpses of the palace's initial stone wealth.

The palace has had a checkered history. Count Orlov (1734–1783) fell out of favor and died before the building was completed, so the state acquired the palace. It had a series of royal residents, who made alterations to the building. (Notably, architect Alexander Bryullov added some Gothic Revival elements—pointed arches, vaults, and rosettes—in the mid-19th century.) With the overthrow of the old regime in 1917, the palace became home to a series of Soviet institutions, the most famous being a Lenin Museum (1937–1991).

In 1992, after the demise of the USSR, the palace was turned into a branch of the Russian Museum, housing two permanent collections: The **Ludwig Museum** in the Russian Museum is the best

collection of post–World War II world art in St. Petersburg; the **Yakov and Iosif Rzhevsky Collection** of early 20th-century Russian paintings (and early 19th-century furniture) complements the Ludwig. The museum also stages temporary exhibitions.

The palace courtyard is home to the equestrian **statue of Tsar Alexander III,** created in the early 1900s by the Italian-Russian-American prince, Paolo Trubetskoy. It used to stand in the center of Vosstaniya Square on Nevsky Prospekt. ∎

The stubborn and hefty equestrian image of Alexander III outside the Marble Palace originally stood in front of the Moscow Railway Station.

Millionaires' Street & the Palace Embankment

Millionaires' Street

⬛ Map p. 52

⬛ Metro: Nevsky Prospekt

MILLIONAIRES' STREET RUNS WEST FROM THE BETSKOY mansion by the Swan Canal to Palace Square. It parallels the Palace Embankment; the great houses on the street's northern side also face the river, presenting different facades to those strolling the Palace Embankment. These thoroughfares give visitors some of the most distinctive and historic impressions of St. Petersburg.

Wedding parties frequently gather on the bridge over the Winter Canal.

Millionaires' Street began life in 1711 as a link between Peter's Summer and Winter Palaces. Before being named after the rich nobility that lived in its grand mansions during the 19th century, this road was called Foreigners' Street because the surrounding area had initially been designated the Foreigners' Quarter. Nowadays, its name notwithstanding, the street seems a bit low key: architecturally nothing appears to stand out, the intersection with Moshkov Lane gets busy with traffic, and, since most of the stately houses have been converted into apartments, the former opulence and sense of society have largely vanished. And yet, the history is palpable.

Heading west along Million-aires' Street from the Marble Palace, take note of **No. 4.** This rather serene two-story building with four Corinthian columns and a pediment was St. Main Apothecary (by Giacomo Quarenghi, 1789–1796). **No. 10,** built in 1852 to 1854, was the home of Andrey Stackenschneider, the gifted architect of the mid-19th-century palaces that give the city much of its present-day character. The four playful reliefs on the facade represent. Stackenschneider and his wife and daughters; they hint of the salons held within during the 1850s and 1860s. The Romanov dynasty came to its formal end at No. 12, **Putyatin's House,** where, on March 3, 1917, Tsar Nicholas II's brother Michael renounced his right to the throne.

Stackenschneider designed No. 19, **New Michael's Palace** (1857–1861), for Tsar Nicholas I's youngest son Grand Duke Michael; the palace's facade on the Palace Embankment is a lavish neobaroque and neo-Renaissance confection that hints at the wealth of ornament inside. (The palace is now part of the Academy of Sciences; *public access limited.*)

PALACE EMBANKMENT

Two other important palaces flank the New Michael's Palace on the embankment side. The **Moldavian Prince Cantemir Palace** *(No. 8)* was Francesco Rastrelli's first building in St. Petersburg (1720s), though it was largely rebuilt in the 1870s.

The **Grand Duke Vladimir's Palace,** No. 26, looks like a Florentine palazzo. Completed in 1874, this Alexander Rezanov-designed building was a 365-room extravagant showpiece of decorative art for the youngest

son of Tsar Alexander II. As president of the Academy of Arts, he bought Repin's masterpiece "The Volga Bargehaulers," which now hangs in the Russian Museum (see pp. 118–125). He is mainly remembered for ordering, as commander-in-chief of the Transfiguration Guards and St. Petersburg military district, the Bloody Sunday massacre of the worker-demonstrators in the Palace Square area in January 1905. Now housing the Gorky House of Scholars, the palace is closed to the public; its arched Renaissance porch, however, covers most of the sidewalk: Note the lizards on the lanterns. ∎

Architect Stackenschneider's own house (No.10) features family portraits on its facade.

Palace Square

Palace Square
Map p. 52
Bus: 7 & 10;
Trolleybus: 1, 7, & 10;
Metro: Nevsky
Prospekt

THIS IMMENSE, GRAND SEMICIRCULAR SPACE IN THE heart of the city represents the zenith of imperial order and ambition. It also celebrates the Russian eclipsing of the Napoleonic empire in Europe. Once the site of parades, festivals, rallies, demonstrations, the Bloody Sunday massacre, and the 1917 storming of the Winter Palace, the square now mainly plays host to disparate groups of tourists, Rollerbladers, students, and other folks relaxing.

Palace Square was given its present form in the early 19th century. The great crescent-shaped **General Staff and Ministries of Finance and Foreign Affairs building** (by Carlo Rossi, 1819–1829) marks the southern edge of the square and faces the Winter Palace. Its length stretches more than 1,700 feet (518 m).

The highlight of the General Staff is the double triumphal arch at its center, which Rossi conceived as a celebration of the victory over Napoleon. A dynamic coppered Victory, riding her six-horse chariot, and flanking Roman soldiers surmount the arch; they are 32.8 feet tall (10 m) and weigh 16 tons. The Glory figures and armorial bearings below were sculpted by Stepan Pimenov and Vasily Demuth-Malinovsky.

The arch stands directly opposite the ceremonial entrance to the Winter Palace and appears to join two identical wings, but the large glass dome to its right reveals the building's internal asymmetry. This dome covers the General Staff's famous library and reading room.

The assassination of Moses Uritsky, the Petrograd Cheka (secret police) chief, in August 1918 in the ministries wing (eastern side) led to the square being renamed Uritsky Square until the end of World War II. At the dawn of the 21st century, art replaced political bureaucracy when the Ministries wing became part of the Hermitage (see p. 76).

With your back to the General Staff, direct your eyes to the **Alexander Column** in the middle of the square. Although it is dedicated to "Alexander I from a grateful Russia," the column really bears witness to his brother Nicholas's vision of a Russia defended by militarism and patriotism.

It was an exercise in strength: 704 tons of red granite were hewn from a quarry near Vyborg, transported along the Gulf of Finland, and raised, in less than two hours, by 2,400 soldiers and workers using an ingenious mechanism of ramps and pulleys. Five years later, on August 30, 1834, the finished column was unveiled. The crowning bronze angel (with Alexander's face) bears a 20-foot (6 m) cross and is trampling a snake, signifying good triumphing over evil.

Bas-reliefs, laurel wreaths, and four double-headed eagles festoon the column's pedestal. The reliefs are crowded with the arms of ancient Russian leader-heroes and pairs of allegorical figures—War and Victory, Wisdom and Abundance, Justice and Peace—and the Niemen and Vistula Rivers, which Napoleon had to cross on his disastrous 1812 Russian campaign.

Reaching to a height of 155.8 feet (47.5 m), the monument was made deliberately taller than the Vendôme Column and its figure of Napoleon in Paris; ironically, though, August Montferrand, the column's sculptor, had been born in Paris, trained at its architec-

tural academy, and decorated for his service in Napoleon's Grand Army before arriving in Russia in 1816. His Alexander Column has an incredible sense of proportion and silhouette actually manages to dominate its monumental architectural backdrop. ■

Carlo Rossi's magnificent double triumphal arch looms over visitors as they enter Palace Square from Bolshaya Morskaya Ulitsa.

The Hermitage & Winter Palace

THE WINTER PALACE, AND WITH IT THE HERMITAGE, IS THE ultimate symbol of the might of the Russian Empire. Its sumptuous rooms contain some of the world's greatest art, much of it collected by generations of tsars. The palace, its magnetism undeniable, is the epicenter of St. Petersburg. A visit to its hallowed halls is a must.

Rastrelli's baroque Winter Palace was designed by Empress Elizabeth. It houses part of the world-famous Hermitage art museum.

Historians argue whether the building we see today is the fourth, fifth, or sixth Winter Palace. Regardless, this iteration is the baroque design of the Italian architect Francesco Bartolomeo Rastrelli (1700–1771); it was built between 1754 and 1762 for Empress Elizabeth and served as the main residence of the tsars from the 1760s until the storming by the Bolsheviks in 1917.

The sheer size and scale of this imposing palace boggles the mind. Designed on a square plan around a central courtyard, its exterior facades measure 656 feet (200 m) long. The principal facade faces Palace Square, another side faces the Admiralty, and yet another stretches along the Palace Embankment. It counts more than a thousand rooms.

Two tiers of white columns rise rhythmically against a green backdrop; the lower columns appear to grow from the ground, while the longer upper columns spring from the first floor entablature. Sculptural figures stand atop the building's cornice, rimming the roof of the palace. Two rooftop projections break the symmetrical, rippling mass of the palace. The golden cupola visible from Palace Square belongs to the church within; the octagonal tower seen on the western facade served as the tsars' observation room and telegraph station from the early 19th century on.

Rastrelli never finished the Winter Palace (he was fired by Catherine II). The interior shows only the beginnings of his and Empress Elizabeth's combined dream; the majority of the design owes to makeovers by a line of their followers. Some of the latter came out of necessity (a huge fire in 1837 wrought immense damage), while others were principally stamps of taste by individual members of the imperial family.

VISITING THE PALACE

Begin your visit by walking through the impressive triple arches at the center of the Palace Square facade. Once inside, unless you take a guided tour, you have to make some tough decisions. The more than 365 exhibition rooms of the Winter Palace and adjoining Hermitage buildings create a labyrinth of dazzling architecture and art. To cover each room, you would have to walk 7 miles (11.2 km); to just glance at each of the 2.8 million objects you would need nine years. Whichever route you choose, some doubling back will be necessary. Get your bearings by first touring the Grand Suite, five state rooms that end at the church.

Grand Suite

The Grand Suite, a gilded wonderland of mirrors, organic forms, volutes, vases, and sculptures, is essentially the product of architect Vasily Stasov's classicizing redesign in the late 1830s. The rooms host-

ed gala celebrations, court festivities, martial ceremonies, and the reception of dignitaries.

Approach the Grand Suite via Rastrelli's **main (Jordan or Ambassadorial) staircase,** which stands in the northeast corner of the palace. As you climb the white Carrara marble steps, note the female allegorical statue of Power on the first landing. At the second floor, the wide doors in the center take you into two halls (Rooms 191–192) that hold temporary exhibitions. Instead, take the smaller doors with the rococo decoration to the left. They lead to the **Field Marshals' Hall** (Room 193). The room's austere white militarized decoration is offset by a gilded, painted carriage, which Peter I acquired in Paris in 1717 for his wife's coronation. Several later monarchs also used it for their coronations.

Walk through to **Peter's (or Small Throne) Hall** (Room 194), August Montferrand's memorial to Peter I. Note the PP (Petrus Primus) monogram on the red velvet walls and elsewhere. The wall paintings depict two of Peter's great victories in the 1700–1721 Great Northern War against Sweden; Jacopo Amigoni's 1734 painting of Peter and Minerva hangs behind the throne.

Next enter the **Armorial Hall** (Room 195), which is ringed by golden Corinthian columns and displays European silver. The coat of arms of the Russian provinces fringe the chandeliers.

From the center of the Armorial Hall, turn into the narrow **1812 Gallery** (Room 197). This hall by Carlo Rossi (1826) commemorates the victorious leaders of the campaign against Napoleon. It features 332 portraits of Russian generals (all painted by English artist George

The Hermitage & Winter Palace
www.hermitagemuseum.org

Map p. 52

Dvortsovaya Naberezhnaya 38

311-3420, 110-9625, or 571-3420

Closed Mon.

$$$$

Metro: Nevsky Prospekt or Gostiny Dvor

PALACE EMBANKMENT

1ST FLOOR

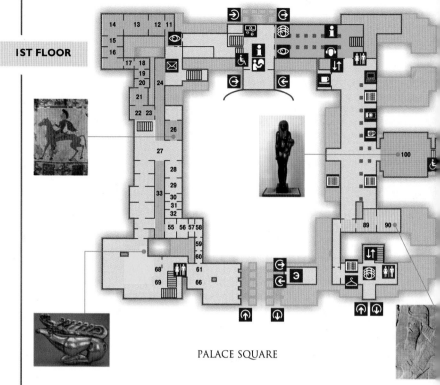

PALACE SQUARE

Dawe, 1819–1828) and images of allies Franz I of Austria (by Peter Krafft) and Friedrich Wilhelm III of Prussia, and Tsar Alexander I (both by Franz Krüger).

The Grand Suite climaxes in the **Great Throne Room,** St. George's Hall, (Room 198), the main ceremonial state room. The marble and bronze of the columns and walls and the rich, twinned decoration of the metal-girdered ceiling and 16-wood parquet floor add majesty. The English-made throne (by George Clausen, 1737) sits under a carved relief of St. George slaying the dragon. It was under the saint's aegis that several tsars proclaimed their reforms and vowed not to bow to their foes.

Before leaving the Grand Suite, walk into the **Great Church**

(Rooms 270–271), whose original baroque luxury was re-created after the 1837 fire. Tsar Nicholas II married Princess Alice of Hesse-Darmstadt (the future Empress Alexandra) here on November 14, 1894. Somewhat surprisingly for a church, the angels are cupidlike (notice the pairs around the cupola) and the gilded decoration is floral and secular, as if making a connection between the power of the monarchy and the sacred mystery of religion.

From the church, several touring options present themselves. In many respects, it makes sense to finish the Winter Palace before moving on to the attached Old and New Hermitage buildings. It's also logical to go through the palace according to the various

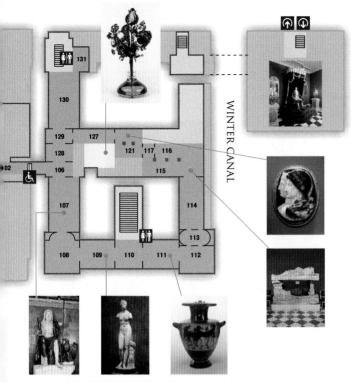

MILLIONNAYA STREET

departments and sections of world art into which the Hermitage museum divides. Bear in mind that you'll have to move between floors a couple of times.

15th- to 18th-c. German art

Continue past the Commandant's Staircase after the church to reach a small suite of rooms (268–263). Previously used by state secretaries, they now house the collection of 15th- to 18th-century German art. Pause before Lucas Cranach the Elder's daringly nude "Venus and Cupid" (1509) to see cupids quite different than those in the church.

French art

The section on French art extends around the German rooms along the Palace Square front and above to the third floor. The second-floor **apartments of Catherine II and her son Paul I** (Rooms 272–281 and 283–297) contain works from the 15th to 18th centuries. The bulk of this collection derives from Catherine's dedication to French culture. Chronologically, it makes sense to walk through the collection from Room 272 to 288 and then back from 297 to 290. Feast your eyes on more cupids (notably by sculptor Étienne-Maurice Falconet), the beautiful ideals of Nicolas Poussin, the caprices of Antoine Watteau and Jean-Honoré Fragonard, the humble piety of Jean-Baptiste Siméon Chardin, Jean-Antoine Houdon's marble sagelike Voltaire, and the fine Louis XIV

PALACE EMBANKM

2ND FLOOR

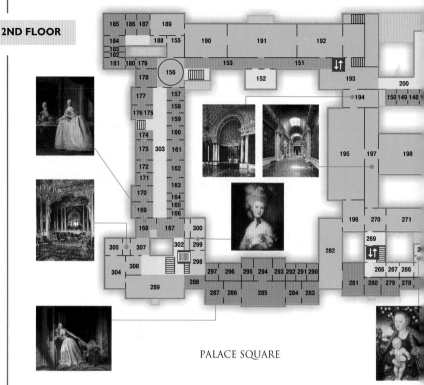

PALACE SQUARE

tapestries, furniture, and porcelain. This celebration of the art of the French ancien régime is interrupted by the fanfare of the double-story **Alexander Hall** (Room 282), whose sky blue fan vaults and bas-reliefs commemorate military success over Napoleon.

Climb the Commandant's Staircase (there is also an elevator nearby) to the third floor and one of the Hermitage's biggest draws: the vast collection of late 18th-century through early 20th-century French art **(Rooms 315–330 and 343–350).** This bounty stems from private collections nationalized after the 1917 Russian Revolution. You might be taken with the cool neoclassic and fiery romantic paintings of the early 19th century, but the strength of the section mostly lies in its Impressionist and post-Impressionist work by artists such as van Gogh, Gauguin, Rodin, Picasso, and Matisse. A moment of reflection on Monet's "Waterloo Bridge," Cézanne's "Mont Sainte-Victoire," or Matisse's "Dance" is always worthwhile.

German & Italian 19th- to 20th-c. art

While on the third floor, take a peek at the rooms that run parallel with the modern French art. These rooms (333–342) are dominated by German and Italian 19th- and 20th-century painting. The Caspar David Friedrichs and early Wassily Kandinskys are particularly outstanding.

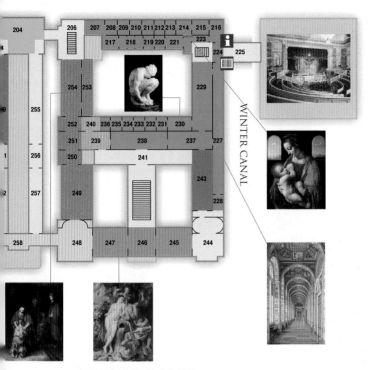

MILLIONNAYA STREET

Eastern art

The third floor former apartments of Nicholas I and Alexander III hold art from the Middle and Far East. The **Middle East Rooms** (381–397) have some excellent Byzantine icons and silverware, Sassanian silver, and Persian rugs. The **Far East section** (Rooms 351–366) has impressive Tibetan Buddhist pieces and Japanese netsuke.

Use the Wooden (October) Staircase to descend to the first floor rooms that hold art from **Central Asia** (Rooms 33–39) and the **Caucasus** (Rooms 55–61). Look for the leaping wildcats in the **Elephant Hall** (Room 36), a room featuring large eighth-century murals from Sogdiana (present-day Uzbekistan).

Archaeology Department

Nearby, in **Rooms 11 to 26,** you can find some intriguing prehistoric artifacts, many for animist rituals, that date from the early Stone Age to late antiquity. Don't miss the Pazyryk burial mound objects, which were unpacked from the Siberian permafrost and date from the fifth to fourth century B.C. They include a carved wooden griffin, the world's oldest pile carpet, and a chariot.

Gold Room

The Gold Room, also on the first floor, is an unsurpassable highlight of the Hermitage. It holds unique and priceless treasures, among them Peter I's collection of ancient Siberian goldware; the astonishingly masterful Scythian,

PALACE EMBANKMENT

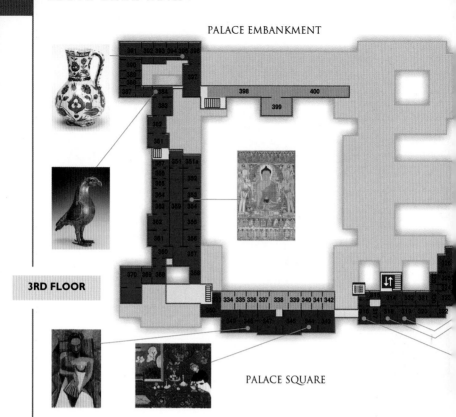

3RD FLOOR

PALACE SQUARE

Sarmatian, and Greek gold adornments from pre-Christian burial mounds north of the Black Sea; and some opulent Indian jewelry. You must join a special guided tour to visit this room.

The best of the rest
On the second floor by the Wooden (October) Staircase, pause in the small **English Collection** (Rooms 298–301) to view Thomas Gainsborough's "Portrait of a Lady in Blue" (late 1770s), mythological subjects by Joshua Reynolds, and the selection of pieces from the exceptional 650-piece Green Frog Dinner Service made for Catherine II by Josiah Wedgwood.

From here, enter the **apartments of Empress Maria Alexandra,** wife of Alexander II (Rooms 289 and 304–308). The first room (289), Alexander Bryullov's **White Hall,** is covered with white plaster ornament interspersed by French romantic landscapes painted by Hubert Robert. The **Golden Drawing Room** (304), inspired by Russo-Byzantine chambers in the Moscow Kremlin, displays carved gems. The remaining four rooms compose an eclectic suite in which the neorococo fancy of the dining room and boudoir stands out.

The **apartments of Tsars Alexander I, Nicholas I, and Nicholas II and rooms of their sons** (Rooms 151–190) surround the **Dark Corridor,** which is lined with French and Flemish tapestries. Devoted to Russian

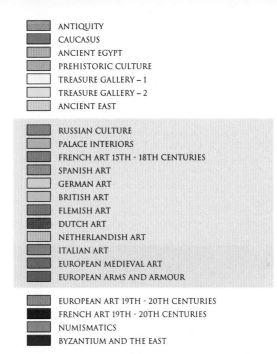

- ANTIQUITY
- CAUCASUS
- ANCIENT EGYPT
- PREHISTORIC CULTURE
- TREASURE GALLERY – 1
- TREASURE GALLERY – 2
- ANCIENT EAST

- RUSSIAN CULTURE
- PALACE INTERIORS
- FRENCH ART 15TH - 18TH CENTURIES
- SPANISH ART
- GERMAN ART
- BRITISH ART
- FLEMISH ART
- DUTCH ART
- NETHERLANDISH ART
- ITALIAN ART
- EUROPEAN MEDIEVAL ART
- EUROPEAN ARMS AND ARMOUR

- EUROPEAN ART 19TH - 20TH CENTURIES
- FRENCH ART 19TH - 20TH CENTURIES
- NUMISMATICS
- BYZANTIUM AND THE EAST

culture, these halls display very few items relating to pre-Petrine Russia, focusing instead on 18th- to early 20th-century developments in decorative art. **Nicholas II's neo-Gothic library** and the tapestry-bedecked small **dining room** (178), as well as the green **Ural Malachite Room** (189), are particularly eye-catching.

Among these apartments is a suite of rooms showing off Russian furniture design. It moves from a refined empire-style drawing room, with Karelian birch furniture, through second rococo, Gothic Revival, and art nouveau to the powerful ruggedness of neo-Russian styles in vogue around 1900. The whole climaxes in the **Concert Hall** (Room 190) with its awesome 1.5-ton silver sepulchre of Alexander Nevsky, made in the St. Petersburg Mint in the mid-18th century for the Alexander Nevsky Monastery. The next room, the **Great (Nicholas) Hall** (Room 191), the largest room (actually the ballroom) in the palace, leads you back to the Jordan Staircase.

SMALL HERMITAGE

The Small Hermitage (by Jean-Baptiste Vallin de la Mothe and Yuri Velten, 1764–1775) adjoins the Winter Palace to the east. Catherine II commissioned the building to house her growing art collection and be a place of retreat and intimate meetings. Built in her preferred neoclassic style, it comprises a northern and southern pavilion, two connecting galleries, and a central hanging garden. Many visitors head for the light-filled **Pavilion Hall** (Room 204, by Andrey Stackenschneider, 1850–58) of the northern pavilion, reached via the second floor of the Winter Palace. This exquisite room combines Moorish, Renaissance, and antique styles. Note the "Roman" mosaic floor; the "Bakhchiserai" Fountains of Tears; and the incredible Peacock Clock (late 18th century), whose moving and

LARGE HERMITAGE

The Large Hermitage adjoins the Small Hermitage; it actually comprises two buildings, the Old and New Hermitages. Yuri Felten built the Old Hermitage block (1771–1787) for Catherine II; Stackenschneider converted it to royal apartments after Nicholas I commissioned Leo von Klenze to build the New block (1842–1851) to serve as Russia's first "public" museum. From Millionaires' Street, you can't miss the ten giant

Rastrelli's ornate Jordan Staircase leads to the Grand Suite of ceremonial halls.

sounding parts resemble a garden. The gallery that runs south from here exhibits **early Flemish paintings** (Rooms 261–262), including the Christ diptych attributed to Robert Campin (1430s) and the snowy Flemish village "Adoration of the Magi" (early 17th century) by Pieter Bruegel the Younger.

granite Atlantes supporting the New Hermitage's portico.

Old Hermitage

Italian Renaissance art dominates the second-floor galleries of the Old Hermitage, which is best accessed via the Council Staircase next to the northern pavilion of the Small Hermitage. The galleries overlooking the Neva include Perugino's sensationally beautiful "St. Sebastian" (ca 1495) and culminate in the grand and extremely refined **Leonardo da Vinci Hall** (Room 214), which holds Russia's only works by Leonardo, the early "Madonna with a Flower" (1478) and the serene "Litta Madonna" (ca 1490). The halls flanking the inner courtyard hold **Venetian art.** The first (Room 217) has a transfixing painting by Giorgione of Judith trampling the head of Holofernes (ca 1505).

The **Raphael Loggias Room** (227) runs into the New Hermitage. This immensely decorative corridor by Quarenghi (1783–1792) re-creates the 13 vaulted bays of Vatican loggias (1513–18) that Raphael painted with 52 biblical scenes and highly symmetrical Roman grotesque ornament. The adjoining **Raphael Hall** (Room 229) contains rare pieces of majolica earthenware and Raphael's "Holy Family" (ca 1506). Next door, the **Cabinet of Frescoes** (Room 230) exhibits the Hermitage's only Michelangelo, the powerful marble "Crouching Boy" (early 1530s). Continue around the inner courtyard of the Old Hermitage to encounter galleries containing works by Bernini and Caravaggio.

New Hermitage

The second-floor galleries and Skylight Halls of the New Hermitage showcase Italian High Renaissance paintings (e.g., Tintoretto and Carracci), 18th-century Italian art (including works by Bellotto and Tiepolo), and art from Spain and the Low Countries.

The **third Skylight Hall** (Room 239) has Velázquez's mustachioed "Count Olivares" (ca 1640), while El Greco's thought-

provoking "Apostles Peter and Paul" (1587–1592) resides next door in Room 240. Close by is one of the Hermitage's megadraws, the unparalleled collection of 20 or so **paintings by Rembrandt** (Room 254). His great "Return of the Prodigal Son" (ca 1668) is bathed in a diffused red spirituality. The **Tent Hall** (Room 249) displays 17th-century Dutch painting; the more enlivened and fleshy **Flemish school of Rubens and Snyders** is located in the halls above the Millionaires' Street entrance (Rooms 245–248).

Before descending the sleek main staircase, look at the weighty armor in the **Knights' Hall** (Room 243) and the graceful, idealized white marble sculptures by Thorvaldsen and Canova in the **Gallery of the History of Ancient Painting** (Room 241). Downstairs, superb collections of ancient **Greek and Roman art** are displayed in a variety of imposing neo-Grecian halls (mostly Rooms 107–130). Equally fine **Egyptian antiquities** are displayed in Room 100. ■

A painting of Tsar Peter with Minerva (by Jacopo Amigoni, 1734) hangs above the throne in Peter's (or Small Throne) Hall.

Golden-winged gryphons hold up the Bank Suspension Bridge over the Griboedov Canal.

A bevy of bridges

If you are going to build a city in a river delta, where the land is divided into a hundred islands formed by 40 rivers and canals, then you're going to need bridges. Peter the shipwright-tsar didn't want them: Bridges impeded the passage of ships. His idea was to travel by boat, have St. Petersburg as a center of shipping, and use the rivers as streets.

Peter only sanctioned the building of bridges to span the boggiest terrain and smallest rivulets. Petersburg's first bridge, the little **John Bridge,** connects his fortress with Petrograd Island. The first bridge across the Neva was a temporary floating pontoon that joined Vasilevsky Island with the Admiralty Side; the temporary pontoon was erected in 1727 after Peter's death.

The bridgebuilding trend continued. Today, Peter's city, against his wishes, counts more than 400 bridges and, in many respects, they define the character of the city, giving it its romantic aura. Graced by some fine metal- and stonework, as well as a wide stock of elegant lampposts, some of the bridges are extraordinarily beautiful. From small to large,

stone to iron, fancy to industrial, chain to rising bascule, the bridges are everywhere, testaments to St. Petersburg's history.

Each time a bridge is built, it becomes a topic of conversation. The Neva's newest bridge, the **Bantovy Suspension Bridge,** climbs over (and also demolished) residential wooden cottages in Novosaratovka. Its ribbon cutting in September 2006 marked the completion of St. Petersburg's 68-billion-ruble ring road. At the same time, the Neva's oldest bridge, the Lieutenant Shmidt Bridge, a great local favorite, was dismantled. In the 1990s, it was rumored that a Japanese company was trying to buy it as a museum piece. It remains to be seen if the original be reassembled in its rightful place

Of the 135 bridges in the center of town, the Griboedov (formerly Catherine) Canal probably has the most picturesque; however, the Fontanka, Moika, Neva, and Winter Canal (see p. 76) all have some special ones, too. On the Griboedov, look for the **Bank** and **Lion Suspension Bridges** (1826), which appear to be held up by the teeth of, respectively, four winged gryphons and lions.

The Fontanka had seven drawbridges erected over its waters in the 1780s; only two, both three-arched and with distinctive granite towers, survive: the **Staro-Kalinkin** and the **Lomonosov.** Two other distinctive bridges along the Fontanka are the **Egyptian Bridge** (1826), guarded by four iron sphinxes, and the much admired **Anichkov Bridge** (1839–1841) with its virile, nude horse tamers.

In the early 19th century, the Moika was spanned by St. Petersburg's first iron bridges, designed by the Scotsman William Hastie. The first was the **Green (or Police) Bridge** (1806), which forms part of Nevsky Prospekt, but perhaps the **Singers' Bridge** (1840) or the **First Engineer Bridge** (1829) are the most attractive.

The Neva, the all-important shipping conduit, received its first permanent bridge in 1850. Eleven now span its banks; most are drawbridges that rise, after midnight usually, to allow shipping to pass. Their open-jaw silhouettes are a St. Petersburg highlight, especially during the White Nights. Note in particular the French-designed **Trinity Bridge** (1897–1903), adorned with highly decorative triple lamp-posts and rostral obelisks. Bridges in the "Venice of the North" are works of art. ■

The Lomonosov drawbridge over the Fontanka River (upper); the Post Bridge over the Moika (middle); the Egyptian Bridge over the Fontanka (bottom)

The Winter Canal and its bridges are one of St. Petersburg's most romantic places.

More places to visit around South Bank Neva

HERMITAGE EXHIBITIONS IN THE GENERAL STAFF BUILDING

In the 1990s, the ministries wing of the General Staff building on Palace Square became part of the Hermitage. The second-floor rooms that once comprised the official residence of the minister of foreign affairs (known as the Nesselrode apartments after the first minister to occupy them) now hold an exhibition called "The Realms of the Eagle." It depicts coolly severe art in the empire style. Elsewhere you'll find the more contemplative idyllic decorative schemes of the French post-Impressionists Pierre Bonnard and Maurice Denis, designed circa 1908 to 1911 for the mansion of the Moscow textile industrialist Ivan Morozov. For those seeking a greater burst of energy, the superb display of modernist applied art should not be missed.
www.heritagemuseum.org ✉ Palace Square 6 💲 $$ ☎ 311-3420, 110-9625, or 571-3420

WINTER CANAL, HERMITAGE THEATER, & PETER I'S WINTER PALACE

The short Winter Canal runs between the Moika and Neva Rivers just east of the Hermitage. Crossed by the Winter and Hermitage Bridges, it is one of the most poetical and Venetianlike corners of the city. St. Petersburgers and visitors alike love the view along the canal from Millionaires' Street toward the two arches of the old granite Hermitage Bridge and the walkway above.

The walkway was built in 1783 to join the Hermitage to the new Hermitage Theater. Catherine II commissioned the Italian architect Giacomo Quarenghi to design the theater in the Palladian style. Concertgoers get the rare chance to see an original, and very beautiful, 18th-century auditorium, replete with statues of Apollo and the nine muses. The theater played a key part in Catherine's court life.

Underneath the Hermitage Theater, on the site of Peter I's Winter Palace (late 1710s), the private rooms in which the founder of St. Petersburg spent his last years have been re-created *(tickets available from Hermitage ticket office)*. Here you can see Bartolomeo Carlo Rastrelli's stiff wax figure of Peter (1725), the tsar's carriage, and reproductions of his dining room and turnery.
www.heritagemuseum.org **Hermitage Theater** ✉ Dvortsovaya Naberezhnaya 32 ☎ 311-3420, 110-9625, or 571-3420 ∎

St. Petersburg's main avenue, Nevsky Prospekt, is also the city's main stage. The streets around its first stretch teem with life. The 19th and 21st centuries meet more vividly here than anywhere else in St. Petersburg.

Neva to Griboedov Canal

High drama on the Mariinsky stage

Cruise ships dock on the Neva's English Embankment, in sight of St. Isaac's Cathedral.

Neva to Griboedov Canal

THE CENTER OF ST. PETERSBURG HINGES AROUND THE ADMIRALTY. THE
city's two most important squares flank it and, seemingly from its glinting needle
spire, the city's key streets radiate out like sun rays. By the time these traffic-
filled streets reach the Griboedov Canal, they have crossed two islands,
Admiralty and Kazan, and have passed some of St. Petersburg's
most symbolic monuments and historic institutions.

Since Peter's new Russian Empire was to be
a maritime one, the capital's focus on shipbuilding and the navy makes sense. The
city's early nautical emphasis can still be felt
today through the buildings of the Admiralty, which began as a fortified shipyard in
1704; St. Nicholas's Church, named for the
patron saint of sailors; the ships moored on
the English Embankment; and the names of
some streets.

Besides its maritime connections, this
area of the city contains some of Petersburg's most emblematic sights. To the west
of the Admiralty stands the Bronze Horseman, Russia's most famous monument and
the image that encapsulates the nature of
the city as well as the Romanov empire.
Behind the monument rises the center's
tallest building, St. Isaac's Cathedral, its vast
golden dome dominating the surroundings.

The area around St. Isaac's is marked by
prime housing and, to the east, what
became the financial core of the city in the

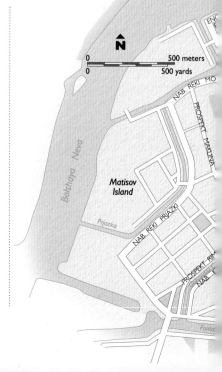

late 19th century. Before money took center stage here, the Mariinsky Theater was built right on the western edge of Kazan Island. Behind this area of high society, across Kryukov Canal on Kolomna Island, is a much poorer, but lively quarter.

One of the best ways to explore this part of town is by boat. Two worthwhile stops along the banks of the Moika are the Yusupov and Stroganov Palaces. The Yusupov is a gem, offering plenty of attractions within; Rasputin was murdered, or more correctly, his murder began, here. The beautiful Stroganov stands at the intersection of the Moika and Nevsky Prospekt, the

most glamorous avenue in St. Petersburg, with fashionable stores, clubs, restaurants, and hotels. On this avenue, especially between the Moika and Griboedov Canal (as well as a little beyond), is where one needs to go to see and be seen. Set back from the avenue, the curving colonnades of the Kazan Cathedral gather in passersby to witness resurgent Orthodoxy and view a memorial to the Russian defeat of Napoleon. ∎

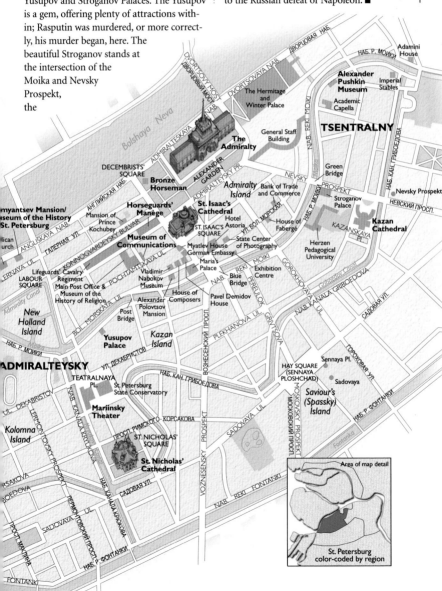

The Admiralty & Alexander Garden

The Admiralty & Alexander Garden

 Map p. 79

Bus: 7 & 10; Trolleybus: 1, 7, & 10; Metro: Nevsky Prospekt

"ALL ROADS LEAD TO THE ADMIRALTY" … OR AT LEAST SO it may seem. Three of St. Petersburg's great axial avenues, including Nevsky Prospekt, radiate in bold straight lines from its central tower with gilded spire, it borders Palace and Decembrists' Square, and, it holds a landmark position on the Neva. One of Tsar Peter's primary considerations in founding the city was Russian access to the sea, and via that to the rest of the world; for Peter the creation of the Admiralty was not only a priority but the key to Russia's future. In many respects it fulfilled this role, if not always in the ways anticipated or desired. With a perimeter of 3,937 feet (1,200 m), it certainly made a brave attempt at announcing Russia's naval prowess to the world.

Peter established the Admiralty as a fortified shipyard for his burgeoning Russian navy in 1704. The first ship for the new fleet, the *Poltava,* rolled down its slipways in 1712; the last, the 256th, left drydock in 1844. The Admiralty's original wooden buildings were rebuilt in stone in the 1730s and then the whole complex was reconstructed between 1806 and 1823 under the aegis of Adreyan Zakharov after new docks were built on islands farther west.

Zakharov's symmetrical plan centered around the main gate and stretched out over 1,312 feet (400 m) to create an essential, link between the city's main squares. Zakharov's genius was to beautify this utilitarian edifice through the use of simple geometric volumes (now colored yellow), eye-catching white Doric and Ionic colonnades, large porticoes and arches, and a gilded cupola with a spire that rises to 230 feet (70 m). The spire's weather vane of a little ship has become the symbol of St. Petersburg. The added sculptural decoration, in particular the life-size nymphs carrying globes and the relief depicting Peter's founding of the fleet in Russia that frame the central arch, make this

building one of the world's most attractive naval institutes. Much attention was lavished on its restoration after it was hit by five bombs in World War II.

ALEXANDER GARDEN

The awesome impression that the Admiralty makes is enhanced by the wooded Alexander Garden, which borders two sides of the complex. German botanist Eduard Regel designed the garden in the early 1870s. The garden is a favorite for visitors and Petersburgers alike.

Broad paths wend through a variety of trees in front of the Admiralty, eventually converging on one of St. Petersburg's most beautiful fountains. Visitors young and old love to stop here for a few moments to enjoy an ice cream and admire the surrounding busts of Gogol, Lermontov, and Glinka. Other interesting monuments in the garden include a statue of the famed 19th-century explorer of Central Asia, Nikolai Przhevalsky, with his saddled camel, and a Farnese Hercules. Representation of connections between the cultures of Russia and antiquity is never far away in this part of town. ∎

Opposite: The city radiates out from the landmark needle spire of the Admiralty.

Bronze Horseman & Decembrists' Square

NO SYMBOL IN ST. PETERSBURG IS MORE MESMERIZING AND provocative than the Monument to Peter the Great, which stands where the Alexander Garden meets Decembrists' Square. Thanks to Pushkin's 1833 poetic interpretation of the haughty majesty, indomitable will, tyrannical rule, and visionary concern of the founder of St. Petersburg, the monument is better known as the Bronze Horseman. The rearing horse and rider have become *the* image of St. Petersburg, as well as of imperial Russia. Tourists and locals are drawn to the horseman. And young newlyweds flock to it to have their photographs taken, as if their vows include lifelong compliance and willing subjection to the monument's force.

The Bronze Horseman was Russia's first monument that embodied the idea of enlightened absolutism. It encapsulates the notion of an all-powerful monarchy with a civilizing mission. That this accorded with the approach to autocratic government of the monument's patron, Catherine the Great, makes the Bronze Horseman as much a memorial to her as to the unbelievably illustri-ous predecessor she was trying to emulate. The linkage is made tangible in the dedication, in Russian and Latin, on either side of the monument: "To Peter the First from Catherine the Second."

You might be impressed, or perhaps even alarmed, by different elements of this apparently very simple monument. It is an expression of domineering command that you have to look up to. Its silhouette commands a lot of space, making the city's architecture appear just a backdrop and the broad Neva River in front of it nothing more than a small hurdle of nature to be leapt over, controlled (ironically there was a bridge here but it burned down in 1916 and was not replaced). Remarkable for an equestrian monument, the magnificent horse has just its two rear feat on the ground (trampling the snake of Treason). In addition, the horse stands not on a right-angled pedestal but on a gigantic 1,600-ton granite boulder with which it forms a pyramid. Known as the **Thunder Rock,** this boulder was discovered in 1768 near the village of Lakhta on the northern coast of Gulf of Finland; it was identified as the boulder upon which Peter reputedly stood and surveyed the scene of his future city. It has been carved and shaped to look like a dramatic crag.

The timeless authority and forward movement of the Bronze Horseman was created by the French sculptor Étienne-Maurice Falconet, recommended to Catherine by her mentor Denis Diderot. It took Falconet 16 years to complete the monument; it was unveiled in 1782. One of its most dramatic features is the laurel-wreathed head of Peter, the work of Falconet's assistant, the outstanding Marie-Anne Collot, who in 1767, at the age of 19, had become the first woman and youngest ever member of the Russian Academy of Arts. She modeled Peter's head on a mask that was made during his lifetime, but she added a furrowed brow, bulging eyes and cheeks, pursed lips with German moustache, and a long, broad, exposed neck. The effect, reinforced by the glaring, slightly downward distant stare is dauntingly powerful.

DECEMBRISTS' SQUARE

Decembrists' Square was previously known as Senate Square for the imposing **Senate and Holy Synod building** on its western side. This building bears a striking similarity to the General Staff and Ministries of Finance and Foreign Affairs building (see p. 62) on Palace Square: They are both twin-function buildings of comparable proportions and definition, with a central arch surrounded by Corinthian columns and allegorical sculptures. In fact, Carlo Rossi began this building (1829–1836) after he finished the General Staff building.

The Senate housed Russia's highest legislative body (established in 1711), while the Holy Synod was essentially Peter's Ministry of Religion, created to oversee his reforms of the Orthodox Church in 1723. The tragic poet Anna Akhmatova captured the building's arch as a place of rendezvous for pre-1917 revolutionary lovers: "Under the Galernaya Arch,/Our shadows remain forever."

The square was not always so conducive to romance: On December 14, 1825, the uprising against the accession of Tsar Nicholas I, led by reform-minded officers and nobles demanding a constitutional monarchy and an end to serfdom, was crushed here. Official figures listed 80 deaths that day; the arrested faced penalties ranging from hanging near the Peter and Paul Fortress to exile in Siberia. The event was a defining moment for Nicholas's subsequent militaristic rule. The square was eventually given its present name to honor these Decembrists, as the uprisers came to be called. ■

St. Isaac's Cathedral

WHEN YOU ENTER ST. ISAAC'S CATHEDRAL, YOU CAN GET AN uncanny feeling for why the 1917 Revolution happened. It has to do with scale, show, and effort. Regardless of whether one thinks its proportions quite work, the cathedral still ranks as one of the world's top architectural splendors of the 19th century.

With the Orthodox feast day of St. Isaac of Dalmatia coinciding with the day of his own birth (May 30th), Tsar Peter made it a priority to have a church dedicated to the saint at the center of his new city. The first wooden one was erected not far from the site of the present (fourth) one as early as 1707. The cathedral we see today took shape after the Napoleonic Wars. Entrusted to August Montferrand, it took 40 years to complete (1818–1858).

The 333-foot-tall (101.5 m) gilded dome of St. Isaac's rises high above the city skyline and can be seen from miles away. Capable of holding 12,000 worshipers, this colossal church is laid out on a symmetrical Greek cross plan; it has four corner bell towers, porti-

himself, clutching a small model of the cathedral.

More than 400,000 workers toiled on the cathedral. Fatalities ran into the hundreds. The total cost was 23,256,000 rubles, making the cathedral six times more costly than the Winter Palace. It is a wonderland of semiprecious stones from across Europe and Siberia (including 14 types of marble, malachite, jasper, prophyry, and lazurite), metals, and decorative arts.

The ground level murals have been labeled in English; the reliefs on the three great oak-and-bronze doors have not been labeled. It helps to know that the doors on the south feature ancient Rus; the north, the life of St. Isaac; and the west, Apostles Peter and Paul. The mosaic icons and murals were installed between 1851 and 1914 when humidity caused some of the original painted works to decay. In the chancel, take note of a rare occurrence of stained glass in an Orthodox church; it depicts Christ Resurrected.

Finally, crane your neck back and stare up at the dome; 262.5 feet (80 m) away hangs what appears to be a **flying white dove.** With a wingspan of 5.4 feet (1.65 m) and made of silvered copper, the bird, lit by the natural light of the dome's lantern, represents the Holy Spirit and acts as the focal point of the cathedral's largest mural, Karl Bryullov's 8,611-square-foot (800 sq m) **"The Virgin in Majesty,"** which shows the Virgin Mary and a circle of saints against a backdrop of the heavens.

Before leaving St. Isaac's, climb up to the **colonnade** (*fee*) that runs around the drum of the dome. It gives unrivaled panoramic views of the city. ■

St. Isaac's Cathedral

www.cathedral.ru

- Map p. 79
- St. Isaac's Ploshchad 4
- 315-9732
- Closed Wed.
- Cathedral $$$; colonnade $$
- Bus: 3, 22, & 27; Trolleybus: 5 & 22; Metro: Nevsky Prospekt

coes adorned with massive bronze reliefs, sculptures of the Apostles and Evangelists, and 48 massive, red granite Corinthian columns.

Before you enter the church, pause to look up at the sculptures in the pediments. The scene over the formal **west entrance** (by Ivan Vitali) is particularly interesting: It purportedly shows St. Isaac blessing the Byzantine emperor Theodosius and his wife Flaccilla, but Theodosius has the face of Tsar Alexander I and Flaccilla that of the tsar's escort, Empress Elizabeth; other recognizable faces include the St. Isaac's construction commission chairman (Prince Peter Volkonsky), the president of the Imperial Academy of Arts (by Alexey Olenin), and Montferrand

St. Isaac's Square

St. Isaac's Square

Map p. 79

Bus: 3, 22, & 27;
Trolleybus: 5 & 22;
Metro: Nevsky
Prospekt

THE UNASSUMING ST. ISAAC'S SQUARE FRONTS ST. ISAAC'S Cathedral (see pp. 84–85). It is perhaps best appreciated for its unobstructed view of the cathedral, but it does have some other interesting features. The square offers an eclectic mix of buildings, an open grassy area, a commemorative statue, and well-organized traffic.

At the center of the square is Baron Peter Clodt von Jurgensburg's **statue of Nicholas I** (1856–59). Nicholas was largely responsible for the square's creation because he channeled state funds into St. Isaac's Cathedral and Maria's Palace, the buildings that close the square to the north and south. Clodt's statue reveals by default the brilliance of Étienne-Maurice Falconet's Bronze Horseman (see pp. 82–83).

Nicholas, who spent his life trying to imitate Peter, also sits on a rearing horse, but his monument has none of the intrinsic expressive power of Peter's. He appears arrogant and stiff, and is cluttered by props, armory, allegorical figures, and scenes narrating his achievements. The last compose the suppression of the 1825 Decembrists' revolt, the 1831 uprising, the 1832 establishment of a Code of Laws, and the 1851 construction of a bridge on the St. Petersburg–Moscow railroad.

To either side of the statue, the buildings fronting the square appear rather severe in comparison to the excesses of St. Isaac's, but looks can be deceiving. The boxish **Maria's Palace,** created by Andrey Stackenschneider in the early 1840s for Nicholas's eldest daughter, Maria, was a glittering showpiece of taste and quality. It has served as the State and City Council since 1884. Group visits are occasionally possible but need to be arranged in advance.

Until the 1861 Emancipation Act, the land in front of Maria's Palace (much of which is actually the Blue Bridge over the Moika) served as a marketplace for the sale of serfs. Walk clockwise from here to the square's secondmost imposing building: the former **German Embassy** (No. 11), built by the outstanding German modernist architect Peter Behrens (1911–13) in a stripped classicist style that almost anticipates post–World War II brutalism. The vast brown granite blocks and severe angles apparently made this the perfect building for Intourist, the state tourist agency during the years of the Soviet Union. Now back in German hands as the Dresdner Bank, the building only lacks its gigantic roof statues of two naked Teutons leading massive horses by bridle (by Eberhard Encke); they were felled and thrown into the Moika by a mob fueled with anti-German sentiment at the outbreak of World War I.

Next door, the **Myatlev House** (No. 9) is the square's oldest building, having been built in the 1760s as the Naryshkin Palace. In the 1770s, Denis Diderot stayed here during his visit to the city at the invitation of Catherine II. The poet Ivan Myatlev bought the house in the early 19th century; it soon became a leading literary salon where many Romantics gathered. The Myatlev stares across the grassy expanse of the square to the **Hotel Astoria.** ∎

Opposite: The fussy, vainglorious monument to Nicholas I in St. Isaac's Square is a fitting memorial to the tsar known as the "Gendarme of Europe."

Horseguards' Manège

🅰 Map p. 79

✉ St. Isaac's Plosh-
chad 1

☎ 314-8859

🕐 Closed Thurs.

🚌 Bus: 3, 22, & 27;
Trolleybus: 5 & 22;
Metro: Nevsky
Prospekt

Horseguards' Manège & Boulevard

TRY TO IMAGINE THE HORSEGUARDS' MANÈGE ("RIDING school") before it was dwarfed by St. Isaac's and without the trees on Alexander Garden. Then its concept becomes clear: It was a key architectural element in the central spaces of St. Petersburg. The adjacent boulevard named for the riding school promises a pleasant stroll outside the hours of rush-hour traffic.

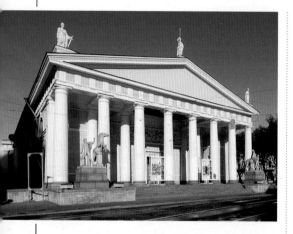

The temple-like Horseguards' Manège is a now a temple to art, serving as an exhibition hall.

Giacomo Quarenghi's Manège (completed in 1807) is essentially a large, minimally decorated, and well-lit rectangular hall with a grand Doric-columned and pedimented portico. Reinforcing the temple-like tone are the frieze over the door, which depicts a frenzied horse-taming competition, and the **sculptures of the Dioscurs** (twin sons) of Zeus, also controlling horses. Italian sculptor Paolo Triscorni modeled the latter on those in front of the Quirinale Palace in Rome.

In the 1840s they were removed to the Horseguards' Barracks when residents of the newly completed Holy Synod next door objected to the statues' nakedness; they were returned in 1954 when the building was reincarnated as the **Central**

Exhibition Hall. The exhibits held here during the late 1970s and '80s were among the city's most daring and relatively independent; today's exhibits can be of mixed quality.

HORSEGUARDS' BOULEVARD

The tree-lined Horseguards' Boulevard runs behind the manège. The boulevard was laid out in the mid-1840s over the canal that had previously run from the Admiralty (see pp. 80–81) to New Holland Island (see opposite). At the boulevard's eastern end, note the **twin granite columns** topped by bronze Victory figures. Designed by Christian Rauch, these were a present from Prussia in 1845 in return for two sculptures of horse tamers by Baron Peter Clodt von Jurgensburg.

The southern side of the boulevard is dominated by the barracks and stables of the **Lifeguards' Cavalry Regiment** (No. 4) while the northern side boasts Harald Bosse's beautiful Renaissance-style **mansion for Prince Kochubey** (No. 7, 1853–57). It was actually rebuilt in its present form, with some superbly decorated interiors, and with the busts of turban-wearing Africans on the garden railings, for a Greek alcohol merchant called

Rodokanakis. A rather pricey restaurant has opened on the ground floor, allowing access to view at least some of the mansion's interior.

At the Horseguards' Boulevard's west end, the last building on the northern side was the palace of Grand Duke Nicholas, son of Nicholas I and commander of the Russian forces that liberated Bulgaria from the Ottomans in 1877 to 1878. Andrey Stackenshneider's Italianate design was completed in 1861. Since 1918 the palace has been the **Trades Union's Palace of Labor.** The beautiful double staircase is worth a glimpse, as is the ballroom, where tourists are entertained "Russian style" in the evening.

The nearby undistinguished **Labor Square** (ploshchad Truda) marks the boulevard's end. It was known as Annunciation Square until the Horseguards' regiment's church in its center was pulled down by the Stalin regime in 1929. From here, you can look across to buildings on New Holland Island.

During the summer, the boulevard offers pleasant areas to sit and enjoy a drink or ice cream; in winter, its icy path is a favorite for fathers pulling children on sleds. ■

New Holland Island

New Holland Island

Ⓜ Map p. 79

The small, triangular-shaped New Holland Island is bordered by the Moika River and the Admiralty and Kryukov Canals. The timberyards here are reminders of Tsar Peter's shipbuilding program begun in the early 1700s.

The navy still has a role in the management of the island so access is extremely limited, but you can walk alongside the canals and look across to the complex of buildings. Probably the best way to appreciate it is from the water on a sightseeing cruise.

The timber houses were initially wooden themselves, but were rebuilt in redbrick (hence the island name's Dutch association) between 1765 and 1789 to designs by Jean-Baptiste Vallin de la Mothe and Savva Chevakinsky. The highlight of the island is the tall **arch** with Tuscan columns that faces the Moika, under which timber-laden barges used to pass. Now,

despite being overgrown and crumbling in its rather desolate surroundings, this mighty arch is one of St. Petersburg's most romantic sights.

The New Holland site is set to undergo reconstruction in the near future; British architect Sir Norman Foster won the international competition to turn it into a hospitality complex. ■

The surprisingly picturesque ruins of a once vibrant 18th-century redbrick shipping yard occupy New Holland Island.

English Embankment

THESE DAYS, THE LARGE PALACES THAT LINE THE ENGLISH
Embankment compete in height with gleaming white international
cruise ships as the central part of the quay has become the passenger
terminal for travelers who choose to visit St. Petersburg by ship.

**Rumyantsev
Mansion/State
Museum of the
History of St.
Petersburg**
www.spbmuseum.ru
- Map pp. 78–79
- Angliskaya
  Naberezhnaya 44
- 571-7544
- Closed Wed.
- $

Most people stroll the English
Embankment to look across the
Neva River at the ensemble of
buildings and ships on Vasilevsky
Island. But the buildings along
here reveal how the English and
Scottish merchants, industrialists,
medics, architects, engineers,
tradesmen, innkeepers, and nan-
nies mixed in this area two centuries ago.

At the western end, where the
embankment meets the New Admiralty Canal, the relatively modest **No. 74** was owned by James
Wylie, president of the medical
academy and physician to Tsars
Paul and Alexander I. **No. 56**

appears a typical classicist mansion, but it is in fact the 1815
Anglican church built by Giacomo
Quarenghi; it has a very ornate
hall of worship (including some
fine late 19th-century stained
glass) on the second floor. A
plaque on **No. 52** reveals that
future chancellor of the German
First Reich, Otto von Bismarck,
lived here when he was the Prussian envoy to Russia (1859–1862).

The **Rumyantsev Mansion**
(No. 44) is now a branch of the
Museum of the History of St.
Petersburg. The magnificent 12-
columned portico was added by
the great collector and Russian

foreign minister Count Nikolai Rumyantsev 1824–26 (by Vasily Glinka), after he purchased the house from its previous owners. Rumyantsev had planned a public museum to display his collections of ancient manuscripts, rare books, medals, coins, and applied art, but all was controversially transferred to culture-hungry Moscow in 1861. Today, three displays of art, posters, photographs, objects, and room mock-ups reveal many interesting aspects of life and culture in

tend to be closed to the public. Note the impressive portico designed by Quarenghi at the **Collegium of Foreign Affairs** *(No. 32)* and the **von Derviz House** *(No. 28)*, designed by Alexander Krasovsky in the late 1890s. The latter, in 1961, became the USSR's first Palace of Weddings, where newlyweds tied the knot. The ornate Gothic Revival hall is quite fine. The impressario of the Ballets Russes, Sergey Diaghilev, lived in **No. 22** before World War I; composer

Leningrad during the 1920s, 1930s, and World War II. The museum also shows well-curated temporary exhibits of historic and contemporary art.

The small **granite monument** (1939) outside the museum commemorates where the cruiser *Aurora* (see p. 181) lay at anchor and famously fired its blanks for the storming of the Winter Palace on November 7, 1917.

The mansions between Labor and Decembrists' Squares used to belong to members of the nobility and royal family; they

Dmitry Shostakovich was often found at **No. 20**. The externally severe **Vorontsova-Dashkova House** *(No. 10)* reputedly served as the lavish setting for the first ball of Natasha Rostova in Leo Tolstoy's *War and Peace*. The last house of note is Countess Laval's Mansion (1809) at No. 4. The countess held popular literary salons in the 1820s: Pushkin read his *Boris Godunov* here in 1828. The mansion is now, with the neighboring Senate and Holy Synod building, the Russian National Historical Archive. ∎

People love to stroll and sit along the Neva's embankments, watching the activity of the river.

Ballet & opera

St. Petersburg is renowned worldwide for its ballet and opera, for that produced today by the Mariinsky Theater, and for the performances of the Ballets Russes a century ago. With the help of the city's Ballet School (founded 1738) and Rimsky-Korsakov St. Petersburg State Conservatory (founded 1862), these companies have forged the reputations of St. Petersburg's great dancing and singing stars.

It all came together toward the end of the 19th century. Gifted Petersburg choreographers blended the refined precision of the French style and the virtuosity of the Italian manner in such a manner that a harmonically blended Russian style of dancing emerged. Marius Petipa (1818–1910), who arrived from the Parisian Opera in 1847, led the way. By 1869 he was chief ballet-master of the new Mariinsky. Petipa, in many respects, was the key to the success of composer Peter Tchaikovsky (1840–1893), choreographing his *Nutcracker* and *Swan Lake* with a balance of orchestrated corps de ballet and miniature divertissements that ever since have remained world favorites.

The Mariinsky had opened in 1860 with a premiere of Mikhail Glinka's opera *A Life for the Tsar*. The popularity of the medieval national theme inspired a new generation of Petersburg composers; pre-Petrine subjects were exotic: Modest Mussorgsky (1839–1881) penned *Boris Godunov;* Alexander Borodin (1833–1887), *Prince Igor;* and Nikolay Rimsky-Korsakov (1844–1908),

Ivan the Terrible (Ivan Grozny) ballet being performed at the Mariinsky Theater

The Snow Maiden. The success of the operas can be largely credited to the lovely bass voice of the singer Feodor Chaliapin (1873–1938), renowned for his Boris Godunov.

National themes of a different sort infused the work of the pre–1917 Revolution musicians. St. Petersburg started producing stage legends, with choreographer Mikhail Fokine (1880–1942), who took up where Petipa left off, and composer Igor Stravinsky (1882–1971) leading the way. The results were explosive when they combined their talents with those of the impressario Sergey Diaghilev (1872–1929), painters from the World of Art group, and dancers such as Anna Pavlova (1881–1931), Vaslav Nijinsky (1889–1950), and Ida Rubinstein (1880–1960). Taken to Paris by Diaghilev, Rubinstein's nude and sexualized performance of the lead in Mussorgsky's *Scheherazade* in Paris 1910 was one thing, Nijinsky's anticanon primitivized lead of Stravinsky's paganistic *Rite of Spring* another. Dance, music, and stage and costume design were free and unfettered during this era.

Then the Soviet era began. The artistic virtuosos were written out of the history books; stage repertoires and routines reverted to the classical tradition. Stalin's favorite ballet was Boris Asafyev's *Bakhchiserai Fountain,* which premiered in the State Academic Theater of Opera and Ballet (the Mariinsky's new name) in September 1934. In it, a Georgian beauty stabs and kills a Western princess, a rival in the harem, and is then herself hurled from a cliff by the Tatar khan. Within months of the ballet's premiere, Stalin had murdered the Leningrad Communist Party boss Sergey Kirov, changed the name of theater to Kirov, and started the mass purges.

In 1992 the Kirov became again the Mariinsky. It has experienced a meteoric revival under the leadership of its new conductor and artistic director, Valery Gergiev (b. 1953). Its success has reinvigorated the city's smaller troupes, notably the Boris Eifman Ballet Company and the Mussorgsky Theater. Try to catch the performances of prima ballerinas Ulyana Lopatkina (b. 1973), Farukh Ruzimatov (b. 1963), and the young Anastasia Lomachenkova. ■

St. Petersburg theater has long been renowned for the lavishness of its stage productions, with their mix of Oriental exoticism and ancient Russian spectacle.

Mariinsky Theater

OUT OF THE ASHES OF A CIRCUS THAT BURNED DOWN IN 1859 grew the Mariinka, as it is known locally, or the Kirov, as it has been known internationally. Officially, it is the State Academic Mariinsky Theater. The theater owes its premier position among world opera and ballet companies to the single-minded vision, energy, virtuosity, and passion of Valery Gergiev (b. 1953), its director and chief conductor since the late 1980s. Performances are sellouts, tickets pricey.

A statue of Nikolay Rimsky-Korsakov stands in the square opposite the Mariinsky.

Mariinsky Theater
www.mariinsky.ru
- Map p. 79
- Teatralnaya Ploshchad 1
- 326-4141 or 714-1211
- Bus: 3, 22, & 27; Minibus: 312

The exterior of the Mariinsky doesn't quite do justice to the spectacles within. Designed by Albert Cavos (son of Italian composer Catarino Cavos), the theater opened in 1860 and was named after Empress Maria, the escort of Tsar Alexander II. Its imposing, eclectic turquoise-and-white main facade and silhouette were largely acquired through alterations made in the 1890s.

The interior of the theater, by contrast, is both elegant and sumptuous. The sparkling, reflective **foyer,** with its bas-reliefs of Russian composers, leads to the Mariinsky's jewel: the five-tiered, horseshoe-shaped, gilded, blue-upholstered **auditorium** capable of seating an audience of 2,000. A huge sparkling cone-like crystal chandelier casts light onto the ceiling's painted circles of golden arabesques and 22 dancing nymphs and cherubs (by Enrico Franchioli). The three-tiered **royal box** commands pride of place directly opposite the stage. Note the incredible petticoats painted on the curtain by the Ballets Russes designer Alexander Golovin in 1914.

The ambitions and drive of the Mariinsky are transforming the surrounding **Little Kolomna neighborhood.** Behind the Mariinsky, on the other side of the Kryukov Canal, a second Mariinsky theater complex is rising. This new theater, whose glass-roofed design by Frenchman Dominique Perreau has engendered some controversy, promises to alleviate some of the cramped backstage space issues of the older theater, as well as provide another stage venue.

The large **St. Petersburg State Conservatory,** designed by Vladimir Nikolya and built in the 1890s, faces the Mariinsky. Founded as the Russian Music Society by the pianist Anton Rubinstein in 1862, the conservatory has produced many of Russia's finest musicians, and is now named for Nikolay Rimsky-Korsakov (1844–1908). A statue of the composer stands in the square, along with one to another famed Russian composer, Mikhail Glinka (1804–1857). ■

St. Nicholas's Cathedral

IN THE MID-1750s, THE ADMIRALTY REQUESTED THAT A church be erected in the neighborhood where sailors and officers of the Baltic fleet lived. The result is the beautiful and gracious St. Nicholas's Cathedral, named for the patron saint of sailors and known as the Sailors' Church: A baroque blue-and-white church with five gilded cupolas. It is one of the few churches in St. Petersburg that remained open and kept its interior intact during the Soviet period. The bell tower for the church stands some 100 yards (91 m) away by the Kryukov Canal. The tower's four tiers taper elegantly into a golden spire, reaching for the sky. The waterside setting of the tower is particularly picturesque.

St. Nicholas's Cathedral

🏛 Map p. 79

✉ Nikolskaya ploshchad 1/3

☎ 714-7085

🚇 Metro: Sennaya; Tram: 3 & 14

For all its lively baroque decoration, certain features of the church's centralized cross plan identify it with earlier Russian traditions, not least the use of three columns at the corners. Also, there are two churches in one here. The **ground level church,** with its low, heavily vaulted ceilings, great pillars, mass of icons, semidarkness, chandeliers, burning candles, and buzz of activity, was originally the winter (or heated) church; up the discreet stairs to the left and right of the entrance is the much more spacious and lighter **summer (Epiphany) church.** The latter's resonant blue-and-gold iconostasis with its columns entwined by garlands is superb, but the chamber is only open for services on Sundays and special feast days. Visitors are welcome at this time, but they need to be respectful of worshipers.

Plaques on the church walls commemorate sailors who have lost their lives at sea. Recently the names of those who died in the *Kursk* nuclear submarine tragedy in August 2000 have been added. Composer Peter Tchaikovsky donated the icon of St. Peter in the upper church and the famed author Anna Akhmatova, whose burial service took place here in

1966, prayed before the touching icon of St. Anne.

The cathedral is a little out of the way for most visitors, but this gem in the middle of the quiet, tree-lined gardens of St. Nicholas's Square is well worth the trip. ∎

St. Nicholas's Cathedral, the so-called Sailors' Church, is one of St. Petersburg's best mid-18th-century churches.

The curvaceous lines, gilded decoration, and painted panels of the theater in the Yusupov Palace were added in the late 19th century.

Yusupov Palace

Yusupov Palace
- Map p. 79
- reki Moiki Naberezhnaya 94
- 314-9883 or 314-8893
- Closed a.m.
- $$$ (by group tour only)
- Bus: 3, 10, 22, & 27; Trolleybus: 5 & 22

THE YUSUPOV PALACE ATTRACTS SCORES OF PEOPLE TO eat at its fashionable restaurant, to marvel at its renowned interiors, to go on the Rasputin murder tour, or to attend a concert of Mozart music. Whatever the reason, a couple of hours here is time well spent.

Viewed from the Moika Embankment, the Yusupov Palace appears a rather dull yellow building that could well be mistaken for a military barracks. Its severe early classicist style is the design of Jean-Baptiste Vallin de la Mothe and dates to the mid-18th century. The interior, however, is another story: It starts with Prince Nikolay Yusupov's purchase of the palace in 1830 from the Shuvalov family. Yusupov was one of the richest men in the country and he also ranked as one of the very top connoisseurs and collectors of art in Russia.

Eighty years old when he bought the house, Yusupov only lived in the palace one year before he died. His descendants, beginning with his son Boris and ending with his grandson Prince Felix Yusupov the cross-dressing assassin of Rasputin, masterminded the decorative feast inside.

Only a smattering of the fantastic Yusupov collection of art remains. Most of it went to enrich the State Hermitage after nationalization took place in 1919 and the palace came under the auspices of the People's Commissariat for Enlightenment.

Since the interiors were completed by several generations of Yusupovs, who had virtually limitless funds and access to and choice of the very best designers and craftsmen, they compose a whole anthology of fashionable St. Petersburg styles from the last 80 years of the tsarist regime. Considering the palace was bombed and used as a hospital during the World War II, they have survived very well.

You may prefer one style over another, but all the rooms are impressive, with several outstanding. The suite of elegant **public rooms** on the second floor—the Green, Red, and Blue Drawing Rooms; Large Rotunda; Ballroom; and White Columned and Nicholas Halls—was redecorated in the 1830s under the direction of Andrey Mikhailov. A **suite of halls** off the Nicholas Hall was largely decorated in the 1890s and housed the Yusupov art gallery. A highly ornate neorococo **theater** seats 180 people. A whole range of other rooms, from the heavy oak dining room to the delicate porcelain boudoir and the exotic Moorish room, reveal other popular styles of their days.

The cellars contain a **waxworks exhibit** devoted to the murder of the charismatic Grigory Rasputin (1869–1916), whose murder began in these rooms. The enormous influence that Rasputin, a Siberian peasant turned mystic, prophet, and healer, wielded upon the royal family (into which Felix Yusupov had married) provoked powerful opponents to employ drastic means to drastic ends. The display tells in graphic detail the story of his poisoning, shooting, and subsequent disposal in the Malaya Nevka on December 16, 1916. ∎

The relatively austere Moika River facade of the Yusupov Palace masks an ornamental treasure trove.

Moika Embankment

**Moika
Embankment**

Map pp. 78–79

COURSING FROM MATISOV ISLAND IN THE WEST TO THE Summer Garden in the east, the Moika River crosses the very heart of the city, defining the southern side of Admiralty Island and the northern edges of Kolomna, Kazan, and Savior's Islands. A short walk along the handsome granite embankments of its eastern half or a boat trip along its entire length are both highly recommended.

Fourteen bridges span the 3-mile-long (4.5 km) Moika, making it possible to start and end a walking tour in numerous places. This is a meandering, slow-flowing river where each turn brings a different view, changing reflections, and atmosphere.

Start at the gigantic arch of New Holland Island and head east.

**Boats cruising
the Moika River
pass some
memorable St.
Petersburg sights.**

The first bridge met is the **Pot-seluev,** one of four iron bridges (1806–1816) constructed over the river by the Scottish architect William Hastie. The permanence of these bridges transformed life in the city. The view northeast from here to distant St. Isaac's Cathedral is grand: In the middle ground you will see the **Communications Workers' House of Culture,** a rare example of an early Soviet building in this part of town, whose tall structure was a radical 1930s adaptation of the 1860s spired Reform church that stood on the site. It stands opposite the 1840 house of architect August Montferrand *(No. 86)* and just after the attractive little pedestrian **Post Bridge,** one of St. Petersburg's first chain bridges (1824). Farther along, rumor has it that Russia agreed to sell Alaska to the United States in **No. 72,** the house of the Russia-America Company in 1867.

After passing St. Isaac's Square, the most significant buildings before you reach Nevsky Prospekt are the fine 18th- and early 19th-century houses that comprise the Herzen Pedagogical University. The **Razumovsky Palace** *(No. 48)* with its pleasant courtyard is particularly attractive.

Farther upriver, on the southern bank, by the Green Bridge, is the **Stroganov Palace** (see pp. 104–105). After passing the rear of the General Staff building, look for the renowned **State**

Academic Capella *(No. 20, tel 314-1058),* set back in a large courtyard on the northern side. It is home to the Glinka Choir; the fine, intimate concert hall was reconstructed with a delicate paraphrasing of the French royal style of Louis XVI in 1886 to 1889. (The Capella's symphony gives regular concerts autumn through spring, while in summer, the entertainment focuses on Russian culture.) This stretch of the Moika offers some of the river's most beautiful views: the beautiful Singers' Bridge, the slice of Palace Square, and the sequence of bridges over the little Winter Canal by the Hermitage.

Continuing past No. 12, the former Volkonsky Mansion and now the **Alexander Pushkin Museum** (see box below), the Moika curves around the back of Millionaires' Street, past two contrasting yet harmonious empire-style buildings: the low-slung **Imperial Stables** (1817–1823) on the southern bank and the taller **Adamini House** (*No. 1,* 1823–27) on the northern. The latter hosted some of Russia's most scandalous avant-garde artistic events in the 1910s, when it was home to the experimental Dobychina Art Bureau and the

bohemian cellar-club known as The Comedians' Halt. Adorned with mementoes to this past, the latter has reopened as a music café.

The Moika's eastern end stars three large parks—Field of Mars, Michael Garden, and Summer Garden—and offers lovely vistas north and south and to the river's last three picturesque bridges. The **Engineers' Castle** (see pp. 126–27) sits near where the Moika joins the Fontanka. Finally, look for the little **Chizhik-Pizhik,** the little bronze bird sculpted by Rezo Gabriadze (1992) where youngsters throw coins for good luck, virtually under the First Engineer's Bridge. ∎

Pushkin's study is the most authentic and touching part of his last apartment. It includes his sabre, a painting of the Daryl Gorge in the Caucasus, and his Blackamoor inkstand.

Alexander Pushkin Museum

This museum dedicated to Russia's greatest poet is divided into two parts. The first is the nine-room apartment where he lived for the last few months of his life; he died here on January 29, 1837, of wounds sustained in a duel. The rooms are arranged with period furniture and some of the writer's cherished art and artifacts. The multilingual audioguide is worth the investment: It explains the details of the rooms, including why the writer's Gothic clock is stopped at 2:45 (the time of his death).

The second part of the museum traces the poet's life and creative work. These rooms contain some fine portraits, as well as landscapes of the places within the Russian Empire where he lived and traveled. This well-conceived exhibit will appeal to fans of Pushkin and his times. ∎

Alexander Pushkin Museum

✉ reki Moiki Naberezhnaya 12

☎ 571-3531

🕐 Closed Tues. & last Fri. of month

💲 $$

🚌 Bus: 7 & 10; Trolleybus: 1, 7, & 10; Metro: Nevsky Prospekt

Bolshaya Morskaya Ulitsa

**Bolshaya
Morskaya Ulitsa**
🗺 Map p. 79
🚌 Bus: 3, 22, & 27;
Trolleybus: 5 & 22

BOLSHAYA MORSKAYA ULITSA (GREAT SEA STREET) RUNS almost parallel to the central 1.5 miles (2.4 km) of the Moika River and, like the river, it is a wayfare full of changing impressions and historic sights. Walking its length from the arch of the General Staff building to the Potseluev Bridge, you may find it hard to believe that you are on the same street, despite the fact that other than a bend that follows the meander of the river, the street is just about dead straight.

The House of Fabergé was home to tsarist Russia's foremost jewelers at the turn of the 20th century.

Walking west from the General Staff arch, take a moment to appreciate the **Azov-Don Bank** (*Nos. 3–5, 1913*) on the right. It signals that you are entering the booming, financial heart of pre-revolutionary St. Petersburg. The Swedish architect Fredrik Lidvall used a powerful neo-empire style for the bank, giving the lines of its light gray granite facade a sense of immaculate precision. In fact, this bank contrasts with the rest of the banks on Bolshaya Morskaya, which, though largely of the same period, are far busier, eclectic, or ponderous in appearance—witness the incredibly overladen neo-Renaissance **Bank of Trade and Commerce** (*No. 15,* by Marian Peretiatkowicz, 1912–15) farther down the street, after you cross Nevsky Prospekt.

Almost opposite this bank is the turn-of-the-century **House of Fabergé** (*No. 24).* Designed by Karl Schmidt, its smooth dark columns and modern Gothic features reek of opulence. Down the street, No. 35 employs an unusual Nordic language on the facade and main staircase; at the back of the courtyard is the **State Center of Photography,** which opened in 2002. It organizes interesting temporary exhibitions of Russian and international photography on its premises and at other venues.

Opposite, the **Union of Artists** occupies the beautiful premises of the former Society for the Encouragement of Art (*No. 38,* 1830s and later). The union is trying to reinvent itself and rid itself of its Soviet origins; its exhibitions are of variable quality. This section of the street ends with another classically refined building by Lidvall, the famous luxury **Hotel Astoria** (*No. 39,*

1912) on St. Isaac's Square. Since it sat opposite "his" German Embassy, Hitler had planned to hold his victory banquet here.

The stretch of Bolshaya Morskaya west of St. Isaac's Square assumes an altogether different character than east of the square. After the mightiness of the German Embassy come some

A little farther down, the **House of Architects** is housed in the 1836 Alexander Polovtsov mansion (*No. 52*). The house has some superbly decorated rooms from the 1860s to 1880s, notably the Bronze and White Halls. They can be visited occasionally since the halls are used for public events. Shortly after

The restrained facades of the Hotel Astoria contrast with its opulent interior.

select 19th-century mansions. August Montferrand designed in the 1830s both the **Pavel Demidov House** (*No. 43*), with the large sculpted Atlantes, Caryatids, and Glories around the entrance, and the Princess Gagarina House (*No. 45*) next door, which is now the **House of Composers,** where chamber concerts are occasionally offered.

No. 47 was the birthplace of the writer Vladimir Nabokov (1899–1977), famed for the erotic bestseller *Lolita*. Rebuilt with art nouveau features in 1901, the house was home to Nabokov until his family fled into emigration in 1917. The house contains a little museum dedicated to Nabokov's life and works.

the Polovtsov house, by the Communications Workers' House of Culture, Bolshaya Morskaya becomes one with the Moika Embankment.

MALAYA MORSKAYA

The much shorter Malaya Morskaya (Little Sea Street) runs parallel to Bolshaya Morskaya between Nevsky Prospekt and St. Isaac's Square. It is a buzzing street these days and in the 19th century was briefly home to numerous leading Russian cultural figures: Tchaikovsky died in **No. 13;** Gogol wrote his St. Petersburg satires *Diary of a Madman* and *The Nose* in **No. 17;** and Dostoevsky was arrested in **No. 23.** ∎

St. Petersburg Union of Artists
☎ 314-4734
🕐 Closed a.m. & Mon.
💲 $

State Center of Photography
www.ncprf.org
☎ 314-1214

Nabokov Museum
www.nabokovmuseum.org
☎ 315-4713
🕐 Closed Mon.
💲 $

Nevsky Prospekt

Nevsky Prospekt
🅼 Map p. 79

NEVSKY PROSPEKT (NEVA PERSPECTIVE OR AVENUE) IS BEST not considered a street but, as its name suggests, a view, a panorama with well-worked-out minor views. It is not really a thoroughfare as that would imply it goes somewhere. It does not. It simply bisects the city, running from the Neva River in the west to the Neva River in the east. Nevsky Prospekt is St. Petersburg's most famous and finest street. It is the arbiter of social and cultural life. It is an orchestrated ensemble comprising distinctive parts. It is a street that calls out for pedestrian interaction.

Nevsky Prospekt is where the whole city comes together and shows itself off.

Originally, in the 1710s, the bent line that is Nevsky was two separate roads across a swampy forest. One started from the Admiralty and headed east, the other left the Alexander Nevsky Monastery and headed west. Both roads linked their respective institutions to the ancient high road that led south to Novgorod. They joined it near present-day Vosstaniya Square.

The stretch from the Admiralty was then the main way into and out of town and was called the

Great Perspective Road, changing to Nevsky Perspective Avenue in 1738 and then, after its joining with the eastern stretch in the 1760s, to Nevsky Prospekt. The distinctiveness of the two early parts is apparent: the grandeur and eloquence of the western section contrasts with the more compact and poorer eastern.

Nevsky Prospekt is 3 miles (4.5 km) long and, for the most part, about 200 feet (60 m) wide. Marked by sunny and shady sides, its character derives from which way you look at it, where you walk on it. Since the Admiralty was the hub of the city, as the street developed so the wealthiest institutions and nobility arranged

All-powerful Nevsky Prospekt!

"The only place in St. Petersburg where a poor man can combine a stroll with entertainment. How spotlessly clean are its pavements swept and, good gracious, how many feet leave their marks on them! Here is the footprint left by the clumsy, dirty boot of an ex-army private, under whose weight the very granite seems to crack; and here is one left by the miniature, light-as-a-feather little shoe of the delightful young creature who turns her pretty head towards the glittering shop-window as the sunflower turns to the sun; and here is the sharp scratch left by the rattling sabre of some ambitious lieutenant—everything leaves upon it its imprint of great power or great weakness. What a rapid phantasmagoria passes over it in a single day! What changes does it not undergo in only twenty-four hours!"

— NIKOLAY GOGOL
"Nevsky Prospekt," 1835

their estates along its western stretches. Although its main growth (1740s–1800s) occurred when the fashion was for displays of baroque and empire, these styles were amply supplemented in later years by different kinds of historical, art nouveau, and 20th-century architectural styles. Particularly important for these additions was the new idea of shopping in style and the need to be seen. Nevsky became all about pleasure. The stretch of Nevsky between the Moika and Fontanka Rivers offers the best sense of the variety of styles. ∎

Stroganov Palace

Stroganov Palace

- 🅜 Map p. 79
- ✉ Nevsky Prospekt 17
- ☎ 571-2360
- 🕐 Closed Tues.
- 💲 $$
- 🚌 Bus: 3 & 7;
  Trolleybus: 1, 5, 7,
  10, & 22;
  Metro: Nevsky
  Prospekt

AN ARCHITECTURAL MASTERPIECE, THE STROGANOV PALACE sits at the Green Bridge on the Moika Embankment, where Nevsky Prospekt crosses the river. The elegant lines of the palace bring to mind the Winter Palace (see pp. 64–73), and rightly so: The two shared the same architect (Francesco Bartolomeo Rastrelli); were built at the same time and by the same workers; and used the same style, high baroque.

THE PALACE

The Stroganov family had become the richest in Russia mainly through their control of the salt industry from the 16th century. Baron Sergey Stroganov (1707–1756), one of Empress Elizabeth's grandees, commissioned the palace (1753–54), but it was his son Alexander (1733–1811) who, 35 years later, transformed the interior into a remarkable celebration of classical art. The redesign was carried out by Fyodor Demertsov and the young Andrey Voronikhin. Count Alexander nurtured Voronikhin from the time when he was a boy serf on the Stroganov salt holdings in

collection—much of it now hangs in the Hermitage, tagged with the provenance "formerly Stroganov Collection"—its physical state deteriorated under the toll of the war and half a century serving as the People's Commissariat for the Shipbuilding Industry. New life was breathed into the palace in 1988 when it came under the auspices of the Russian Museum (see p. 118).

A long-term restoration was begun, and currently nine rooms are open to visitors. The busily decorated **Great Hall** on the second floor (or piano nobile) is the only extant original Rastrelli interior in St. Petersburg. Entitled "The Hero's Escapade," the extravagant celestial allegories and *trompe l'oeil* gallery of the ceiling painted by Guiseppe Valeriani in the 1750s are particularly eye-catching. Count Alexander's **Mineral Study,** with its cupola and gallery for his mineral collection, the **formal dining room,** and the **Arabesque Hall** are particularly fine examples of classical-style interiors. The onetime showpiece of the palace, the long art gallery, still awaits reconstruction.

RUSSIAN MUSEUM EXHIBITS

Currently, the Russian Museum stages **exhibits of Russian art** in the palace, focusing particularly on art representative of the Stroganov school of religious art from the 16th and 17th centuries, which the family encouraged in the Russian north and east before the founding of St. Petersburg.

A separate **waxworks display,** reached through an entrance in the courtyard, charts the history of the Romanov royal family. ∎

Before St. Petersburg was established, the Stroganov family had made their fortune from salt and founded a school of ecclesiastical art.

the Urals to when he became Russia's first empire-style architect. Alexander was also president of the Academy of Arts and a great collector; he assembled probably the best private art collection in the country.

Outside, the palace's **Nevsky** and **Moika facades** rival one another for being *the* face of the palace. The Nevsky side probably just edges out the other because of all the decorative elements that accentuate the main entrance. Look closely at the bow-shaped pediment to find the Stroganov coat of arms, with its bear's head and flanking sables.

The 20th century did not serve the building well. It was stripped of its magnificent art

Kazan Cathedral

WHEN YOU STAND BEFORE THE LONG EMBRACING ARMS OF the Kazan Cathedral's colonnade, you stand before a masterpiece that very strategically opened the period of empire-style architecture and art in Russia. It was designed by Andrey Voronikhin, a former serf of Count Alexander Stroganov, and completed in 1811. It also happens to be a unique symbol of the Russian role in the defeat of Napoleon.

The Kazan Cathedral appears more colonnade than church and serves as a memorial to Russia's victory over Napoleon.

On December 31, 1999, the Museum of the History of Religion and Atheism housed in the Kazan Cathedral since 1932 ceased to exist. The clearing out of the museum had started in 1990, when the first service in almost 70 years took place among the displays of Marxist materialism and Darwinist empiricism. Since then, the cathedral's religious reawakening has been proceeding apace.

The sacred, miracle-working icon of Our Lady of Kazan, after which the cathedral is named, was returned in 2001, new bells have been cast, and a new iconostasis is being made to replace the one made from 3,600 pounds (1,633 kg) of silver brought back from France after 1812 and removed by the Bolsheviks in 1922.

Large gold inscriptions on either side of the west entrance indicate that the cathedral was started by Tsar Paul and finished by Tsar Alexander I. Paul decreed that the church emulate Bernini's

St. Peter's in Rome; hence the **great colonnade.** But here the forest of 96 columns hides all of the church save its 236-foot-high (72 m) dome. Complying with patriotic conditions, the colonnade and church are constructed from local limestone. The **Nevsky facade** is embellished with sculptural decoration (including bronzes of St. Andrew, St. Vladimir, John the Baptist, and Alexander Nevsky); the doors feature ten bronze reliefs of biblical scenes that imitate Lorenzo Ghiberti's for the Florence Baptistry.

Though supported by 56 monolithic granite Corinthian columns, the internal space of the Latin cross-plan church is not overly grand and ostentatious like that of St. Isaac's (see pp. 84–85), St. Petersburg's other great 19th-century cathedral. In addition, the return of crowds of believers, the lighting of candles, the delivery of the liturgy, the choral chants, and the praying before the icons (the bejeweled **Our Lady of Kazan** hangs to the right of the iconostasis), have added a more pervasive atmosphere of devotion.

The Kazan also serves as a memorial for the 1812 war. The relatively modest **tomb of Field Marshal Prince Mikhail Kutuzov** (1745-1813), who died while leading the Russian army toward Paris, occupies a corner of the northern transept. It is low and surrounded by gilded railings, a small icon, a painting depicting the religious celebrations in Moscow's Red Square after the ending of the Polish occupation in 1612 (believed to have been made possible by the intercession of the Kazan icon), captured French banners, and the keys from 8 European fortresses and 17 cities freed from Napoleon's control by the Russians. ∎

Kazan Cathedral
www.kazansky.net
⚠ Map p. 79
✉ Kazansky Ploshchad 2
☎ 571-4826 or
314-5856
🚌 Bus: 3 & 7;
Trolleybus: 1, 5, 7,
10, & 22;
Metro: Nevsky
Prospekt

A walk around Nevsky West End

For all its expansiveness, Nevsky (as the prospekt is lovingly known in Russia) begins a little as it ends—in a surprisingly condensed way. The first reason is that its westernmost neighborhood was originally home to the tradesmen and laborers engaged on the ship-building projects in the Admiralty docks and they were not afforded a great deal of space. Another reason was the real estate pressure, resulting from the neighborhood's subsequent transformation into the financial "city."

One of the best ways to appreciate Nevsky is to walk up it (south) on the shady side and then back down (north) its sunny side, at any time and on any day.

Start your walk on Admiralty Prospekt in order to see how Nevsky works as one of the three rays emanating from the Admiralty. The other two arterial roads, Voznesensky (Ascension) Prospekt and Gorokhovaya Street, have none of Nevsky's panache. The house at the far end of Admiralty Prospekt, **No.12 ❶**, built between 1817 and 1820 and occupying a large triangular plot of land by St. Isaac's Cathedral, was designed by the cathedral's architect, August Montferrand, for the Princes Lobanov-Rostovsky. The two large but friendly-looking marble lions by Paolo Triscorni sitting outside its great portico so impressed Alexander Pushkin he mentioned them in his "Bronze Horseman" poem.

The neighboring No. 10 house has gone down in art history as being the home of the **Artel cooperative of artists,** a group of indignant students who, in 1863, engendered a massive crisis in the academy of art. They refused to take part in its medal competition due to the stipulated ancient mythology subject matter; they wanted something contemporary. Setting themselves up as an alternative, independent group, the Artel broke the monopoly the academy (and hence the state) had on art production in the Russian Empire.

The nearby Quarenghi-designed **Wittinghof House ❷** (*Admiralty Prospekt 6, 312-2742, closed Sat.–Sun., $*), better known as Gorokhovaya 2, served as the headquarters of the notorious St. Petersburg secret police. From 1875 to 1917 it housed the city administration with various legal

---

- 🅜 See map p. 79
- ▶ St. Isaac's & Admiralty Prospekt
- ↔ 1.3 miles (2.1 km)
- ⊕ 1 hour
- ▶ Church of St. Peter, Nevsky 22–24

NOT TO BE MISSED
- Wittinghof House
- DLT
- Meltser House
- Singer Building

The fountains in front of the Admiralty are a favorite place for rendezvous.

departments, the governor's office, the police, and the recently created Okhrannoye Otdeleniye (Secret Police Department). The latter's agents were responsible for the collection of information on those suspected of connections with revolutionary or social movements. Visit the four sad rooms of the **Gorokhovaya 2 Museum** *($)* within (a

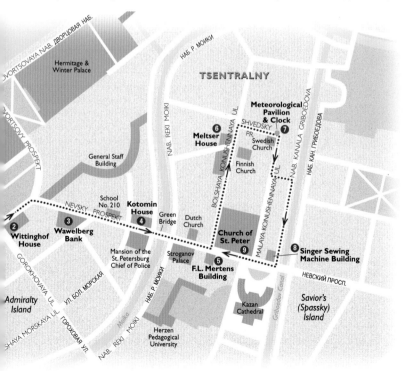

branch of the Museum of Russian Political History) to understand how this political role was carried out. Although not everything is explained in English, the display charts the development of the political police from their 1879 register of St. Petersburg prostitutes (3,592 in total, including 4 Danes, 58 Swedes, 1 Turkish, 164 Germans, 1,028 peasants, and 574 soldiers'

The Literary Café makes much of its connection with the fate of Pushkin.

wives and daughters) to the 1917 arrival on the scene of the Bolshevik's own secret police, the Cheka. Also based here, the Cheka were led by the "iron" Felix Dzerzhinsky; a large plaque outside honors him, and his study can be seen inside.

Continuing on your walk, turn right (east) onto Nevsky Prospekt, where the 1912 **Wawelberg Bank** ❸ (No. 7), designed by Marian Peretiatkowicz, immediately stands out. Its ponderous arcade is strung over the pavement and looks like a heavily rusticated Renaissance palazzo. Since Soviet days, the

building has housed Aeroflot and its successor companies. This area (and nearby Bolshaya Morskaya Ulitsa; see pp. 100–101) quickly became dedicated to an increasing number of Russian banks and insurance companies in the early 20th century. The 1915 Moscow Bank was torn down in 1939 to make way for the severe-looking **School No. 210** (Nevsky Prospekt 14), which was erected in a record 54 days (by Boris Rubanenko). The school is the only Soviet building in this area.

Farther up the street, on the left, look for the **Kotomin House** ❹ (Nevksy Prospekt 18), which dates back to 1815. Many Petersburg 19th-century literary figures used to meet upstairs here in the café of the confectioners Wolf and Béranger. Pushkin, in fact, after downing a stiff drink and his second in tow, set out for his fateful duel from here at 4 p.m. on January 27, 1837. You can enjoy something of that early atmosphere in the **Literary Café,** which now occupies the same room.

On the site opposite the Kotomin House, Francesco Bartolomeo Rastrelli erected a wooden structure that served as a temporary Winter Palace while the great Winter Palace we know today was being built. It was pulled down in 1762 and replaced with the **mansion of the St. Petersburg Chief of Police Nikolay Chicherin** (Nevsky Prospekt 15). Its exterior is noticeable for its two tiers of columns that wrap around the street corner. The interiors were altered by the Eliseyev family around 1860. With facades along Nevsky Prospekt, Bolshaya Morskaya Street, and the Moika Embankment, this large house became home to a variety of leading entertainment clubs and artistic institutions both before and after the 1917 Revolution. It is currently being converted into a luxury hotel.

After crossing the Moika by means of the Green (or Police) Bridge, you pass the **Stroganov Palace** (see pp. 104–105) on the right and the house of the **Dutch Church** on the left (No. 20; by Paul Jacquot, 1834–39) before you reach the 1912 **F. L. Mertens building** ❺ (Nevsky Prospekt 21). As home to the most fashionable of furriers, this building made a huge statement about modern style in prerevolutionary St. Petersburg. While Marian Lalewicz's three great arches hint at classical tradition, the architect's use of reinforced concrete and expanses of windows ushered in the new.

From here, leave Nevsky and walk up the center of the tree-lined Bolshaya Konushennaya (Great Stables) Ulitsa. Notice the **DLT** department store with the spire on the left (Nos. 21–23; by Ernest Virrikh, 1913). Originally the Retail House of the Guards' Economic Society, this building was the city's largest retail premises of the early 20th century. Its remarkably large and open interiors are also made possible by the use of reinforced concrete. Just past DLT, the 1905 **Meltser House 6** *(Bolshaya Konushennaya Ulitsa 19),* by contrast, looks like an interpretation of some northern castle. It is full of different textures, colors, and materials. The Swedish identity of its architect, Fredrik Lidvall, reveals that you are entering the old Swedish quarter.

Pass the Finnish Church *(Bolshaya Konushennaya Ulitsa 6a)* on the right and turn down Shvedsky Pereulok (Swedish Lane) to enter a world of Scandinavian decorum. Where the lane ends and turns into Malaya Konushennaya Street, you walk into a recently pedestrianized zone. This area hasn't quite come to terms with its new character and, despite a couple of new sculptures and cafés, it can feel a bit barren. Still, the neo-Romanesque **Swedish Church** and Lidvall's nordic art nouveau apartment house *(Nos. 1–3)* for the church on your right are interesting. And you might stop to check the temperature, air pressure, humidity, wind direction, or just the time on the elegant **Meteorological Pavilion and Clock 7** (by Nikolay Lansere, 1914), which stands in the center of the street.

Turn left onto the short Cheboksar to reach the Griboedov Canal Embankment where you'll find an extremely picturesque view of the **Church of the Savior on Spilled Blood** (see p. 116). Next, walk up the embankment to the sunny side of Nevsky to admire **Nevsky Prospekt 28 8**. This 1904 art nouveau building, with a regulation-height-exceeding globe,

The Singer building is an outstanding example of art nouveau.

was built for the American Singer Sewing Machine Company. Note the lovely touch of modern sewing accoutrements (even machines) to some of the sculpted, winged female figures on the prows of ships that jut out of the building at its attic level.

As you head back down Nevsky toward where you began your walk, you'll notice a church set back from the line of the street. This was built as the German Lutheran **Church of St. Peter 9** *(Nos. 22–24;* by Alexander Bryullov, 1833–38). Unfortunately for the building, the twin-towered neo-Romanesque exterior and the sculptures of Sts. Peter and Paul hide an interior that was converted into a swimming pool from the 1950s to 1991. ■

More places to visit in the Neva West End

ALEXANDER POPOV CENTRAL MUSEUM OF COMMUNICATIONS

Founded in 1872, the Museum of Communications is ironically one of the most up-to-date and hi-tech museums in St. Petersburg. Reopened in 2003 after a 30-year hiatus, it is housed in the magnificent (but outwardly modest) 18th-century palace of Prince Alexander Bezborodko (1747–1799), Catherine the Great's chancellor of the Russian Empire, who, among his many other roles, was head of the Postal Department. Architect Giacomo Quarenghi skillfully united two earlier mansions to create the palace, producing in the process interiors that show some of his best work. The decoration of the **ballroom** (or ceremonial hall) has survived and is exceptional. The educational aspect of the museum

Diners in the Museum of Communications enjoy their meal beneath a Luch satellite.

uses a variety of well-considered and tasteful interactive displays (some of which are in English) to journey through the still evolving history of communications. Beyond postboxes and stamping machines, you can see the development of radio and satellite technology through Russian eyes, view some Soviet-period TVs and record players, and really get into the history of telephones, including cell phones. Finally, in the two vast, glazed ceiling atria, which were originally the courtyards of the old houses, you can enter a virtual sphere and go for a virtual ride through space, dine next to a giant Luch satellite, come to terms with cable transmissions and flat screens, or catch up with your e-mail.

www.rustelecom-museum.ru

✉ Pochtamtskaya Ulitsa 7 (entrance at Pochtamtsky Pereulok 4) ☎ 571-0060
🕐 Closed Sun.–Mon. & last Thurs. of month
💲 $ 🚍 Bus: 3, 22, & 27; Trolleybus: 5 & 22

MAIN POST OFFICE

The rather beautiful Main Post Office (1782–89), designed by Nikolay Lvov, stands just up the street from the Museum of Communications (see above). The main transactions hall used to be the courtyard before it was glazed over and given an art nouveau face-lift in 1903. The proportions and light of this square space are exquisite. Outside, a gallery arch, added in 1859, connects the building to the State Museum of the History of Religion (see below) on the other side of the street. In a sign of the times, you might well find it more convenient to send a letter from the Museum of Communications' post office rather than from here.

✉ Pochtamtskaya Ulitsa 9 ☎ 312-8302
🚍 Bus: 3, 22, & 27; Trolleybus: 5 & 22

STATE MUSEUM OF THE HISTORY OF RELIGION

The State Museum of the History of Religion is the reinvented Museum of Religion and Atheism that was housed in the Kazan Cathedral until the end of 1999. The museum opened in 2001, and its informative displays cover a variety of religions from Siberian shamanism and antiquity to Judaism, early and modern Christianity, and, especially, Russian Orthodoxy.

✉ Pochtamtskaya Ulitsa 14/5 ☎ 571-0495 or 314-5838 🕐 Closed Wed. 💲 $ 🚍 Bus: 3, 22, & 27; Trolleybus: 5 & 22 ∎

The creation of Nevsky Prospekt in the late 1700s extended the city from the shores of the Neva to the Alexander Nevsky Monastery. The street and the suburb to its north grew into realms for the favored and fashionable.

East of Griboedov Canal

Detail of lamppost outside the Stieglitz Institute

East of Griboedov Canal

THE FONTANKA RIVER MARKED THE SOUTHERN BORDER OF ST. PETERSBURG until the mid-18th century, making a 4-mile (6.4 km) arc around the five main islands of the city. The eastern border of the outer Savior's (Spassky) Island is edged by the Griboedov Canal. This waterway was formed along the course of a small river during the reign of Catherine II and was originally called Catherine's (Ekaterininsky) Canal. In 1923, the canal was named after Alexander Griboedov, a renowned early 19th-century playwright who had lived on its banks.

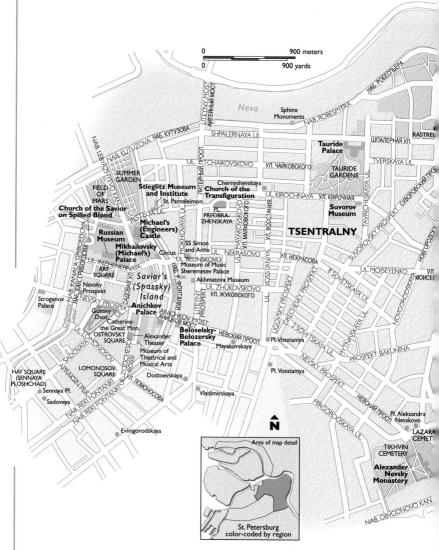

Gostiny Dvor (Trading Rows) was imperial St. Petersburg's largest retail premises.

Also during Catherine's reign, Nevsky Prospekt was created as St. Petersburg's main arterial road, linking the Admiralty on one stretch of the Neva to Peter's spiritual guardian of the city, the Alexander Nevsky Monastery, on another stretch of the same river (the Neva makes a large bend here). Dominated by the baroque Smolny Convent, the low-lying corner of land to the monastery's north grew into a large, respectable residential quarter. Russian president Vladimir Putin was born here in 1952. Savior's Island has two faces. South of Lomonosov Street, life bustles around the marketplaces of Hay Square (Sennaya Ploshchad) and Apraksin Dvor. A somewhat rundown neighborhood (it's the setting for much of Fyodor Dostoyevsky's *Crime and Punishment*), the area is showing signs of improvement and remains the place for bargains. By contrast, the area north of Lomonosov Street brims with style. Nevsky Prospekt cuts across the island here and the area abounds with vogue boutiques, clubs, hotels, and restaurants. The empire-style Arts and Ostrovsky Squares, the masterworks of Carlo Rossi, architecturally define the quarter.

The three main sights of northern Savior's Island break with the neoclassic character of the area in different ways. The Russian Museum externally agrees with Rossi's scheme, but inside it offers the best of Russian art, from the 18th to 20th centuries. Michael's Castle looks like a quasi-medieval fortress. And the Church of the Savior on Spilled Blood is the city's most colorful and decorative church.

An appealing set of palaces cluster near the Anichkov Bridge, which now carries Nevsky Prospekt across the 230-foot-wide (70 m) Fontanka. Occupied by state institutions during the Soviet days, the palaces are regularly opened for scheduled group visits. The horn of land created by the bend in the Neva holds the unique, but worn, Stieglitz Museum of applied art, and to its east, architect Rastrelli's masterful Smolny Cathedral. A mile (1.6 km) upstream along the Neva, the active Alexander Nevsky Monastery is open to visitors, and on its edges lie two cemeteries with the graves of many of St. Petersburg's cultural greats from the 18th and 19th centuries. ■

Church of the Savior on Spilled Blood

THE SPARKLING, MULTICOLORED CHURCH OF CHRIST'S Resurrection, popularly known as the Church of the Savior on the Blood, was built as a memorial to the "tsar liberator" Alexander II on the very spot he was assassinated. The church's silhouette harks back to the Russo-Byzantine styles of Muscovy and Yaroslavl from the 16th and 17th centuries.

The medieval appearance of the Church of the Savior on Spilled Blood belies its turn-of-the-20th-century construction.

Alexander III introduced a new wave of repression and the fostering of neo-nationalism. The old Russian style of the church is one of the most visible marks of the latter. It fostered a wave of Russian Revivalist architecture across the country and beyond.

Designed by Alfred Parland, the church was completed in 1907; it took 24 years to build and cost a staggering 4.5 million rubles (the vast majority coming from the state purse). The complex asymmetry of the plan is complemented by an amazing compilation of expensive materials, intricate forms, and symbolic motifs. It reaches to 265 feet (81 m) and is the most important monument of mosaic art in Russia.

Treat the church like a piece of jewelry; let it speak to you through whatever catches your eye. It might be the textures of its **stonework** (the granite and limestone of the exterior, or the marbles, jasper, porphyry, and rhodonite of the interior). Or the intricate shapes of the domes, window casings, steeple, bell tower, porches, and gables. Or the 20 **gilt plaques** listing the "deeds of Alexander II" on the base outside. Or the 144 mosaic coats of arms of the Russian Empire's regions, provinces, and towns that surround the bell tower.

Most likely, the explosion of colorful **mosaics,** covering some

On March 1, 1881, a bomb was lobbed under the carriage of Tsar Alexander after it turned onto the embankment of the Catherine (now Griboedov) Canal. The tsar emerged unscathed but was killed by a second bomb thrown by Ignacy Gryniewicki, a member of the People's Will, a revolutionary group intent on overthrowing the tsarist regime and asserting democratic freedoms and rights.

Alexander II had freed the serfs and could well have introduced a constitution; instead, his successor

69,970 square feet (6,500 sq m), will draw your attention. The scheme of the mosaics was inspired by the painted interior of St. Vladimir's Cathedral in Kiev. Many of Russia's leading artists made contributions: You can find a meek Alexander Nevsky by Mikhail Nesterov in the northern icon case, while Christ Pantocrator by Nikolay Kharlamov covers the central cupola, and Viktor Vasnetsov's most widely reproduced Virgin and Child is on the main **iconostasis.**

Closed by the Soviet authorities in 1930, the church reopened as a state museum in 1997 after nearly three decades of restoration work. ■

A polychromatic feast of religious mosaics awaits visitors to the Spilled Blood.

The empire-style Michael's Palace designed by Carlo Rossi houses the main branch of the Russian Museum.

Russian Museum

THE EMPIRE OF THE STATE RUSSIAN MUSEUM HAS GROWN significantly in recent years. Its five branches—the Mikhailovsky (Michael's), Stroganov, and Marble Palaces; Michael's (Engineers') Castle; and the Summer Garden—together form the most complete ensemble of Russian art that exists. They hold some of the very best visual culture that Russia has offered the world, particularly since its Western orientation that began with the founding of St. Petersburg. Mikhailovsky Palace is the core of the Russian Museum; it is the original home of the museum, and its largest part.

MIKHAILOVSKY PALACE

Mikhailovsky Palace was, and still is, a key and dominant feature of Carlo Rossi's superb urban plan for the quarter bound by the Griboedov Canal, Moika River, Sadovaya Street, and Nevsky Prospekt. Created in the wake of the Napoleonic Wars, the whole ensemble is an expression of high empire style. Approaching the palace from Nevsky Prospekt, you

get a good view of its nicely refined central portico. Lying behind some distinguished, tall railings and a *cours d'honneur* (ceremonial courtyard), the columns and pediment of the portico fittingly complement the rest of the facade.

The palace was built to Carlo Rossi's design in 1819 to 1825 for Grand Duke Michael (1798–1849), the younger son of Tsar Paul and brother of Tsars Alexander I and Nicholas I. The ceremonial White Hall (Hall 11) and the exquisite double staircase of the palace's main entrance best reveal Rossi's original white, gold, and mauve-gray neoclassic interior decor.

The duke's widow looked after the palace until her death in 1873, after which it was eventually bought by the state and reconstructed as the Russian Museum of Alexander III. Appropriating Russian works of art from the Hermitage, Academy of Arts, and royal palaces, it opened in March 1898. It now contains almost 400,000 items. You see but a fragment; the rest is in storage or is touring the world.

THE ART

The Mikhailovsky Palace has two entrances, one on the right of the Arts Square facade, the other to the Benois wing on the Griboedov Canal Embankment. To follow the chronological order of the exhibited works, enter from Arts Square and then climb the main stairs to the second floor, where you'll find the first room. If you'd like to start with a more modern bang and work backward in time, use the Benois door and reverse the order of rooms.

Rooms 1–4: Old Russian art

If there is a weakness of the Russian Museum is its collection of pre-Petrine art—essentially icons created before the founding of St. Petersburg. (Moscow's Tretyakov Gallery or the Kremlin have the premier collections.) Nevertheless, the Russian Museum does have some real gems.

You can see (in chronological order) the doleful-eyed little "Archangel Gabriel with the golden hair" from the 12th century; the event-packed "Battle between Novgorod and Suzdal" (a 16th-century Novgorod icon); Dionisy's "Doubting Thomas" (ca 1500); the laconicly spiritual life-size Sts. Peter and Paul by Andrey Rublev (1408, from the Assumption Cathedral in

Russian Museum

www.rusmuseum.ru

⬛ Map p. 114

✉ Inzhenernaya Ulitsa 4

☎ 595-4248; tour office 314-3448 or 595-4240

🕐 Closed Tues.

💲 $$$ (for Mikhailovsky Palace) $$$$ (for all branches)

🚇 Metro: Nevsky Prospekt & Gostiny Dvor

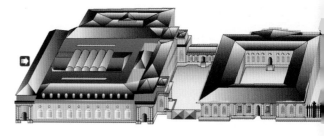

Vladimir); and Simon Ushakov's "Virgin and Child" (1662). These works mark the main shifts in the essentially Byzantine approach to icon painting. The expressiveness of Rublev's work is particularly striking.

Rooms 5–17: 18th- & early 19th-century art

When Peter became tsar, he oriented art in a new direction. Instead of principally looking south toward Constantinople's religious order for direction, he focused the gaze westward toward Rome, the German lands, the Low Countries, and Paris, and in particular toward their secularized court-dominated cultures. Pragmatism went before vanity in this rise of the self-conscious image. You can see the development of portraiture from its rather Byzantinist origins in **Rooms 5 and 6.**

Peter's purposeful collection of Western art and his invitation to foreign artists to come and work in Russia brought about the emergence of homegrown masters, who took their cues from the new arrivals. The initial stiffness of their painting gradually disappears. You might appreciate Ivan Nikitin's "Peter I on His

Deathbed" (1725), Ivan Vishnyakov's portraits of the English youngsters Sarah and William Fermor (1750s), or the imperious baroque presence of "Empress Anne with African Pageboy" (1731–1741) by Bartolomeo Carlo Rastrelli.

Turn the corner into **Room 8.**

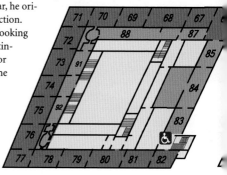

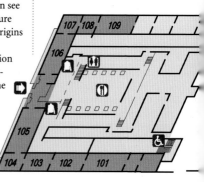

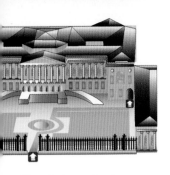

Rooms 1-4 Old Russian Art 12th -17th century icons.

Rooms 5-10 & 12 18th century (Petrine & Post-Petrine)

Room 11 White Hall

Rooms 13-17 & 18-23 Art of the first half of 19th Century

Rooms 24-48 & 54 Art of the second half of 19th Century

Unnumbered rooms connecting 48 are Folk Art

Rooms 66-82 Art from the turn of the 20th Century

Room 83-109 20th Century Art

The paintings and sculptures here tell the story of the mid-18th-century founding of the Imperial Russian Academy of Arts, and its (Catherine's) program of neoclassicism. Look in particular for the rather charming heroic passions and virtues

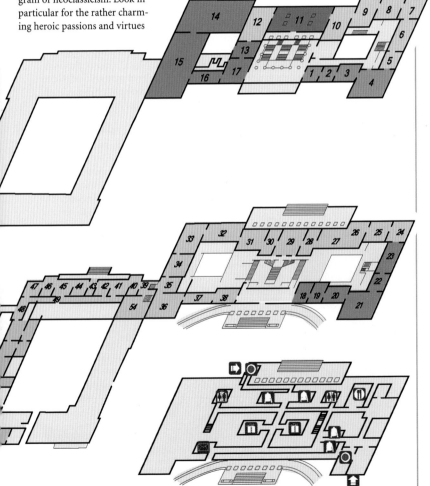

in Anton Losenko's paintings and Mikhail Kozlovsky's sculptures.

Two painters stand out from the late 18th century, Dmitry Levitsky and Vladimir Borovikovsky, and their works dominate **Rooms 10 and 12.** Note the sensitivity of Levitsky's female portraits (particularly of young noblewomen) and Borovikovsky's staunch "Murtaza-Kuli Khan" (1796). **Room 11** is Rossi's majestic **White-Columned (or White) Hall;** it is a model of graceful order.

The pictures exhibited in the next few rooms rotate periodically, as they are under more demand (and more likely to be loaned) elsewhere. Keeping that in mind, you'll come across paintings that reveal Russia turning Roman, and, reading between the strokes, heading toward similar crises. This is most clear from Karl Bryullov's vast doom-laden "The Last Days of Pompeii" (1830–33) in which you might spot at least one self-portrait. Other classics of this period include Fedelio (Feodor) Bruni's large-scale "Death of Camilla, Sister of the Horatii" (1824) and "Copper Serpent" (1837–1841); Alexander Ivanov's studies for "Appearance of the Messiah" (1837–1857), a work that cost him 20 years of his life and a loss of faith (you might prefer the lighter touch of his young male nudes and landscapes); Ivan Aivazovsky's marinescapes, not least the devastating "Ninth Wave" (1850). Calm is really only restored in this part of the Russian Museum with the arrival of Silvestr Shchedrin's exquisite Italian landscapes (look at his light), Orest Kiprensky's relaxed portraits, and Alexey Venetsianov's harmonies of Russian country life.

Rooms 18–48 & 54: Late 19th-century art

Returning downstairs, follow another counterclockwise tour of the rooms if you want to track the chronological development of Russian art through the remainder of the 19th century. The whole of the palace's first floor is given over to this period, together with a sequence of rooms in the Rossi Wing.

The start is small-scale with a few satirical and melancholy little paintings by the emotional Pavel Fedotov. This mood is countered by some academic and salon showy painting before things get

A plaster study of "grief" for the tomb of sculptor Mikhail Kozlovsky by Stepan Pimenov, 1802

serious again with the increasingly realistic images by Vasily Perov, Ivan Kramksoy (the leader of the Artel cooperative), and Ivan Shishkin. Nikolay Ge (Gay) emerged as an outstanding "spiritually" expressive painter at this time.

The Russian Museum's collection of paintings **(Rooms 25–35 & 54)** by the outstanding group of artists called the Wanderers (Peredvizhniki) is second only to that in the Tretyakov Gallery in Moscow. You can get an idea of the group's drive for democraticization and the contemporary in the arts by looking at the paintings of Viktor Vasnetsov, Nikolay Yaroshenko, and, to an extent, Russia's beloved Ilya Repin. The most powerful work by Repin is the epic "Volga Bargehaulers" (1870–73), which hangs in **Room 33**. It encapsulates the struggle (against the odds) of the various peoples of the Russian Empire.

Vasily Surikov and Vasily Vereshchagin had similar concerns, but often couched them in great "realist" pictures of Russian history. Surikov's large "Yermak's Conquest of Siberia" hangs in **Room 36.** In contrast try to get inside the minds of the evocative, atmospheric landscape painters Isaak Levitan **(Room 41)** and Arkhip Kuindzhi **(Room 40)** or the consumptive Maria Bashkirtseva **(Room 31).**

Folk art

The last ten unnumbered first-floor rooms of the Rossi Wing are devoted to Russian folk art, from whole carved house gables to ceramic whistles and lace to enamelware. This excellent exhibit is low profile and seems underrated by the museum, yet it attracts a good number of visitors.

Rooms 66–85:
Late 19th- & 20th-century art

The paintings hanging in the rooms in the Benois Wing constantly rotate because of the high demand abroad for 20th-century Russian art. Still, whatever is on the walls you should leave with an impression of a very vibrant, questing art scene that was full of experiment and variety (until the 1930s). **Rooms 66 and 67** feature the demon-obsessed genius

The 1882 "Outlaws" by Konstantin Savitsky

of Russian art of Mikhail Vrubel and the quieter spiritualism of Mikhail Nesterov. Their work leads into an era dominated by symbolism and a St. Petersburg group known as the World of Art (Mir Iskusstva), who, as the name suggests, drew on all kinds of approaches and aspects for their work. World of Art member Léon Bakst designed stage sets and costumes for the Ballet Russes; his work is on display in **Room 68.** Nikolay Roerich is best remembered for his eloquent, generalized Oriental-type of mysticism.

Rooms 80 to 82 focus on the so-called avant-garde, exhibiting some excellent early paintings by Wassily Kandinsky, Kazimir Malevich, Pavel Filonov, Vladimir Tatlin, Natalya Goncharova, Mikhail Larionov, and Olga Rozanova. The styles they use mix certain neo-Russian "primitive" qualities with the kind of formal experiments that were then taking

place elsewhere in Europe, not the least of which was cubism and the move toward abstraction.

Rooms 83 to 85 often reveal the idealism, optimism, and trauma of the postrevolutionary period: On display are works of agitprop (agitational propaganda); constructivist works by Tatlin, Alexander Rodchenko, and Lyubov Popova; and finally, the socialist realist paintings of artists such as Isaak Brodsky and Alexander Gerasimov, for whom the call of the Lenin and Stalin cults proved all too strong. Sometimes there are also works on display that show something of a middle ground. Keep an eye out for paintings by Alexander Deineka, Vladimir Lebedev, and Alexander Samokhvalov.

The first-floor rooms of the Benois Wing showcase temporary exhibits, usually ones focusing on a certain period of Russian history and drawing on the museum's vast permanent collection. ∎

Ilya Repin spent almost three years painting the "Centenary Meeting of the State Council" (1901–03), an image of the late tsarist Russia's legislators.

Michael's Castle stands out among the palaces of St. Petersburg for its mysterious medieval associations. It is now a branch of the Russian Museum.

Michael's (Engineers') Castle

Michael's (Engineers') Castle
www.rusmuseum.ru

🅰 Map p. 114
✉ Sadovaya 2
☎ 570-5112 or
570-5175
🕐 Closed Tues.
💲 $$
🚇 Metro: Nevsky Prospekt

TSAR PAUL WAS BORN AND DIED ON EXACTLY THE SAME site. While born to Catherine the Great in Empress Elizabeth's Summer Palace, he died in Michael's Castle. Replacing the former, the latter was Paul's unique contribution to St. Petersburg. It is a palace that stands apart from the general order of things, a palace with more than its fair share of innovation and intrigue, mystery and murder. The ghost of Paul, in his nightshirt, is said to be regularly seen at the window of his bedroom (Sadovaya facade, first floor, last on the left).

Michael's Castle (1797–1801) is named after Archangel Michael, whom Paul regarded as his heavenly protector. He had it built not only as his new family residence in the Russian capital, but also as the headquarters of the Maltese Order of the Knights of St. John, whose grand master he had (disputedly) become in 1798. The palace is riddled with allusions to the medieval world, as well as inversions of his detested mother's taste. Its long and complicated genesis, novelties, and history have led it to become St. Petersburg's most argued over building. The question of architect has exercised historians for decades: The balance of opinion has recently shifted in favor of the Italian Vincenzo Brenna, but there is still a strong body of support for the palace being the work of (or at least inspired by) the Russian freemason Vasily Bazhenov.

Unlike most other palaces in St. Petersburg, Michael's Castle stands alone and has something of a castle-like appearance—even more so in the past, when it was surrounded by moats on two sides and rivers on the others, entered only via drawbridges, and defended by cannon. A church sits on the palace's west side. The center of the main, **southern entrance** is covered in marble and full of pomp. Note the enormous flanking obelisks with relief war-trophies, the pediment relief on the subject "History Enters Russia's Glory into Her Annals," and the inscription "Your home is befitting of an object of worship for days to come."

To build the castle, Paul razed his mother's palace at Pelle, outside St. Petersburg, and used its materials as well as marble intended for St. Isaac's Cathedral. The pomp Paul desired can still be seen in the marble staircase, the throne and oval-shaped halls, the **Raphael Gallery,** and the church *(not always open to public).* Worthy of attention are Paolo Triscorni's sculpture of "Dying Cleopatra" on the stairs and Jacob Mettenleiter's "Temple of Minerva," painted on the ceiling of the Raphael Gallery (most prominent among the celestial creative spirits is the commanding architect drawing the plans of Michael's Castle itself).

The **apartments of Paul's family**—his wife Maria and sons Alexander and Konstantin—are less immodest (those of Nicholas and his sisters even more so). Paul and his family lived in the castle for a mere 40 days. The fortress-like building was supposed to provide protection for the paranoid tsar, but such was not the case. His own military leaders conspired to have him replaced by his son Alexander and murdered him in his bedroom at midnight on March 11, 1801.

His family moved out, and in 1819 the Engineering College for the training of military engineers and sappers was installed, giving rise to the alternative name of Engineers' Castle. The most famous of the college's students was Fyodor Dostoyevsky.

The Engineering College moved out in the 1960s, and in 1994 the building came under the purview of the Russian Museum. After major renovations, the most interesting rooms opened to the public. The permanent exhibits include **"Subjects of Antiquity in Russian Art,"** which showcases many classical nudes; Italian baroque sculptures taken from the Summer Garden; and **"Foreign Artists in Russia from the 18th to the First Half of the 19th Century",** which has many pleasant surprises, including the penetrating portraits of Giovanni-Battista Lampi the Elder and François Jouvenet's "Muzhik with a Cockroach" (1723).

Alexander's **personal apartments** contain an information area with an electronic gallery of the Russian Museum. And you can't miss the newly installed tragicomic bronze **monument of a seated Tsar Paul** in the center of the octagonal, interior courtyard (by V. E. Gorevoy, 2003). ∎

The extensive arcades of Gostiny Dvor provide perfect window-shopping opportunities.

A walk around the Nevsky/ Sadovaya Axis

About halfway between the Griboedov Canal and the Fontanka River, Nevsky Prospekt is bisected by Sadovaya (Garden) Street. Created between the 1730s and 1820s, Sadovaya traversed the whole of Savior's Island and was a vital means of cross-city communication. Architect Carlo Rossi completed the street's northern extension to the Field of Mars and created the two main architectural ensembles that give the areas around the Nevsky/Sadovaya axis their definition.

Begin your walk at the **equestrian monument to Peter the Great ①** that stands in front of Michael's Castle. Less visited than the Bronze Horseman (see pp. 82–83), this Peter is a far more baroque vision (with all the military trappings) of a triumphal and severe Roman emperor. He is even placed above reliefs depicting scenes from his greatest land and sea battles (Poltava and Hangö). Modeled by Bartolomeo Carlo Rastrelli while Peter was still alive and cast during the reign of Peter's daughter Elizabeth, the statue remained in the casting store until 1800, when Tsar Paul decided to set it on a pedestal in front of his new palace with an inscription "To Great-grandfather from Great-grandson." Its installation screamed of Paul's obsession with countering the symbols of state left by his mother Catherine the Great.

From the monument, walk down the center of tree-lined Klenova Street, past Michael's Castle's twin lodges, to the palace's **manège (riding school) ②** and **flanking stables** on Manezh Square. (The riding school is now the Winter Stadium.) These buildings were given their present empire-style appearance by Rossi in 1824.

Cross the wedge-shaped square to the corner of Italianskaya and Malaya Sadovaya Streets. On the left is the oversize and showy 1914 **Merchants' Club House** *(Italianskaya 27),* now the studios of the popular Channel Five TV station, and on the right is the rather refined, early 1750s palace of Count Ivan Shuvalov, a favorite of Catherine's and president of the Academy of Arts. It houses the Center of Medical Prophylaxis and with it the little visited **Museum of Hygiene ③**

(Italianskaya 25, tel 571-4227, closed Sat.–Sun.; $), which exhibits diseased organs in jars, a display dedicated to Ivan Pavlov and his salivating dog, and a striking early 18th-century mummy of a woman in well-preserved clothes.

Walk down the pedestrianized **Malaya Sadovaya Street** toward Nevsky, into which the street ends. The view ahead is tidily closed by the **Alexander Theater** (and **Catherine Monument**) on Ostrovsky Square across Nevsky. With its benches, street lamps, fountain, lilac, and occasional buskers, Malaya Sadovaya offers a pleasant respite from the hurly-burly of Nevsky. At the far end, you can take your photo with the new bronze **monument to Karl Bulla** (by B. A. Petrov, 2001), the photographer of prerevolutionary St. Petersburg.

At the corner with Nevsky, enter the unmistakable **Gastronome** ❹ *(Nevsky Prospekt 58).* This fine food and wine store takes up a large part of the grand, multi-functional **Yeliseev building,** one of St.

🗺 See area map p. 114
▶ Peter the Great statue, Michael's Castle
↔ 2 miles (3.2 km)
🕐 1.5 hours
▶ Mikhailovsky Gardens

NOT TO BE MISSED
- Yeliseev building
- Gostiny Dvor
- Arts Square
- Russian Ethnographic Museum

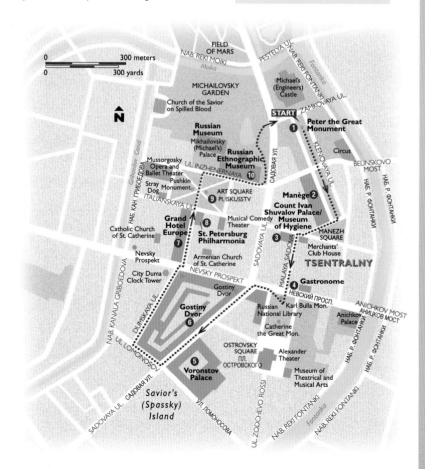

Petersburg's best examples of art nouveau. Built at the turn of the 20th century, its generous structural use of concrete, iron, and glass open up the interiors. In the first-floor delicatessen (which sells a top range of chocolate, tea, and alcohol), you can still see the magnificent mirrors, marble counters, chandelier, lights in the form of flowers, and stained-glass panels. Upstairs held the Farce Theater (since 1929 the Akimov Comedy

1798 and had Giacomo Quarenghi build an Orthodox church and Catholic chapel here. In 1810, it became an elite officers' military school, the Corps des Pages, today's Suvorov Military Academy.

Now cross to the other side of Sadovaya and enter **Gostiny Dvor (Trading Rows)** ⑥ *(Nevsky Prospekt 35)*, which began life as a merchants' inn. Rastrelli started the project in the mid-1750s, but cost overruns

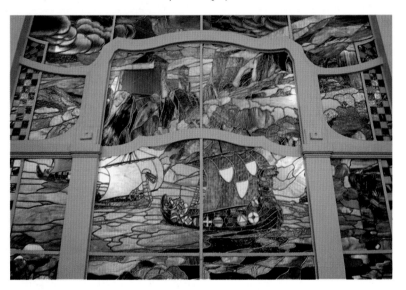

Detail from Latvian designer Karlis Brencens' art nouveau stained glass, Grand Hotel Europe

Theater) and a casino. On the exterior, a great arch wraps around the stained glass of the upper floors and the large allegorical sculptures of Trade and Industry, Art and Science.

At this point, cross over (or under) Nevsky. If you wish, visit the adjoining **Ostrovsky Square** (see p. 132) then return to this point. From here, walk down Nevsky and follow the curved corner of the **Russian National Library** to head south along Sadovaya Street. Where Sadovaya Street meets Lomonosov Street, glance through the railings of Rastrelli's mid-18th-century **Vorontsov Palace** ⑤ *(Sadovaya Ulitsa 26)*, with its fussily decorated entrance. Tsar Paul gave the palace to the Chapter of the Maltese Order of the Knights of St. John in

soon prompted the hiring of Jean-Baptiste Vallin de la Mothe and a design change. The result is four remarkably long, unadorned strings of two-tiered arcades around a building that takes up the whole of an irregularly shaped block. Ever since the 19th century this has been St. Petersburg's most important mall, where people promenade as much as shop.

Make your way through the mall to the metro stop near the 1804 hexagonal clock-tower-cum-beacon of the **City Duma** *(Nevsky Prospekt 31–33)* and take the pedestrian underpass to the other side of Nevsky. Two neoclassic churches, both built between the 1760s and 1780s and both dedicated to St. Catherine, stand not too far apart: the Yuri Felten–designed **Armenian Church**

(Nevsky Prospekt 40–42) and Vallin de la Mothe' Roman Catholic **St. Catherine Church** *(Nevsky Prospekt 32–34).*

At the corner of Nevsky and Mikhailovskaya Street, admire the Rossi-designed 1839 Nevsky facade of the **Grand Hotel Europe** ❼ *(Mikhailovskaya 1–7).* Ignore the later Mikhailovskaya facade, which disrupts the architectural harmony of the area, and wander into the hotel to appreciate Fredrik Lidvall's art nouveau interiors (1908–1910). A visit to the restaurant is worth it for a view of the superb mushroom-shaped stained-glass panel of Helios.

Continue down Mikhailovskaya Street to where it meets Arts Square and Nevsky Prospekt. The last building on the right is the 1839 former Nobles' Club and is now, since 1921, the **St. Petersburg Philharmonia** ❽ *(Mikhailovskaya 2).* Designed by Rossi and Paul Jacquot, its white-columned hall has superb acoustics. Tchaikovsky's "Sixth Symphony" premiered here in 1893, and the Philharmonic continues to offer some of the finest classical music in St. Petersburg.

Arts Square (Iskusstv Ploshchad) ❾ forms the core of Rossi's plan for this part of the city. In the center stands a statue of Alexander Pushkin, one of the best sculptures of 1950s Leningrad and probably the most expressive of Pushkin. Notable addresses around the square include the **Mussorgsky Opera and Ballet Theater** *(Ploshchad Iskusstv 1),* one of three surviving imperial theaters; the **Musical Comedy** *(Italianskaya 13);* and **Stray Dog** *(Ploshchad Iskusstv 5),* a restaurant named for the earlier cabaret café here where the most daring performances of the early Russian avant-garde artists and writers took place.

Cross Arts Square toward the dominating Mikhailovsky Palace (the Russian Museum, see pp. 118–125). On the palace's right is the **Russian Ethnographic Museum** ❿ *(Inzhenernaya 4, closed Mon. & last Fri. of month, $$).* Built in the Rossi style, it actually dates from the early 20th century (by Vasily Svinin, 1900–1915) and is worth seeing for its central Marble Hall, replete with glazed ceiling, marble colonnades, and the relief of "The Peoples of Russia," which wraps around three walls.

A statue of Alexander Pushkin proudly commands the heart of Arts Square.

The museum's impressive "Parade of Peoples" exhibit reveals the ethnicities living across the entire breadth of the Eurasian Russian Empire, showcasing a rich diversity of life, from Siberian reindeer herders to Caucasian mountain dwellers. Temporary exhibitions often relate to textiles.

Conclude your walk with a restful pause in the **Mikhailovsky Palace Gardens,** landscaped by the Scottish architect Adam Menelaws in the early 1820s. Enter on Sadovaya Street, to the east of the palace. ■

St. Petersburg's sole monument to Catherine the Great stands in front of the recently restored Alexandra's Theater.

Ostrovsky Square

THE ENSEMBLE OF OSTROVSKY SQUARE, COMPRISING A landscaped square, a theater complex, and a beautiful street, is a creation of Carlo Rossi. Completed it 1834, it runs between Nevsky Prospekt and Lomonosov Square. Originally named after Tsar Nicholas I's wife, Alexandra, the square was renamed, after the playwright Alexander Ostrovsky (1823–1886), in the Soviet period.

Ostrovsky Square
 Maps pp. 114 & 129

Museum of the Theatrical and Musical Arts
www.theatremuseum.ru

✉ Ostrovskogo Ploshchad 6
☎ 571-2195
🕐 Closed Tues. & last Fri. of month
💲 $
🚌 Bus: 3 & 7; Trolleybus: 1, 5, 7, 10, & 22; Metro: Gostiny Dvor & Nevsky Prospekt

The 49-foot-high (15 m), bell-shaped **statue of Catherine the Great** (by Mikhail Mikeshin, 1873) in the square's center is the only monument to her in town. Clad in a sweeping ermine robe, she stands haughtily above a circle of nine of her worthies. The multicolumned **Russian National Library** (1834), with its allegorical statues, lines the west side of the square, while on the east side, two **pavilions** (1818) provide entrance to the Anichkov Palace garden.

Behind Catherine rises the monumental 1832 **Alexandra's Theater,** home to St. Petersburg's oldest and most important theater company. Its six-columned portico surmounted by a dynamic bronze group offers a sense of celebration and harmony to the square. The **Museum of the Theatrical and Musical Arts** sits behind the theater and is worth a visit for its historic images of the leading lights of the Russian stage.

The locally loved **Zodchevo Rossi Ulitsa** (Architect Rossi Street) is remarkable for its precise proportions: It is as wide (72 feet/21.6 m) as the buildings are high and ten times as long. Waves of white columns rise in tiers the length of the street. Ensconced at **No. 2** since 1836, Russia's finest ballet school, now the **Russian Academy of Ballet,** counts among its alumni Rudolf Nureyev and Mikhail Baryshnikov. The neo-Byzantine apartment house at **No. 5,** designed by Nikolay Basin, outraged many when it was completed in 1879 because it violated Rossi's architectural order. ■

Anichkov & Beloselsky-Belozersky Palaces

THE ANICHKOV AND BELOSELSKY-BELOZERSKY PALACES appear to face one another across the Fontanka River on the southern side of Nevsky Prospekt in a dramatic architectural contest. The powerful, regulated white Ionic columns of the Anichkov seem to challenge the flights of ornamental fancy set against a reddish ground of the Beloselsky-Belozersky.

The palace interiors rival their exterior, offering breathtaking tours through the changing times and fortunes of St. Petersburg. Much has been lost, but what remains tells a vivid story. *(Access to both palaces and events.)*

As the street's oldest palace—completed in 1754—the Anichkov Palace predated the Nevsky's "perspective" idea and hence orientation to the river was more important. Its Nevsky side is even closed by Giacomo Quarenghi's and Rusca's multicolumned chancellory building, the Kabinet (1803–1811). Originally designed for Empress Elizabeth's favorite Count Alexey Razumovsky (1709–1771) as a baroque edifice by Mikhail Zemtsov, Grigory Dmitriev, and Bartolomeo Francesco Rastrelli.

A **suite of rooms** on the first floor retains the luxurious appearance of tsarist times. Look for the magnificent "pineapple" chandeliers and the exquisite Crimson, Gold, and Blue Salons. Post-revolutionary fervor transformed the walls and ceilings of two rooms: In 1936, a team of folk artists from the village of Palekh (renowned for its enamelwork) painted them with the Russian fairy tales of Alexander Pushkin and Maxim Gorky in all-consuming compositions of vibrant color and action.

The Beloselsky-Belozersky

Palace acquired most of its current neorococo appearance in 1847 (by Andrey Stackenschneider). Its **formal rooms** and **staircase** offer a feast of plaster

The unadorned exterior of the Anichkov Palace disguises some extravagantly decorated interiors.

putti, caryatids, arabesques, and painted panels by French masters. Concerts take place in its substantial **concert hall** and the former library. Sold to the state in 1884 by its owners—the Beloselsky-Belozersky family—the palace became home to Tsar Alexander III's younger brother Grand Prince Sergey and his wife Elizabeth, the granddaughter of Queen Victoria of Great Britain. You may feel Elizabeth's influence in the English touches in the **library** (by Meltser, ca 1900) and the displays detailing the palace's use as Queen Alexandra's English-Russian Hospital during World War I. ∎

Anichkov Palaces
- 🅰 Map p. 114
- ✉ Nevsky Prospekt 39
- ☎ 310-4395
- 🕑 4 tours/month, check outside palace
- 💲 $
- Ⓜ Metro: Nevsky Prospekt

Beloselsky-Belozersky Palace
- ✉ Nevsky Prospekt 41
- ☎ 315-5236
- 🕑 Details for tours at kiosk in left foyer
- 💲 $
- Ⓜ Metro: Mayakovskaya or Nevsky Prospekt

Fontanka Embankment

**Fontanka
Embankment**
 Map p. 114

**Horse tamers
guard the
Fontanka's
Anichkov Bridge.**

UNTIL THE MID-18TH CENTURY, THE FONTANKA MARKED the southern boundary of St. Petersburg. As it flows from the Neva (by the Summer Garden) to the Neva (close to its mouth), it arcs around the historic center of the city, becoming the third concentric waterway after the Moika River and Griboedov Canal. Peter's creation of the Summer Garden at its start gave the river its name: Fontanka derives from the fountains that he introduced to St. Petersburg there.

Museum of Music
✉ Sheremetev Palace,
Fontanka
Naberezhnaya 34
☎ 272-4441
🕐 Closed a.m.,
Mon.–Tues., & last
Wed. of month
💲 $
🚇 Metro: Gostiny Dvor
& Mayakovskaya

**Anna Akhmatova
Memorial Museum**
www.akhmatova.spb.ru
✉ Liteinyi Prospekt 53
☎ 272-2211
🕐 Closed Mon. & last
Wed. of month
💲 $
🚇 Metro: Mayakovskaya

The construction of the river's granite embankments in the late 18th century spurred development. The banks north of Nevsky Prospekt developed first.

The 1841 **Anichkov Bridge,** which carries Nevsky Prospekt across the Fontanka, is perhaps St. Petersburg's most distinctly decorated bridge: four bronze men taming dramatically rearing horses guard the span. Completed in 1850, the sculptures by Baron Peter Clodt von Jurgensburg have become some of Russia's best known, frequently copied, and poetry-inspiring monumental works. They have come to signify heroic victory through struggle both of the city and the nation. In fact, the groups on the bridge are

very early copies themselves: Tsar Nicholas I gave the originals to the kings of Prussia and Naples.

Head north along the left (east) bank of the Fontanka from here, pass the rather serene, 1807 Giacomo Quarenghi–designed facade of the **Catherine Institute for Noble Girls** (No. 36), and stop in front of the **Sheremetev Palace** (No. 34), otherwise known as the Fountain House. Set back from the street behind some refined railings (1838), this beautiful Elizabethan baroque mansion was designed by the talented Savva Chevakinsky around 1750. It was built for Count Pyotr Sheremetev on the estate given to his father by Tsar Peter in 1712. Despite many additions and alterations, a considerable amount of the early interiors has survived, which you can admire in the **Museum of Music** *($)* that occupies a portion of the palace. The museum offers a very rich collection of musical instruments from around the world, including serpent-shaped horns, mini-violins, and Persian instruments. The fine Etruscan Drawing Room holds an exhibit dedicated to the founder of Russian classical music, Mikhail Glinka (1804–1857).

Part of the northern wing of the Sheremetev Palace houses St. Petersburg's most evocative literary museum, the **Anna Akhmatova Memorial Museum,** founded in 1989 in the apartment that the great Russian poet called home from 1927 to 1952. With ample explanatory notes in English, the tribute to Akhmatova (1889–1966) provides insight into her star poet status and reveals the difficult conditions of life for creative spirits in the USSR. In addition, the museum holds the "American Study of Josef Brodsky," a later (1940–1996) great of Russian poetry.

Farther north along the embankment, near the Belinsky Bridge, the octagonal cupola and multitiered bell tower of the 1734 **Church of SS Simeon and Anne** make a pretty picture. The circular building on the opposite bank, whose dome spans an incredible 163 feet (49.7 m), is Russia's first permanent circus, the **Gaetano Ciniselli Circus** (by Vasily Kenel, 1877). It stands on the site of the former Elephant Court, where the elephants sent to Catherine II by the shah of Persia were kept. Closed during the summer, its humorous and daring live acts still attract crowds during the cooler months.

North of the Church of Sts. Simeon and Anne, the Fontanka Embankment is lined with a series of mansions dating from the alexander Pushkin era, save two: **No. 12** is a classic example of Stalinist empire style and the baroque **Church of St. Panteleimon,** near the elegant bridge of the same name, dates from the late 1730s.

The smartest old house on the Fontanka south of Nevsky Prospekt is Nikolay Lvov's 1750s U-shaped **mansion of the poet Gavrila Derzhavin** *(No. 118),* which is now a museum *($)* dedicated to Russian literature of the early 19th century. ∎

Museum of Gavrila Derzhavin

✉ Fontanka Naberezhnaya 118

☎ 740-1922

🕓 Closed Tues. & last Fri. of month

💲 $

🚇 Metro: Tekhnologichesky Institut

The Sheremetev Palace houses the music and Akhmatova museums.

Cathedral of the Transfiguration

Cathedral of the Transfiguration

Map p. 114

Preobrazhenskaya Ploshchad 1

THE CATHEDRAL OF THE TRANSFIGURATION IS POSSIBLY the most obviously militant of St. Petersburg's military churches. The striking fence is made of upright cannon barrels tied in massive iron chains and topped by imperial double-headed eagles. But notice the cannon point downward and bear Arabic inscriptions. The fence celebrates Russia's victory in the 1828–29 war with the Ottoman Empire—the 102 cannon were trophies from captured Turkish forts.

The striking silhouette of the Cathedral of the Transfiguration rounds off Pestel Street at its eastern end.

The cathedral itself pre-dates the war. Empress Elizabeth commissioned the church as Russia's first regimental church in 1742. It was built (1743–1754) for her father Peter's favored Transfiguration Regiment in its part of town and in reaction against the tribulations of "foreign" rule that had blighted the reign of Anne, Elizabeth's predecessor. Its architects Mikhail Zemtsov and Pietro Trezzini created the first centralized cross-plan church with five cupolas (following the example of the cathedrals in Moscow's Kremlin) in St. Petersburg.

Severely damaged by fire in 1825, the cathedral was rebuilt in the late 1820s in the empire style. Architect Vasily Stasov designed the cannon-chain fence and created the compact appearance of the church in the middle of Pestel Street. Notice his large frieze-like **bas-reliefs on the exterior** with their fan-like fusions of Christian symbols and military trophies.

The cathedral was one of the few churches that held services throughout the Soviet period. Its interior is intact, if demilitarized due to the dispersal of its collection of banners, arms, and trophies to the Hermitage and the Artillery Museum and the disappearance of its sets of imperial uniforms. The gilded triumphal arch of the **iconostasis** will draw your eye, as will the light-giving **central cupola** with images of angels carrying the tools of the Passion and the four Evangelists, painted by top professors at the Academy of Art in the early 19th century.

The venerated, jewel-encrusted **"Savior Not Created by Hands"** adorns a lectern in the right-hand choir. This captivating Russian image of the head of Christ is said to have been created in 1676 for Tsar Alexey by the famous Moscow icon painter Simon Ushakov. Handed down to Alexey's son, Tsar Peter, it accompanied him everywhere—his military campaigns, the founding of St. Petersburg, and even his deathbed. It has stood in the cathedral since 1929. ■

The daring iron-and-glass ceiling of the Stieglitz Institute was one of the wonders of late 19th-century St. Petersburg.

Stieglitz Institute & Museum

THE FABERGÉ AND IMPERIAL PORCELAIN FACTORY DESIGNers acquired their amazing skills, and the decorators of the St. Petersburg's palaces, mansions, banks, and stores were trained, at the Stieglitz School of Technical Design, which was one of the world's best endowed and cutting-edge art schools around the turn of the 20th century. An adjoining museum showcased the school's work and the amassed collection of its benefactor, multimillionaire financier Baron Alexander Stieglitz.

Applied Arts Museum of the St. Petersburg Art-Design Academy

🅰 Map p. 114

✉ Solyanoy Pereulok 15

☎ 273-3258

🕐 Closed Sun.–Mon. & Aug.

💲 $

For all the artistic flair and renown of the Stieglitz designers of the past, the museum and school are now remarkably low key. Yet this building by architect Maximilian Messmacher, completed in 1896, encloses a uniquely captivating realm of artistry. Stieglitz opened his decorative arts school in 1879. The 30 halls of its museum were to display his collection of 30,000 works detailing the development of applied art.

The museum's **facade** reads like the contents page of a compendium of art history. On top of the Renaissance and baroque borrowings of its forms, there are allegorical sculptures representing the arts, medallions with portraits of great masters, and mosaic panels with the names of even more national and international greats. The lusciously decorated interior glorifies the arts. A huge **exhibition hall** with palazzo-like arcade-galleries and an innovative, glazed ceiling was designed to show off the students' work.

Most of the collection was transferred to the Hermitage (see pp. 71–73) after 1917, and the museum and school were renamed. But enough remains to reveal the original intent: To operate as an elaborate and coordinated style directory for the students and visitors. The displays offer rich tastings of decorative arts from Pompeii, Louis XV, Farnese, Flemish, Muscovy, Wedgwood, 1980s Leningrad, and more. ∎

The art of decoration

Tea cups are revolutionary things. Likewise vases, inkpots, figurines, and sugar bowls. Especially radical are the coffeepots with the dainty white handles. China services aren't so threatening; it's the porcelain ones that need watching—they're the leaders of the gang. That's the way with St. Petersburg.

From its inception, St. Petersburg was intended as the center of Russian refinement. It would lead the country and the empire into a hitherto unknown sphere of polite society where grace, etiquette, and fine-quality articles were the norm. Hence Peter's ideas for the developments of the arts, realized in part by his daughter Elizabeth and then more fully by Catherine II, were that all its fields be united in one tremendous effort to raise Russian standards and international prestige to new heights.

The decorative arts were as important as the fine arts. The Imperial Academy of Arts, established in 1764, offered all varieties of arts and crafts. Within 70 or so years of the city's founding, it had major tapestry, mosaic, glass, metalware, furniture, and, most important, porcelain workshops, many of which were factory scale. (Enterprises working under the patronage of the royal court bore the imperial designation.) In 1879, Petersburg financier and collector Baron Alexander Stieglitz opened what rapidly became one of the world's most advanced private decorative arts school, the Stieglitz School of Technical Design (see p. 137). It, together with the academy, produced the masters who produced the goods.

With the overthrow of the tsarist regime in 1917, the imperial manufactories were turned into state operations. Private ventures vanished (including the world-famous St. Petersburg jeweler Carl Fabergé) or were nationalized. Thus the Imperial Porcelain Factory, founded in 1744 by Empress Elizabeth, immediately became the State Porcelain Factory and then in 1924 the Lomonosov State Porcelain Factory, honoring Russia's first academic scientist. (The new name ignored the fact that it was chemist Dmitry Vinogradov, 1720–1758, Mikhail Lomonosov's friend, who uncovered the "Chinese secret" of how to make porcelain.)

Porcelain reigns supreme in St. Petersburg decorative arts. The Lomonosov factory continued the tradition set by its earlier iteration. The head designer during the Stalin years was Nikolay Suetin (1897–1954). His work began daringly, with tea services decorated with abstract "victory over the sun" color bodies and serene architectonic forms that can be considered socialist art deco. However, by the 1930s, simple stylized figures of workers and tractors started to appear on plates and jugs. Porcelain was being molded as Soviet propaganda. These items are now real collectors' pieces, and Suetin's best are in the Russian Museum. The Lomonosov houses a branch of the Hermitage: A small **museum** (*Obukhovskoy Oborony Prospekt 151, tel 326-4620, closed Mon., metro: Lomonosov-skaya*) traces the history of this most noble of the city's applied arts. The magnificent royal services comprise hundreds of pieces covered in refined patterns or classical scenes, notably the Arabesque, Yachting, Hunting and Cabinet (Study) services. Those sets dedicated to the construction of Soviet-style socialism—complete with images of industry, labor, and banner-waving optimism—are equally delightful.

The unheralded art nouveau works and those of the 1950s to 1970s include some gems; of the former style, look for Rudolf Wilde's underglaze painted dishes, while for the latter, seek out Anna Leporskaya's vases and coffee services.

Two other museums highlight the importance of porcelain in St. Petersburg: The **Museum of the History of St. Peters-** **burg** (see pp. 90–91) shows how porcelain fits in with the development of the city; the **Museum of Russian Political History** (see pp. 176–77) reveals its political brief. ■

Left: The Gossipers' Vase (c.1807); Above: "Hearken the Whispering Sea" (Amandus Adamson, 1904); Below: Display in the Stieglitz Museum

ΦTЪЗAΔ ΦYBOPOBЯ BЪ ПОXOΔЪ 1799 ГOΔЯ.

Suvorov Museum

FOR MILITARY HEROES WITH CULT STATUS IN RUSSIA, LOOK
no further than Generalissimo Alexander Suvorov (1729–1800). He
was the first person for whom a memorial museum was especially created. He gained an unparalleled renown for being an attack-minded
tactician and leader in a military career that lasted half a century.

The Russian adulation of Gen.
Suvorov, whose statue was erected
in the Field of Mars (see p. 58)
just after he died, prompted Tsar
Nicholas II, a hundred years later,
to gather donations for the construction of what he regarded as
a "temple monument." Built 1901
to 1904 to the design of Alexander von Hohen, the museum was
made to look like an ancient
Russian fortress; the tower form
of the entrance was inspired by
the Moscow Kremlin.

The two mosaic panels on the
main facade were the first non-
religious mosaics to adorn any
St. Petersburg building. The left
panel shows Suvorov leading his
suffering men across the snowy
Alps in the 1799 campaign
against Napoleon in northern
Italy; the right panel, his depar-

ture for the campaign from his
equally snowy Russian village.

Inside, the **main hall** advances
the temple-like atmosphere. The
great man's swords rest on an
altar-like podium, behind which
a modern stained-glass panel
depicts Suvorov going to war
under the protection of the Virgin
and Child and two winged angels
of victory. To either side are
mock-ups of the various rooms in
which he lived. The **other halls**
contain war trophies, portraits of
family and foes, banners, battle
models, medals, documents, and
keys to the forts and towns taken
or freed by Suvorov.

Briefly an aeronautical museum (1925–1941), Stalin reverted
the building back to the Suvorov
Museum during World War II,
devoting much space to that war. ■

**State Memorial
Museum of
Alexander Suvorov**
www.suvorovmuseum.ru
🅰 Map p. 114
✉ Kirochnaya Ulitsa 43
☎ 279-3914
🕐 Closed Tues.–Wed. &
  last Mon. of month
💲 $$$ (guided tours
  in English available)
🚇 Metro:
  Chernyshevskaya

Tauride Gardens & around

THE TAURIDE GARDENS AND THE SURROUNDING AREA were once the realm of the upper echelons of society in the late tsarist period. The gardens are now public while the streets host "new" (monied) Russians and international diplomats. An amble here reveals a unique and select side of St. Petersburg, albeit one whose doors are, apart from the restaurants, mainly closed to casual visitors.

Tauride Gardens
Map p. 114

The grid-plan leafy avenues that approach the gardens from the west, especially Tchaikovsky and Furshtatskaya Streets, are lined with mansions redolent of class. Standouts include the 1909 art nouveau **Prince Kochubey Villa** (Furshtatskaya 24), the 1860 **Burturlina Mansion** (Tchaikovsky 10), and the 1904 French Renaissance **Kelch Mansion** (Tchaikovsky 28).

The extensive and picturesque Tauride Gardens sit on a very flat and sandy horn of land around which the Neva makes a great meander. In the 1780s, English landscape gardener William Gould introduced little hillocks, winding paths, ponds, streams, bridges, English fruit trees and bushes, succulent grasses, and even a few cows. Turned into the City Children's Park in 1957, the gardens today are a haven of relaxation for all ages. These gardens were originally attached to the Tauride Palace (see box at right).

The **Tauride Palace** faces the redbrick complex of St. Petersburg's Main Waterworks, erected in the early 1860s. In 2003, this reopened having been turned into the pristine **St. Petersburg Aquaworld** (Shpalernaya 56, closed Mon.–Tues., $) in which you can learn about everything from the development of the city's drainage systems to toilet fashions and Rasputin's favorite baths.

Tauride Palace

The Tauride Palace is now cut off from its gardens. A masterpiece of severe classicism, designed by Ivan Starov, it was built in the 1780s for Catherine the Great's lover Grigory Potemkin (1739–1791). It served as a prototype for countless other palaces on Russian country estates. Potemkin received it, the gardens, and the title of Prince of Tauride as tokens for gaining Russian control of the Crimea (ancient Tauris).

The palace now houses the Intra-Parliamentary Assemblies of the Commonwealth of Independent States and the Eurasian Economic Commonwealth and is off-limits to the public. You can not imagine the scale of the interior grandeur from the seemingly modest exterior visible from Shpalernaya Street. ■

Head west along Shpalernaya and then turn right on Chernyshevskogo to reach the Neva and **Robespierre Embankment.** Two divided and emaciated bronze sphinxes, whose beautiful faces turn into skulls, stand deliberately positioned opposite the Kresty Prison. This is Mikhail Shemyakin's 1995 **Monument to the Victims of Political Repression,** which serves a reminder of dark times in this bright area around the Tauride Gardens. ■

Smolny Convent & Institute

The exterior of the Smolny Cathedral is Rastrelli's greatest achievement in St. Petersburg.

EAST OF THE CENTER OF PETER'S NEW CITY, ON THE shores of the Neva just opposite where it is joined by the Okhta River, a village called Smolnaya grew up. Its name derived from its function as the "tar yard" for the caulking of the ships being built in the Admiralty wharfs. Peter had a little summer cottage here, which in 1720 was turned into the Smolny Palace. It was to serve as the country residence of his daughter Elizabeth.

Smolny Convent

🅼 Map p. 115

✉ Rastrelli Ploshchad 3/1

☎ 571-9182

🕐 Cathedral closed Thurs., bell tower closed Wed.

💲 $ (bell tower)

🚎 Trolleybus: 5 & 22; Metro: Chernyshevskaya

Despite its early history, for the last 200 years "the Smolny" has popularly meant two very different things: a cathedral and the heart of local government.

Smolny Cathedral was Francesco Bartolomeo Rastrelli's masterwork. It forms the centerpiece of Empress Elizabeth's Convent of the Resurrection (1748–1757), which was built on the razed site of her palace. Elizabeth aimed to retire here. Rising to a height of 308 feet (94 m), the silhouette of

the cathedral dominates its surroundings, but not as intended. Rastrelli's model, which you can see in the Academy of Arts, shows that the whole convent complex was to be dwarfed by a colossal bell tower entrance, one some 147 feet (45 m) taller than the bell tower that stands today. Cost overruns and other events resulted in a scaled-back version, and as such, it is the remarkably graceful lines of the cathedral that catch the eye.

Note how the cupolas (the four surrounding ones are belfries) are diagonally fused together, how the architect used white three-quarter columns set against azure blue walls in a way that celebrates movement, especially upward and celestial. Rastrelli's combination of the five-cupola cross-in-square traditions of ancient Russian churches and the sense of the energy of Italian high baroque created a unique, fully three-dimensional building that rises up at the very center of another cross-in-square plan, that of the nuns' living quarters. Climb the **northwestern belfry** for some superb views across St. Petersburg.

The exterior and the interior contrast with each other. The internal work was interrupted by the Seven Years' War (the cathedral was a huge drain on the national finances) and only completed some 80 years later by Vasily Stasov in a more subdued, white style. Deprived of its fine icons and ecclesiastical garb (though services have resumed, it was closed as a church in 1931), the cathedral now hosts exhibitions and concerts.

SMOLNY INSTITUTE

Most Russians identify the Smolny with the rule of the Communist Party from 1917 or the rule of the incumbent St. Petersburg governor. In fact, the Smolny was originally the convent's Institute for Young Noblewomen, founded in 1764 as the first school for Russia's most privileged girls by Catherine II. In 1808 it got its own premises in the southern part of the convent grounds: a well-proportioned, solemn example of Giacomo Quarenghi's severe classicism. The large assembly hall in the south wing completes the air of orderly finesse.

The building became home to the Petrograd Soviet in 1917 and witnessed some of the most formative political moments of the early 20th century. It was here that the Bolsheviks established their grip on power on the night of October 25 and here that Lenin lived and ran the new Soviet government (until March 1918). One of the most expressive (and most copied) monuments of Lenin (by Vasily Kozlov, 1927) stands in front of the portico. Subsequently, the Smolny became the headquarters of the Communist Party in Petrograd/Leningrad and was the scene of the assassination of the party's general secretary, Sergey Kirov, on December 1, 1934.

Today the institute is the St. Petersburg Government Office. It is closed to the public except for a **museum** in the rooms where Lenin spent his time. You may walk in the **gardens,** however. ■

Smolny Institute Museum
☎ 576-7461
🕐 Open Fri.; prearranged group tours 10 a.m.–4 p.m., individuals at 3 p.m.
💲 $$$$ (group tour)

Alexander Nevsky Monastery

Alexander Nevsky Monastery

🅐 Map p. 115

Church of the Annunciation— State Museum of Urban Sculpture

www.gmgs.spb.ru

🅐 Map p. 115

✉ Aleksandra Nevskogo Ploshchad 1

☎ 274-2635 or 277-1716

🕐 Closed Mon. & Thurs.

💲 $ (Annunciation Church)

🚇 Metro: Aleksandra Nevskogo Ploshchad

THE OLDER BROTHER OF THE SMOLNY CONVENT ALSO LIES on the western banks of the Neva, just over a mile (1.6 km) south of the convent at the eastern end of Nevsky Prospekt. Tsar Peter founded the monastery in 1710 to serve as the spiritual guardian of his country's new capital. Very symbolically he named it after Prince Alexander of Novgorod (1220–1263), who had repelled the colonizing Swedes from the Neva in 1240, thereby preserving access to the Baltic Sea for the ancient Russian principalities. The heroic prince became known as Alexander Nevsky and was canonized in 1381.

An **equestrian monument to Alexander Nevsky** (by V. Kozenyuk, 2002) stands in the center of the square bearing his name. A neoclassic arch rises in the south and serves as the gateway into the red-and-white heart of the monastery. As you pass through the gates, you enter one of Russian Orthodoxy's highest ranking monasteries, a *lavra;* there are only three others similarly designated. Peter's head architect, Domenico Trezzini, laid out the monastery complex in 1715.

Immediately on your left is the picturesque single-cupola **Church of the Annunciation,** completed in 1723 as the first stone church in St. Petersburg. It is now the **State Museum of Urban Sculpture.** The three-story church was conceived by Peter as a Russian pantheon. To this end he ceremoniously brought the relics of Alexander Nevsky here on August 30, 1724, the third anniversary of the Nystad Peace, thus making a connection with his own victory over the Swedes. While the relics lay in the upper church, the lowest part became the burial vault for rulers' relatives and leading courtiers.

The remarkable silver sepulchre containing Nevsky's relics was removed to the neighboring Trinity Cathedral in 1790 and to the Hermitage in 1922 (where it can be viewed today), but you can still see the pathos-filled memorial stones of the great and the good from around 1800. You might pause before the entwined hearts and English epitaph for Elizabeth Chichagova (née Proby), the beloved asthmatic wife of Admiral Chichagov, whose elegiac gravestone hints at an amazing international love story. There's no greater contrast than with the orderly "Here lies Suvorov" memorial opposite.

At the center of the monastery is the **Trinity Cathedral,** (1776–1790), which Catherine II commissioned Ivan Starov to build in her favored neoclassical style. Completed in 1790, it has a single dome, and two bell towers mark the western facade. It is a very active church with a fine white marble, bronze, and agate iconostasis; pictures attributed to Van Dyck, Rubens, and Guercino; and a new reliquary for the remains of Alexander Nevsky.

(Since being brought to St. Petersburg, Nevsky's relics have led a peripatetic existence: They were moved from the nearby Church of the Annunciation to here, then to the Hermitage, then to the Museum of the History of

Religion and Atheism, and then here again in June 1989.)

To feel the scale and atmosphere of the monastery, stroll the grounds to either side of the Trinity Cathedral. To the east lies the Nicholas Cemetery, while to the west the War Cemetery and the domestic, metropolitan's, and seminary buildings. To the south there is a wing with a church dedicated to Alexander Nevsky's younger brother, Prince Feodor, in which are buried members of the Georgian royal family. The shady **Metropolitan's Garden** outside the monastery walls exudes a certain non-Petersburgian quality, something that relates the lavra to earlier Russian times. ∎

Staying true to Peter's intentions, the Alexander Nevsky Monastery plays a key role in the spiritual life of St. Petersburg.

Tikhvin & Lazarev Cemeteries

Tikhvin & Lazarev Cemeteries

🗺 Map p. 115

✉ Aleksandra Nevskogo Ploshchad 1

💲 $$ (one ticket for both cemeteries)

🚇 Metro: Aleksandra Nevskogo Ploshchad

YOU MIGHT FIND YOURSELF DYING TO VISIT THE ALEXander Nevsky Monastery for one reason alone: a grave lying next to one of Russia's most famous and celebrated personalities in the Tikhvin or Lazarus Cemetery. These days, for most, the goal is the more spacious, green, and modern Tikhvin.

Dostoyevsky is one of the many illustrious Russians buried in Tikhvin Cemetery.

The Lazarus Cemetery is St. Petersburg's oldest graveyard; Peter founded it in 1713 and later buried his favorite sister, Natalya, and his three-year-old son, Peter, in the Lazarus Mausoleum (their remains were reinterred in the Annunciation Church in 1723).

Since Soviet times, the cemetery has also been referred to as the 18th-century Necropolis. It is crowded with the gravestones of Russian aristocracy, scientists, architects, and statesmen, particularly of the late 18th and early 19th centuries. Many were moved here in the 1930s, both because other cemeteries were being demolished and the Alexander Nevsky graveyards were being turned into a museum. A leaflet in English (*available at entrance kiosk*) details were you can find Mikhail Lomonosov, the great Russian scientist; empire-style architect Carlo Rossi; the Romanovs' toughest finance minister, Sergey Witte; and many others.

Most visitors flock to the Tikhvin Cemetery (*English leaflet available at entrance kiosk*)—or the Necropolis of the Masters of Art as it has been known since Soviet times. More widely spread and more inventive in style and form than those of the Lazarus, the 174 grave-markers here pay homage to Mussorgsky, Dostoyevsky, Rubinstein, Glinka, and a host of other leading Russian artists, actors, singers, and literary figures from the late 19th through 20th century. The gravestones of Tchaikovsky and Rimsky-Korsakov have a special sense of artistry akin to their distinct musical sensitivities.

The former **Tikhvin Church** close to the cemetery's northern wall has a well-organized display of models of the chief public monuments of St. Petersburg, from the earliest to some of the most recent. ∎

The ceremonial Strelka of Vasilevsky Island celebrates St. Petersburg's place at the heart of a new maritime and commercial empire. From the late 18th century on, the city's most talented brains and hands have gathered on this island of knowledge and art.

Vasilevsky Island

Detail of one of the Rostral Columns that stand in front of the Stock Exchange

Celebrating Navy Day (last Sunday in July) on the Strelka of Vasilevsky

Vasilevsky

THE LAST ISLAND IN THE NEVA DELTA IS ALSO THE largest. The Finns called it Hirvisaari (Elk Island), the Russians Vasilevsky. Who is the Basil (Vasily) it was named after? The consensus says that it is Vasily Selezin, a settler from Novgorod who owned the island in the late 15th century. Others claim the honoree is Capt. Vasily Korchmin, who ran Peter's artillery battery on the island at the time of the city's foundation, and folklore holds that it is Basil the Blessed, the 16th-century Moscow saint whose prophesies reputedly helped save Ivan the Terrible's Muscovy from the eastern hoards. Perhaps the answer is all of them.

In the 1710s, Peter decided to make Vasilevsky Island the center of his new Russian capital. A grid plan was drawn up, dividing the land by lines of canals and widely spaced straight streets, in keeping with what Peter had seen and admired on his visit to Amsterdam. Peter's plan didn't quite happen as intended but the streets do form a regular grid. Essentially the most populated eastern side of the island is divided by three main east–west avenues —Bolshoy, Sredny, and Maly Prospekts. These are crossed by streets called Lines, which number from 1 near the Strelka to 29 in the west. Despite their ostensible sameness, they offer lovely strolls.

Home to St. Petersburg University, the Academy of Arts, and the Central Naval College, and with major family-friendly museums, Vasilevsky is a very youthful place. Although there are lots of higher education institutes in other parts of the city, this area is the student quarter. It has a character all of its own. Joined to the left bank by two great bridges whose spans rise at night, its embankments are romantic places.

The main thrust of the island seems to be its pointed nose, which sticks into the Neva River, splitting it into its Bolshaya (Great) and Malaya (Little) branches. Development during Peter's time first centered around this area of land, which came to be known as the Strelka (Spit), and extended down the adjacent bank of the Bolshaya Neva, which today is known as University Embankment. The Kunstkammer, Twelve Colleges, and Menshikov's Palace were all built during Peter's time. The first two, later becoming part of the Academy of Sciences and the

university respectively, marked the start of Peter's organization of a new Russia largely free from its medieval past. They were to educate and regulate. Menshikov's Palace, on the other hand, was to impress and entertain. It was the grandest building of the Petrine era.

The Strelka is one of the faces of St. Petersburg. In the 1730s it was turned into the city's commercial port. The obligatory customhouse, warehouses, and jetties soon appeared. In the early 1800s, Russia's Stock Exchange (Birzha) took up residence in a remarkable building. Looking like an ancient Greek temple, this bourse now houses the much-loved Naval Museum. Its flanking red Rostral Columns, former navigational beacons, are an emblem of the city. Today, the working port no longer exists here; if you want to experience the maritime quality of Vasilevsky, you have to depart from its more lively eastern end and head to its bracing and remote-seeming western shores. ∎

Serny Island

Malaya Neva

Dekabrist Island

LUTHERAN CEMETERY

URALSKAYA UL. УРАЛЬСКАЯ УЛ.

NAB. MAKAROVA НАБ. МАКАРОВА

NAB. REKI SMOLENKA

Customs House/ Institute of Russian Literature (Pushkin House)

Academy of Science

STRELKA

SMOLENSK CEMETERY

VASILEOSTROVSKY

МАЛЫЙ ПРОСП.

6-7 ЛИНИЯ

14-15 LINIYA

СРЕДНИЙ ПРОСП.

Vasileostrovskaya

6-7 ЛИНИЯ

Central Naval Museum (Stock Exchange)

Rostral Columns

NALIKNAYA UL.

MALYI PROSPECT

Vasilevsky Island

14-15 ЛИНИЯ

SREDNY PROSPECT

Cathedral of St. Andrew

St. Petersburg University

Menshikov's Palace

Zoological Museum

Kunstkammer

НАЛИЧНАЯ УЛ.

БОЛЬШОЙ ПРОСП.

Academy of Arts

Academy of Science

Church of the Assumption of the Virgin Mother

Central Naval College

NAB. LEYTENANTA SHMIDTA

Bolshaya Neva

BOLSHOI

Mining Institute

Ice-Breaker Krasin

0   900 meters
0   900 yards

Area of map detail

St. Petersburg color-coded by region

The colonnaded
Stock Exchange
has symbolic
"rising sun" semi-
circular window
highlighting the
attic sculptural
group—"Poseidon
Triumphant."

The Strelka

THE SIGHT OF WHAT APPEARS TO BE A MASSIVE GREEK temple flanked by two tall red columns on Vasilevsky's Strelka (Spit) is a trademark view of St. Petersburg. When referring to the Strelka, Petersburgers mean one of two things: One, the area, the actual 1,837-foot-long (560 m) nose of the island that cleaves the Neva in two; and two, the Stock Exchange complex, one of St. Petersburg's grandest architectural ensembles, designed at the turn of the 19th century by the French architect Jean Thomas de Thomon.

The Strelka
🗺 Map p. 149

**Central Naval
Museum**
www.museum.navy.ru
🗺 Map p. 149
✉ Birzhevaya
Ploshchad 4
☎ 328-2502
🕐 Closed Mon.—Tues. &
last Thurs. of month
💲 $$$
🚌 Bus: 7 & 10;
Trolleybus: 1, 7, & 10;
Metro:
Vasileostrovskaya &
Sportivnaya

In fact, from the 1730s to 1885 the Strelka was St. Petersburg's commercial port and was surrounded by merchant ships from near and far. Prior to the founding of the city, a small village had been here, while during Peter's time there were windmills, sawmills, and the artillery battery of Capt. Vasily Korchmin, after whom the island could be named (if you believe one legend).

The **Stock Exchange (Birzha)** group of buildings was to be the centerpoint of Tsar Alexander I's new mercantile empire and as such was built on a gargantuan scale. The 1810 bourse itself is a supremely simple rectangular building set on a granite podium, surrounded by Doric colonnades, and capped with sculptural groups that are allegories of Russia's maritime prowess and wealth. It is a modern interpretation of the Greek Temple of Hera and Poseidon at Paestum in Italy, even down to its alignment with the grid plan of the coastal town behind it.

The exchange faces east toward the center of an artificially created semicircular square with ramps designed by de Thomon as an ice-cutter quay. The ornamentation of the great twin **Rostral Columns** on either side of the square also signals nautical supremacy, but here the vocabulary is derived from the Romans.

They rise to a height of 105 feet (32 m) and originally served as navigational beacons; fires were lit in the metal braziers that stand atop the columns. They are adorned with limestone bases sporting immense sculpted sea gods and goddesses said to represent Russia's most important trade rivers—the Volga, Dnieper, Volkhov, and Neva. Metal ship prows—rostra, hence the name Rostral—jut out of the columns, pointing to the four compass directions. They are adorned with different protective symbols: winged mermaids, tritons, wolves, and sea horses. Today, the beacons are lit on special occasions.

Since 1940, the Stock Exchange building has housed the **Central Naval Museum.** One of its prized possessions is the "Grandfather of the Russian fleet," the little wooden boat on which Peter learned to sail. The museum also has 2,000 ship (and submarine) models that trace the development of the Russian Navy from the 18th to 20th century, some excellent figureheads created by sculpture professors from the Academy of Arts, and a variety of displays dedicated to Russian and Soviet battles at sea. It also holds temporary exhibitions of marine paintings.

In June 2006, a **fountain** was inaugurated in front of the Stock Exchange. Set in the Neva, it covers an area wider than the length of a football field and jets water twice as high as the columns. With hundreds of spouts and thousands of lights, the fountain performs laser music-light shows (*summer only*). The most impressive shows take place at midnight.

To either side of the Stock Exchange sit the large, former bonded warehouses of the **customs depot.** They were built in the late 1820s. In 1895, after the port had moved west to Gutuev Island, whose deeper waters were capable of taking the larger modern ships, the warehouses were transferred to the Academy of Science.

The southern warehouse, which made use of the walls of a palace built for Peter's sister-in-law, Praskovia Feodorovna, around 1720, also contained a large hall for exhibitions of Russian-made goods. The academy reconstructed the hall as the **Zoological Museum.** Especially popular with children, this attraction is one of St. Petersburg's most visited museums. It currently shows around 30,000 animal species, ranging from insects to the world's only stuffed mammoth. Dioramas bring many of the animals to life. Most interesting, however, may be the skeletons extracted from the Siberian permafrost or Peter's collection of animals, which includes his horse and dog, both of whom he called Lisetta. The northern warehouse now houses a **soil museum** (*tel 328-5402, closed Sat.–Sun., $, pre-arranged tours only*) and the trendy Plaza club and restaurant.

Next door on Makarov Embankment, the customhouse, with its nicely proportioned dome and Ionic-columned portico crowned by a figure of Mercury, has been home to the **Institute of Russian Literature** since 1927. Known locally as the Pushkin House due to its collection of all the known Alexander Pushkin manuscripts, this archive holds unique manuscripts by world-famous writers. A **Literary Museum** (*tel 328-0502, closed Sat.–Sun., $, prearranged tours only*) contains the memorabilia of Russian writers from various eras. You can imagine Tolstoy sitting at his desk and Turgenev writing with his quill. ∎

Zoological Museum
www.zin.ru
- Map p. 149
- Universitetskaya 150 Naberezhnaya 1
- 328-0112
- Closed Fri.
- $
- Bus: 7 & 187; Trolleybus: 1 & 10; Metro: Vasileostrovskaya

Kunstkammer

Kunstkammer

www.kunstkamera.ru

⊠ Map p. 149

✉ Universitetskaya
Naberezhnaya 3

☎ 328-1412

⏲ Closed Mon. & last
Tues. of month

⑤ $$

🚍 Bus: 7 & 187;
Trolleybus: 1 & 10;
Metro:
Vasileostrovskaya

THE MOST DISTINCTIVE SILHOUETTE ON UNIVERSITY Embankment, the Kunstkammer holds St. Petersburg's "collection of rarities," otherwise known as the Cabinet of Curiosities. This was Russia's first museum, originally founded and set up by Peter in the newly built Summer Palace in 1714. He transferred to it all the collections he had gathered on his foreign travels and began to systematize them. Regarded as an encyclopedia museum, the Kunstkammer aimed to further and disseminate knowledge.

The Kunstkammer was built between 1718 and 1734 to designs by Georg Mattarnovi. The heart of Peter's Academy of Science, it contained an observatory, museum, anatomical theater, laboratory, and library. It was opened in an unfinished state but with great ceremony in 1728. Stripped of its sculptures and decorated curvaceous gables, the building retains its baroque feel in its dynamic three-tiered astronomical tower.

Russia's **first planetarium**—a globe, 10 feet (3.1 m) in diameter, designed by the German geographer Adam Olearius and made in 1664—was presented to Peter in 1717 by his daughter Anna's future husband, Karl-Friedrich, duke of Holstein-Gottorp. The globe could seat 12 people inside and rotated on its axis. Its internal map of the planets and stars offered a virtual experience of the solar system according to contemporary knowledge. Later damaged, restored, moved, stolen, and recovered, it was restored once again and now sits on the fifth floor of the tower. It can be visited in small group excursions.

Due to fires and changes of use, little of the Kunstkammer's original interior decoration remains. You can see some early stucco work on the first floor, two allegorical bas-reliefs from the 1770s in the eastern hall, and early 19th-century decorative painting in the rotunda, observatory, and Egyptian hall.

From the outset, the museum was accessible to the public. Entrance was free, and visitors were enticed in by offers of free cups of coffee, glasses of vodka, or bread and lard. The giveaways

have ended, but there's still plenty of reasons to go inside.

The Kunstkammer is actually three museums in one. The tower holds a small **museum dedicated to Mikhail Lomonosov** (1711–1765), Russia's first world-ranking scientist, a truly pioneering man of letters and the arts.

Samples from **Peter's collections** form some of the city's most alluring and disturbing exhibits. The scientific study of physical abnormalities collection is not for the weak-stomached. The specimens—purchased from Frederik Ruysch, the Dutch professor of anatomy, in Amsterdam in 1697 to 1698—relate to anatomy and embryology, of humans and other creatures. Among the various sights are a stuffed two-headed calf and glass jars containing pickled conjoined twins, human parts, and parasitic body growths. The exhibits compose just a tiny fraction of Peter's "Enlightenment" collections.

The rich, diverse exhibits of the **Museum of Anthropology and Ethnography** display some superb works of applied art, courtesy of various Russian world expeditions in the 18th and 19th centuries. They include a striking, feathered Californian American Indian raven spirit costume, Siberian pipes made of mammoth ivory, ritual masks from the Congo, and Javanese shadow puppets. ■

Viewed from the Winter Palace, the Kunstkammer is one of the most distinctive buildings on the northern shore of the Great Neva.

University Embankment

A STROLL DOWN THE LENGTH OF UNIVERSITY EMBANKMENT walks you through the St. Petersburg world of learning. It is here, during the academic year, that you will encounter some of Russia's brightest young sparks.

University Embankment

 Map p. 149

The rather plain **Academy of Sciences,** completed in 1789 by Giacomo Quarenghi, lies immediately west of the Kunstkammer. Designed to house the academy's printing house and professors' apartments *(not open to public).*

A weighty **monument to Mikhail Lomonosov**—Russia's first premier world scientist—sits at the end of Mendeleev Line. The **Twelve Colleges,** oriented south-north along Mendeleev Line, marks the end of the Strelka. The building's red-and-white facade, courtesy of Domenico Trezzini, runs 1,300 feet (440 m) and links the other baroque buildings of the embankment. Finished in 1742, it originally housed (and streamlined) under one roof Peter's 12 bureaucratic departments, which were then called colleges, as well as the Holy Synod, Senate, and Audience Chamber. The highly decorated **Peter Hall** of the Senate is among the best of St. Petersburg's

interiors from the 1730s.

The large-scale reform and growth of Russian bureaucracy in the early 19th century resulted in the ministries, the Senate, and the Synod gaining new buildings. The Twelve Colleges was turned into the newly founded **St. Petersburg University** (1828-1838). The western facade's long arcade served as a corridor, linking various departments. It was here, as students, that future Russian leaders Lenin and Putin headed for their lectures, not to mention the scientist Ivan Pavlov and the writer Alexander Blok. The arcade leads to a square now dedicated to the remarkable inventor of the hydrogen bomb, Andrey Sakharov (1921–1989). A recently installed, highly expressive bronze monument to the gaunt fighter for truth and Nobel Peace Prize winner sits in the center of the square, fronting the severe functionalist **Academy of Sciences Library** (1920s). ∎

Menshikov's Palace

THE OLDEST STONE BUILDING OF ST. PETERSBURG, AND THE grandest constructed during Peter's reign, was not built for the tsar of Russia, but for his friend Alexander Menshikov (1673–1729). Additionally, it is located on Vasilevsky Island, where there seems to be no other palaces and the aspect is one of well-calculated humane order. These facts may seem odd, but in actuality they fit with Peter's scheme of things, his personal distancing from pomp.

Menshikov's Palace

www.hermitagemuseum.org

🅰 Map p. 149

✉ Universitetskaya Naberezhnaya 15

☎ 323-1112

🕐 Closed Mon.

💲 $$

🚌 Bus: 7 & 187; Trolleybus: 1 & 10; Metro: Vasileostrovskaya

Peter turned Menshikov, a son of a Polish stableman, into the most powerful man in the empire after himself. From being a good soldier and Peter's orderly in the mid-1690s, Menshikov rose to become St. Petersburg's first governor, governor of Izhora province, president of the Military Collegium, Most-Illustrious Prince of Russia, Vice-Admiral, and Generalissimo. This man needed a big palace, and quickly.

Menshikov regarded Vasilevsky Island as his domain. His palace faced the Neva River, since the Neva then functioned as St. Petersburg's main street. Built to the design of Francesco Fontana and Johann Gottfried Schedel, the palace became the center of St. Petersburg's political and social life. Great receptions and assemblies took place here, as did the city's biggest parties, including the one to celebrate the victorious end to the Great Northern War in 1721, which coincided with the completion of the palace. The palace's defining three tiers of pilasters and the vaulted, arcade-like vestibule with Roman statues give the building a bit of an Italian palazzo feel.

Since the 1970s, under the aegis of the Hermitage, the palace has been an interesting, well-paced **museum** dedicated to early 18th-century Russian culture. The second floor, which was mainly occupied by family apartments, holds the museum's highlights, including four rooms completely covered in blue-and-white Dutch tiles, a **study** faced in Persian walnut, and the gilded **Grand Hall.** In the 1740s, the hall was turned into a church for the elite Cadet Corps, which occupied the palace after Menshikov fell from favor after Peter's death, was stripped of his possessions, and banished with his family to Siberia. ∎

Rags to riches

Tsar Peter's right-hand man, Alexander Menshikov, was vague about his humble origins. Menshikov proved himself willing and in some respects able and even diligent in his work for Peter. That he should also be able to match the tsar's love of brash, crude humor, and alcohol was also an advantage. Likewise he would devoutly observe Orthodox ritual while at the same time reveling in impious entertainment. His acquisition of property, art, and land was second only to Peter's. By the mid-1720s this former sergeant was running a virtual state within the state, possessing 3,000 villages and 7 towns across Russian, Baltic, Ukrainian, and Polish territories. He owned 300,000 serfs, along with crystal and glass factories, salt and iron mines. ∎

Academy of Arts

Academy of Arts

⬛ Map p. 149

✉ Naberezhnaya
Universitetskaya 17

☎ 323-3578

🕐 Closed Mon.–Tues.

🚌 Bus: 1, 7, & 47;
Tram: 1, 11, &31;
Trolleybus: 1 & 10;
Metro:
Vasileostrovskaya

THE MOMENT WHEN CATHERINE THE GREAT APPROVED the charter and statutes of the Imperial Academy of Arts on November 4, 1764, marked a watershed not just for Russian art and architecture but also for Russian society as a whole. Henceforth the arbiter of what a modern city, town, or country house was to look like, what styles of interior were appropriate, and which trends in painting and sculpture were worthy, was to be the academy. It might seem slightly paradoxical that the dedication above the main door to the new Academy building was "To the Free Arts."

Catherine's notion of freedom meant enlightened and authorized progress. Erecting the vast edifice of the academy (by Alexander Kokorinov and Jean-Baptiste Vallin de la Mothe, 1765–1788) on a prime site and in an unprecedented neoclassic style made a huge statement of intent. From now on the arts in the Russian Empire were to be used for the development of noble character, students were to be drawn from lowly backgrounds at a young age, and the international prestige of Russia was to be incomparably raised by the talents thus nurtured in Europe's largest and arguably most influential art school.

The academy building is a massive temple to art. Guarded by a pair of ancient Egyptian sphinxes on the Neva River landing stage and by a bronze statue of Minerva on the cupola, it stands alone on the Neva embankment and is one of the most imposing sights of St. Petersburg. Its departments, studios, halls, and museum sections —known officially as the **Scientific-Research Museum of the Russian Academy of Arts** —are arranged symmetrically around a circular courtyard.

Although it is still very active as an art school, the public can visit the academy's four-part **museum.** Elsewhere in the city,

and beyond, it also runs five memorial museums of leading artists, including Ilya Repin's estate at Penaty (see p. 235). The museum within the academy's walls relates the history of Russian painting, sculpture and architecture from the 18th to 21st centuries. The sections can be visited in any order and with separate tickets.

A good starting place is the suite of ceremonial rooms that look out over the Neva on the first floor. These essentially are the round **Conference Hall** and the long **Raphael and Titian Halls,** where temporary exhibitions of historic works from the academy collections are shown. It's worth craning your neck to see the ceiling painting of heavenly joy orchestrated by Apollo on the cupola. It depicts "The Celebration on Mount Olympus on the Occasion of the Establishment of the Fine Arts in Russia" (by Vasily Shebuev, 1833). Note the 1764 date being held up by the flying Glory in the foreground. If you then enter the Raphael and Titian Halls you'll see walls covered by life-size copies of works principally from the Vatican and by Raphael and Titian. These were commissioned from academy postgraduates sent on Italian tours during Tsar Nicholas I's reign (1825–1855). Especially significant is Karl Bryullov's "School of

In 2003, after a break of more than a century, the academy was recrowned with a sculptural group depicting Minerva, the Roman goddess of the arts.

Athens." The sheer monumental size of the plaster copies taken from Greek sculptures of heroes and gods and the 1776 copy of the baptistry doors in Florence is impressive. There is a whole section of **plaster casts** from the best known ancient statues downstairs in 33 rooms that partially circle the academy's round courtyard.

On the second floor is the **"History of the Russian School of Art" exhibition,** which includes paintings, sculptures, and graphic art by both professors and students. Be prepared for a trip from neoclassicism to socialist realism in which anatomical perfection, idylls, and mythmaking play a major part. One of the pleasures of taking in this exhibition is that you frequently encounter today's students and you can quietly check out the copies they are making from the originals. In the early summer, it's also possible to see the graduation exhibition.

The academy was also founded as an architectural school and boasts an excellent collection of original **architectural models,** some of which are very large and eye-catching. Notice how impressive Francesco Bartolomeo Rastrelli's Smolny Cathedral bell tower would have looked had he had time to build it. ■

Named for one of their own, the Lt. Shmidt Embankment is popular with sailors.

Lt. Shmidt Embankment

THE NEVA EMBANKMENT THAT STRETCHES BETWEEN Trezzini Square at the northern end of Lt. Shmidt Bridge and the 23rd Line is unlike the others that St. Petersburg visitors encounter. It is really one big passenger- and cargo-ship landing stage designed and built at the same time as the bridge. On warm days and nights, people leisurely stroll the inviting embankment, enjoying the wide quay with its bollards to rest on, the lack of water-edge railings, and the boulevard created between the 12th and 21st Lines.

Lt. Shmidt Embankment (Nab. Leytenanta Shmidta)

Map p. 149

Created at the end of Nicholas I's reign (1847–1854), both the bridge, the first permanent one across the Neva River, and the embankment were named after Nicholas—until 1918. Then it was considered more fitting to honor Lt. Pyotr Shmidt (1867–1906), the young naval officer who had been executed for leading the mutiny of the Black Sea fleet during the 1905 revolution. Shmidt had studied at the **Central Naval College** (No. 17), which was completed in 1799 on the site of a sugar fac-

tory owned by the Englishman John Cavanaugh.

Opposite the Naval College stands one of the best works of public sculpture to adorn St. Petersburg from the late 19th century: Ivan Shreder's relaxed and assured **Monument of Admiral Ivan Kruzenstern** (1770–1846), commander of the first Russian circumnavigatory expedition (1803–06) and subsequent head of the Naval College.

Three more highlights await farther down the embankment. The glittering neo-Byzantine pile of the **Church of the Assumption of the Virgin Mother** sits on the corner of the 15th Line and the embankment. Originally built as a town church (by Vasily Kosyakov, 1895–1903) for the ancient Kievan Caves Monastery, it was handed over in 1991 to the newly reopened Optina Monastery from south of Moscow. You can't miss the distinctive aluminum-covered central dome surrounded by smaller green ones, nor the intricate combination of white sandstone, mosaics, and tiles. The architect used concrete in the construction, so the internal space of the church didn't require as many support columns. Unfortunately, this openness allowed the postwar authorities to open a skating rink in the church. Today, the boldly painted organic designs on the walls are being restored, services have resumed, and a gift shop sells religious choral CDs.

Next, take in the incredible 12-columned portico of Andrey Voronikhin's 1811 empire-style **Mining Institute** (*No. 45, tel 328-8429 for group visits*). Its giant sculptures of Pluto raping Proserpine and of Hercules suffocating Antaeus are dramatic to say the least. Getting inside is not easy but the reward is some exultant painted ceilings dedicated to Russian mineralogy and a **mineralogical museum.**

The embankment ends at the 23rd Line with a unique museum deserving of some time: the icebreaker **Krasin,** which is moored by the gates to the Baltic Factory shipyard. Originally named *Svyatogor,* this ship with the bulging hull was built in Newcastle, England, in 1916 for Russian Arctic service. It had only just arrived in iced-up Archangel when the Russian Civil War

occurred. When the British intervened, the *Svyatogor* fell into their hands. The icebreaker was repurchased, for £75,000 ($140,000), under the Soviet-British trade agreement negotiated by Leonid Krasin, after whom it was renamed in 1927.

The icebreaker's refitted interiors offer a delightful slant on 1950s style. Exhibitions and a short film detail the exploits of the ship, including its rescue of a crashed Italian zeppelin crew in 1928 and its participation in the perilous polar convoys designed to feed starving Russia (one of the best achievements of allied cooperation in World War II). ∎

Krasin

🏛 Map p. 149

✉ Naberezhnaya Lt Shmidt/23–Liniya

☎ 325-3547

🕐 Closed Mon.–Tues.

💲 $ (tours in English by appt.)

🚌 Bus: 7

After years of servitude as a skating rink, the Church of the Assumption is being restored and services have resumed.

A stroll around Bolshoy Prospekt

On the face of it, going for a wander on Vasilevsky Island is difficult. The straight, flat, and broad lines and prospekts militate against the discovery of hidden corners or picturesque surprises. Yet, in typical St. Petersburg fashion, there is more to see than what first strikes the eye. In pre-1917 Revolution times, many Petersburgers regarded Vasilevsky as a German quarter and a walk through its eastern parts reveals why.

The classical Church of St. Catherine was finished in 1771.

Start at the east end of Bolshoy Prospekt. The modest, single-domed **Church of St. Catherine** ❶ *(Bolshoy Prospekt 1, tel 323-1852),* completed in 1771, is a remarkably early example of classicism by the talented German architect Georg Velten (known in Russia as Yuri Felten). After years of serving as a recording studio for the Soviet record company Melodiya, the church was returned to the Lutheran parish in 1992. Restoration to its basilica-plan interior and choir progresses. The church possesses a very good (German) organ; regular recitals of ecclesiastical music are offered.

Head west along Bolshoy Prospekt. At the junction with 2nd–3rd Lines, look to your right to see in the distance the pointed spire and silhouette of another Lutheran church, St. Michael's. Continuing along the the wide boulevard at the corner with 4th Line, turn right to look at the 1901 **art nouveau mansion** *(4th Line 9)* built for the shipping merchant P. Forostovsky by the German architect Karl Shmidt. It has a spire and very fine stone and metalwork; peep inside to see a couple of nice art nouveau tiled stoves.

Return to Bolshoy Prospekt where one block farther down, opposite the **Cathedral of St. Andrew** (see p. 162), you'll see the low-slung arcades of **Andrew's Market** (1790) ❷, whose Bolshoy facade stretches between Volzhsky Lane (Pereulok) and 6th Line. With its separate food hall (1892), it is probably the liveliest place on the street.

The **Order of St. Andrew Obelisk** (2001) stands at the juncture of Bolshoy and 6th–7th Lines. Continue southwest on Bolshoy and discover the **monument of Lenin** ❸ standing outside the redbrick **St. Catherine's School** *(Bolshoy Prospekt 55);* it's a sublime example of early Soviet sculpture (Vasily Kozlov, 1930).

Retrace your steps and turn right on 6th–7th Lines. This newly pedestrianized and tree-lined section draws throngs of Vasilevsky society, who stroll the avenue, mingle in the cafés, and shop in the fashionable boutiques. The architecture is comparatively varied. Immediately after the Cathedral of St. Andrew is the humble-looking 1745 **Church of the Three Prelates** ❹, which after years as a laboratory now belongs to the Georgian Orthodox community. **No. 15** was once the famous Larin Gymnasium; it now houses the Chintamani vegetarian café and the Biergarten. A rather pretentious **statue of Capt. Vasily Korchmin** sitting on his cannon (by G. Lukyanov and S. Sergeev, 2003) faces it across the street. Presumably there was no room for it on the Strelka (see pp. 150–151).

The pedestrianized section of 6th–7th Lines ends at the bustling Srednyi Prospekt by the Vasileostrovskaya metro station. To continue the walk turn right onto Srednyi Prospekt, and proceed past **St. Michael's Church** (*Srednyi Prospekt 18*), the church you viewed earlier. For all intents and purposes it looks like a German Gothic Revival church. Designed by K. Bulmering and completed in 1877, the church served as a warehouse for the local tobacco factory after the World War II. It resumed services again in 1993.

Turn right and stroll down 2nd–3rd Lines or the paralleling Repin Street toward the Bolshaya Neva. Many of Russia's famous artists and architects of the late 19th and early 20th centuries called this area home. Toward the bottom of 3rd Line 2A, you'll find the Academy of Art's **Mosaic Atelier** (*Universitetskaya Naberezhnaya 17*) and the run-down but romantic **Academy Garden** ❺ with its **Apollo Column** (1847). Repin

Street ends at a park where all eyes are drawn to Vincenzo Brenna's **Rumyantsev Obelisk** (1799) ❻, one of the city's best such monuments. It honors Field Marshal Pyotr Rumyantsev (1725–1796), the hero of Catherine II's wars with Turkey. Beyond the park lies the University Embankment. ■

🅼 See area map p. 149
► Church of St. Catherine
↔ 1.4 miles (2.3 km)
⊕ 1 hour
► University Embankment

NOT TO BE MISSED
- Church of St. Catherine
- Cathedral of St. Andrew
- Andrew's Market
- 6th–7th Lines

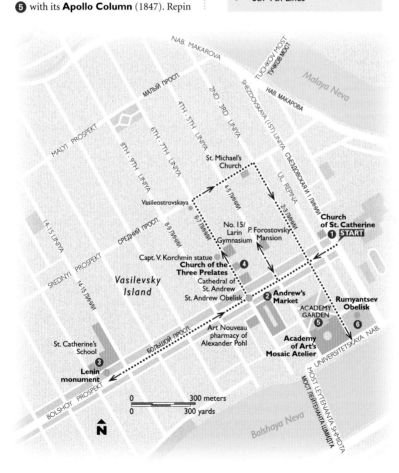

The Cathedral of
St. Andrew is a
favorite choice for
church weddings,
with brides and
grooms often
arriving in white
stretch limos.

Cathedral of St. Andrew

ST. ANDREW HAS A SPECIAL SIGNIFICANCE FOR RUSSIANS.
Legend has it that the saint preached in the lands that became Kievan
Rus. Tsar Peter regarded him as his heavenly protector, established the
Order of St. Andrew as the Russian Empire's highest decoration,
made the diagonal cross of St. Andrew into the blue-and-white flag of
his fledgling navy, and placed his relics in the foundations of the Peter
and Paul Fortress. Peter's plan for the Strelka called for a great Church
of St. Andrew that would imitate and rival St. Peter's in Rome.

**Cathedral of
St. Andrew**

Map p. 149 & 161

Bolshoy Prospekt 21

Metro:
Vasileostrovskaya

The pale-pink-and-white
Cathedral of St. Andrew—a
somewhat simplified copy of
Francesco Bartolomeo Rastrelli's
Smolny Cathedral (see pp.
142–43)—is a replacement: The
first, erected in 1732, burned
down in 1761. Begun in 1764, this
cathedral can be regarded as a
belated baroque fling. Of the five
apparent cupolas, only the large
central one is real. The architect,
Alexander Wist, was arrested for
incompetence when it collapsed
in 1766. Not surprisingly, construction dragged until 1780.

Besides its picturesque appearance, the cathedral is noted for its
gilded **iconostasis,** one of the
oldest in the city. This 56-foot-tall

(17 m) gate and partition
triumphs as a lavish piece of
baroque carving and painting.
Its two oldest icons, those of St.
Nicholas and Alexander Nevsky,
were gifts from the church within
Menshikov's Palace (see p. 155).

St. Andrew's suffered after the
1917 Revolution. In the 1920s,
the Bolsheviks removed many of
the valuables, including the bells;
in 1938, services were stopped; it
was badly damaged during the
World War II; and, after restoration in the 1970s, it served as a
storehouse for the Institute of
Anthropology and Ethnography.
It was reconsecrated in 2001 and
is now one of the most active
churches in the city. ∎

The islands and landmass north of the Neva River have three different faces. They contain the oldest part of the city, its garden islands, and its bustling modern quarters. They're also home to St. Petersburg's football club, Zenit FC, and with it a variety of stadiums, sports grounds, and arenas.

Petrograd Side & beyond

Military memorabilia, Artillery Museum

Petrograd Side & beyond

THE RIGHT BANK OF THE NEVA RIVER IS WHERE IT ALL BEGAN. HAVING seized in May 1703 the Swedish fort of Nyenshants, which was situated at the confluence of the Okhta River with the Neva, Peter advanced a couple more miles downstream and laid the foundations of his dream city on the first islands he came to. While the Swedish fort was razed and its site subsequently turned into a shipyard, the new Russian town began to make its appearance on Hare and Birch Islands. Birch Island changed its name, first to Town Island and ultimately to Petrograd Island.

Although he'd chased the Swedes out of the Neva Delta, security remained uppermost in Peter's mind. So he commenced building with the SS Peter and Paul Fortress, which would wind up covering just about the whole of Hare Island in the widest stretch of the river. Nowadays, it's a building site for more dream castles, since in August the new Art-Beach Festival takes place on its beach and international teams gather to compete in a sand-sculpture competition.

The Peter and Paul Fortress was its own kind of Russian revolution. It had the spirit of a medieval kremlin, but its structures and art were noticeably West European. The baroque style had arrived in northern Russia along with the Italian-Swiss architect Domenico Trezzini and the German sculptor Hans Conrad Osner. The beautiful slender gilded spire of the cathedral in the center draws the eye from many viewpoints around St. Petersburg. It draws people to the premier attraction of the city: the small church that contains the tombs of the tsars, which, for whatever reason, everyone wants to visit. Another somewhat macabre visitor selling point of the fortress is its political prison, the jail of many famous figures and scene of some horrendous crimes by the pre- and postrevolution regimes.

The much larger Petrograd Island cradles tiny Hare Island and offers an almost opposite picture. For while the somber Hare has no cars and no residents and closes down at night, Petrograd is buzzing and modern. After Peter changed his mind about siting the town here (really the only reminder of his plans is his wooden cottage), the island (which from the 1730s–1914 was known as Petersburg Island) lay undeveloped until the turn of the 20th century. Then it developed at a fast clip. It became a center for strands of the Petersburg middle class, with art nouveau apartment blocks and popular entertainment in the landscaped Alexander Park. After some years in the doldrums, the island once again is becoming a respectable address for city dwellers, offering a variety of parks, shopping areas, and sights.

The green islands to Petrograd Island's north are the playground of the city. These are the garden suburbs and island parks

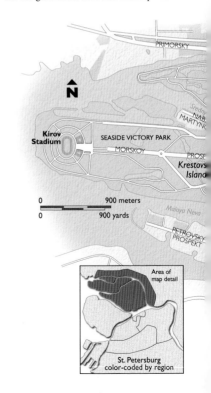

The landscaped parks of St. Petersburg's northern islands are a haven for relaxation.

where Petersburgers relax. There are four, the first of which, Aptersky is more or less a continuation of Petrograd. Kamenny, Yelagin, and Krestovsky Islands are distinc-tive retreats from the city rush to their south. The uninhabited Yelagin is the most picturesque, while Krestovsky has a certain sense of brash new money about it. ■

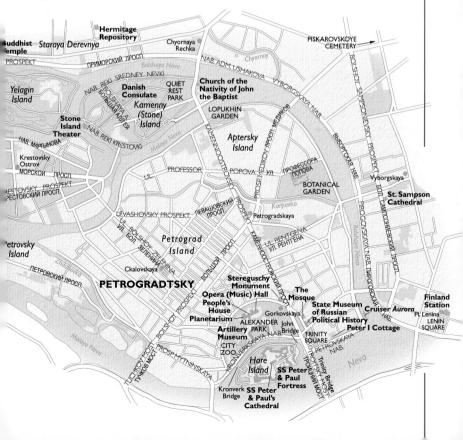

SS Peter & Paul Fortress

**SS Peter &
Paul Fortress**
www.spbmuseum.ru
🅐 Map p. 165 &
168–169
✉ Petropavlovskaya
Krepost 3
🕐 State Museum of St.
Petersburg History
buildings closed
Wed. (except
cathedral in
summer)
☎ 498-0511/0243 or
232-9454
💲 $$ for separate sites
Ⓜ Metro: Gorkovskaya

Note: Helicopter rides
($$$$) over the fortress
and city take off from
a helipad located beyond
the fortress's Basil Gate.

**Opposite:
Trezzini's
cathedral in the
center of the SS
Peter & Paul
Fortress, which
marked a revo-
lution in Russian
architecture, is
the last resting
place of the tsars.**

MODERN RUSSIA HAS ITS BEGINNINGS ON HARE ISLAND,
one of the smallest islands in the Neva Delta. Only 820 by 435 yards
(750 by 400 m), it is located in the widest stretch of the Neva River.
Peter came across the island as he advanced against the Swedes up the
Neva Delta in a decisive moment of the Great Northern War. He
deemed the natural defenses good, so he decided to put down St.
Petersburg's roots here: On May 27 (May 16), 1703, he called for the
construction of a fortress. It was originally the St. Petersburg Fortress,
then Petrograd Fortress, and in 1917 finally became Peter and Paul.

The fortress in many ways epito-
mizes Peter's personality and
reveals his aspirations and cho-
sen direction for Russia. On
Hare Island (Enisaari to the
Finns), Peter continued the tra-
dition of building medieval
Russian kremlins—a fortified
citadel complete with impenetra-
ble walls, cathedral, prison, and a
soldiers' garrison—however, he
did not turn it into a royal resi-
dence and he ordered it built
using West European styles, par-
ticularly Dutch and Italian. As a
result, upon entering the fortress
you enter a world that is West
European in appearance, but
which exudes a quintessentially
Russian spirit.

The fortress covers most of
the island. Its hexagonal plan
with six pentagonal bastions at
each corner is reminiscent of
the "ideal" plans of Italian
Renaissance fortress towns.
Zigzag ramparts placed at the
east and west ends provide fur-
ther defense. Originally made
from wood and earth to designs
by French and German military
engineers brought to Russia by
Peter after his first trip across
Europe, the fortress was later
rebuilt, beginning in 1706, in
brick and faced with granite
slabs under the supervision of
the Swiss-Italian architect
Domenico Trezzini.

PETER'S GATE

Enter the fortress via the main,
ceremonial entrance. To reach the
island, cross the Kronverksky
Strait using the pedestrianized
Ivan (John) Bridge, the oldest
bridge in St. Petersburg, which
joins the island from the east.
Pass through the outer, yellow-
and-white **Ivan Gate** of an out-
lying rampart. The Peter Gate
(1708–1717), the only triumphal
arch of Petrine times, rises
straight ahead. As one of the
most important and beautiful
structures of the fortress, it sets
the mark for the curvaceous,
voluted Baroque style used by
Trezzini elsewhere. But it does
much more.

The gate announces with
much pomp the Russian victory
(albeit slightly prematurely)
over Sweden and associates Tsar
Peter with St. Peter. Take a look
at the wooden reliefs in the
rounded pediment. They depict
the God-blessed Peter the
Apostle expelling Simon Magus
from heaven. Simon is falling
toward a spire of a cathedral
being presented by Tsar Peter in
Roman tunic and wearing a lau-
rel wreath. This allegory for
tsarist divine right and glory
was created by Hans Conrad
Osner, a German sculptor from
Ulm. Osner's work forever
changed Russian sculpture.

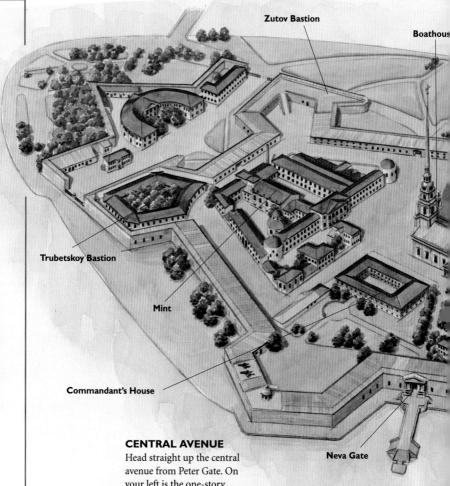

Zutov Bastion

Boathous

Trubetskoy Bastion

Mint

Commandant's House

Neva Gate

CENTRAL AVENUE

Head straight up the central avenue from Peter Gate. On your left is the one-story **Engineers' House** (1748 –49), where 2nd Lt. Fyodor Dostoyevsky began his career after graduating from the Nicholas Military Engineering College. It now houses the **Museum of Old Petersburg** with its extremely rich collections dedicated to the changing fashions and lifestyles of the city. There are tasteful installations of period furniture, dress, and applied and fine art.

Farther along the avenue, you pass Mikhail Shemyakin's intriguing, and hotly disputed, **monu-ment to Peter I** (1991), which shows the tsar frozen in his seat, bald (the face was taken from Rastrelli's wax death mask), and tragically grotesque. (Shemyakin hasn't quite changed Russian sculpture as much as Osner but he's made a stab at it.)

Next on your left is the **Commandant's House** (1743–46), perhaps the most sinister of the fortress's buildings since this became the heart of what's now known as the Russian Bastille (see pp. 172–73). In the early 1790s, part of the house

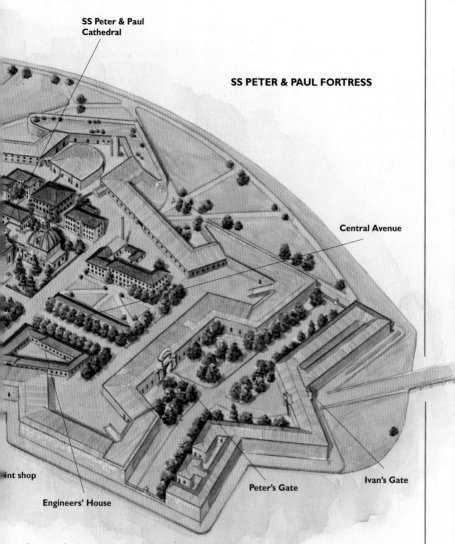

SS Peter & Paul
Cathedral

SS PETER & PAUL FORTRESS

Central Avenue

int shop

Engineers' House

Peter's Gate

Ivan's Gate

became the Supreme Criminal Court and it began to host the Secret Committees of Enquiry. It was here that political prisoners were interrogated, summarily tried, and then sent to meet their fate.

Today, the house serves as a museum. The main hall on the first floor shows how the investigation into the Decembrists uprising in 1825 was conducted.

Now the house is mainly given over to a 28-room multimedia exhibition dedicated to the tsarist history of St. Petersburg (1703–1918), with some revealing old newsreels. There are sections on ceremonial St. Petersburg, Nevsky Prospekt, kitchen and apartment life, trade, fashion, art nouveau, leisure, and transport. Particularly eye-catching are the old shop signboards. Especially thought-provoking, and a great new favorite, is Lenin's car, a Rolls-Royce said to have previously belonged to Rasputin.

SS PETER & PAUL CATHEDRAL

No visitor can miss the **gilded spire** of the SS Peter and Paul Cathedral. At the heart of the fortress that signaled the first realization of Peter the Great's dream for a northern maritime capital for Russia, this spire is one of the key emblems of the city. Rising high above the low and spreading embankments of the Neva River, it is also a central landmark. Capped by a cross-bearing winged angel, which has served as a weather vane since the 1770s, the remarkably slender structure pierces the sky like a needle. It reaches a height of 394 feet (122.5 m), making the Peter and Paul Cathedral the tallest building in St. Petersburg, the tallest cathedral in Russia, and, by some rankings, the sixth tallest in Europe. As such, it announced Peter's westernization of Russia.

Design, build, & sound

The gleaming copper of the spire draws visitors' eyes to what was conceived by Peter as a modern alternative to the multicolored and multiple onion domes of old Muscovy. This radical change to the Russian skyline proclaimed Peter's reforms of the Russian Orthodox Church and was matched by the plan of the cathedral which, instead of being based on a Greek cross, is actually that of a basilica with a rectangular nave and two aisles.

Despite a certain awkward boxiness to its mass, SS Peter and Paul Cathedral has an elegance unmatched by any other ecclesiastical building in Russia.

This is derived not only from the belfry's soaring spire, but also from the eastern facade's large volutes and Corinthian pilasters and the overall proportions of the cathedral, which from across the Neva appears like a ship sailing west.

Peter entrusted the job of designing this first church for his new capital to his chief architect, Domenico Trezzini. The massive stone foundations were laid in 1712; the consecration took place 21 years later. What we see today is a partial re-creation of Trezzini's original project. The cathedral suffered three fires in the mid-18th century—the third, in 1756, caused the most damage. Then the spire was struck by lightning and fell, bringing down with it the original Dutch carillon and smashing the white marble porch below. The subsequent rebuild was completed in 1776 with the installation of a chiming clock, which was commissioned from Barend van Oort Krass, a Dutch master working in Cologne, Germany.

After four decades of ringing out the Soviet anthem, since 2002 the bells have returned to playing the old Russian church and national anthems, as well as occasional summer concerts. Tours of the **belfry** are possible May through October.

The cathedral interior

The interior of the cathedral is remarkable for three things. First, due to its large **windows,** it has considerably more light than is common for Russian Orthodox churches, giving it a certain Protestant quality in keeping with the reformist direction of Peter's vision. This is countered by the second element: the decorative work, which includes origi-

nal ceiling paintings on Gospel themes, a gilded and painted pulpit with figures of SS Peter and Paul, and reproductions of Swedish and Turkish standards taken in battle. But most important in this respect is the 98.4-foot-tall (30 m) **iconostasis,** which rises into the space of the dome. Apparently cramped by the plan of the church, this masterpiece of baroque woodcarving was created in the mid-1720s by a team of Moscow artisans under the supervision of the Ukrainian master Ivan Zarudnyi. The unusually sculptural, gilded holy partition contains 43 icons. Note the Virgin and Child and Jesus Enthroned to either side of the royal gates: Dressed like a 17th-century tsarina, the Virgin was said to be a portrait of Peter's wife, Catherine I, while Jesus is depicted in a patriarchal mitre and the dress of Peter's predecessors, the Moscow tsars.

The connection with the Russian court is furthered by the third feature of the interior: the **royal tombs.** Peter turned the

cathedral into the burial church of the Romanov dynasty. This fact draws tourists by the droves and turns the small cathedral into a heaving mass of (living) bodies. White Carrara marble sarcophagi, designed in the mid-1860s, mark the grave sites of the tsars (and their closest kin). The exceptions are those of Alexander II and his wife Maria (from 1906), which copy ancient Orthodox forms and are made of green jasper and pink rhodonite respectively.

The tombs of the 18th-century Romanovs, including Peter and Catherine II, are in the southern aisle, while those of the 19th-century, starting with Paul, are on the northern side. The remains of Nicholas II and his family, doctor, and trusted servants, shot in Yekaterinburg on July 17, 1918, were interred in the Catherine chapel in the northwestern corner of the cathedral on July 17, 1998. The remains of Nicholas's mother, the Danish wife of Alexander III, were brought from Copenhagen and interred here on September 24, 2006.

The Resurrection stained-glass panel in the Grand Ducal Mausoleum was made in Darmstadt, Germany, in 1905. Destroyed during World War II, it was re-created in 2006.

Crowds of people throng SS Peter and Paul, St. Petersburg's most iconic cathedral, to experience its spectacular interior.

Grand Ducal Mausoleum

The Grand Ducal Mausoleum, attached to the cathedral via a gallery, was designed at the turn of the 20th century for the last tsar's cousins. (The cathedral was reaching capacity, and only the most important royals would still

be buried there.) Thirteen royals were interred before the overthrow of the tsarist regime. On May 29, 1992, the Grand Duke Vladimir, Alexander II's great-grandson, who had died in Miami, Florida, became the first

person buried here since the 1917 Revolution. In 1995, the remains of Vladimir's parents were interred alongside him after their transfer from Coburg, Germany.

RUSSIAN BASTILLE

The Peter and Paul Fortress might be a beacon of beauty, but it's also the basement of barbaric brutality. Russia has its fair share of notorious prisons—St. Petersburg itself has the Kresty on the Vyborg Side, where the victims of Stalin's purges were taken—but none quite match the history and reputation of Peter and Paul's. No one ever escaped from within its walls.

It began with prisoners of war and others being forced into building the fortress in the first place. Then came Peter's imprisonment of his son Alexey in the fortress's safest corner, Trubetskoy Bastion, in 1718. The tsarevich died, apparently by the hand of his father, in Gosudarev Bastion on June 26, 1718. (He's buried below Peter in the cathedral.)

During Empress Anne's reign of terror ($R.$1730–1740) the fortress gained its reputation for the detention of political prisoners. The many who fell into disfavor with the regime were interned in the casemates of the bastions and curtain walls. You can see two examples of their cells in the **Zotov Bastion.** In addition, she had the forerunner of the so-called Secret House (destroyed 1895) built on the Alexey Ravelin (Rampart), to house solitary-confined prisoners. Among those detained there were the Decembrist Pavel Pestel (executed July 13, 1826); Fyodor Dostoyevsky (sent to Siberia in 1850 for his involvement in the reformist Petrashevsky Circle); the anarchist Mikhail Bakunin (sent to Siberia in 1857); the revolutionary writer Nikolay

Chernyshevsky (sent to Siberia in 1864); and the would-be assassin of Alexander II Dmitry Karakozov (executed September 3, 1866).

The most infamous prison of the Peter and Paul Fortress is that of the **Trubetskoy Bastion,** which specialized in incarcerating the victims and champions of the numerous changes of regime from the meek tsarevich Alexey on. In the mid- to late 19th century, the rise of movements demanding regime change continued unabated—the bastion needed more room. In 1872, a two-story block for 69 prisoners was erected in its yard. Mainly used for those on remand, its cells were stark, but not as grim or as small as the ones in the walls of the bastion. The exception is the dark jail, which has no light source. The bastion was turned into a **prison museum** in 1924 and now greets voluntary visitors.

OTHER FORTRESS POINTS OF INTEREST

The outlying Ivan Rampart wall contains the **Gas Dynamics Laboratory Museum,** which explores the history of Russian rocket building. It features a Soyuz 16 spaceship descent vehicle and cosmonauts' spacesuits. The **Boat House** in the center of the island, serves as the ticket office for the nearby Cathedral. It was built (1766) by Catherine II to celebrate Peter's little "Grandfather of the Russian Fleet" sailboat (now in the Central Naval Museum, see p. 151). Opposite the Boat House is Russia's **mint,** which takes advantage of the island security. Completed in 1805, it is still the most important money-making factory in Russia. Exit through the impressive **Neva Gate** to reach a cobbled **beach** speckled by sunbathers in summer; hardy swimmers even cut through ice here in winter. ■

A who's who of Trubetskoy Bastion

A full list of its prisoners has yet to be compiled, but some incarcerees stand out:

Artemy Volynsky, the leader of the campaign to remove Empress Anne (executed June 27, 1740); Princess Elizaveta Tarakanova, who claimed the Russian throne from Catherine through being Empress Elizabeth's secret daughter (died of TB here in 1775); the Chechen Muridist Ushurma Mansur (1792); and Tadeusz Kosciuszko, the fighter for American and Polish Independence (held 1795–96).

Prisoners held in the new penitentiary block prior to 1917 were predominantly social revolutionaries, including the anarchist Prince Pyotr Kropotkin (1874, escaped from hospital in 1876) and members of the People's Will group, like Andrey Zhelyabov (executed April 3, 1881), Lenin's brother Alexander Ulyanov (executed May 8, 1887), and Nikolay Morozov and Vera Figner who both, despite more than 20 years of solitary confinement here and elsewhere, went on to live to be 90.

After 1917, the Trubetskoy Bastion housed tsarist ministers, then members of the Provisional Government. By the winter of 1918-19 it was overflowing with Bolshevik opponents in the winter of 1918 to 1919. Many were taken outside and summarily shot. They included four Romanov grand dukes, killed in what was termed retaliation for the execution of German communists Karl Liebknecht and Rosa Luxemburg. ■

Alexander Park

Alexander Park
⚿ Map p. 165

Artillery Museum
www.artillery-museum
.spb.ru
✉ Alexandrovsky Park 7
☎ 232-0296
🕐 Closed Mon.–Tues. & last Thurs. of month
💲 $$
🚇 Metro: Gorkovskaya

THE ALEXANDER PARK HAS LIGHT AND DARK SIDES. IT'S either fun or war games. It comprises a large crescent-shaped space that seems to grow into Petrograd Island from the SS Peter and Paul Fortress. It was the idea of Tsar Alexander I and opened on Alexander Nevsky Day, August 30, 1843, hence the name. Here you can delve into St. Petersburg popular culture or trace the development of the Russian military machine. A sprinkling of both is probably best.

THE KRONVERK

The SS Peter and Paul Fortress was considered most vulnerable to land attack from nearby Birch (Petrograd) Island to its north. So the defensive Kronverk (Crown Work) was created (1705–1709) on the southern shore of Birch, across the Kronverksky Strait from the fortress. High earthen ramparts were surrounded by a water-filled moat that in plan looked like a crown. Stone escarpments and curtain walls were added.

The Crown Work became home to the Provisions, Artillery, and Cannon Yards; a wharf; a barracks; and the arsenal of Peter's elite Transfiguration Regiment. In the mid-19th century, Nicholas I turned it into the main city arsenal; a horseshoe-plan, redbrick building was raised and made to look something like a medieval fortified castle (Pyotr Tamansky). Today, this building houses the fascinating Artillery Museum.

Military-Historical Museum of the Artillery, Engineers, and Signals Corps

This military museum, Russia's oldest (founded 1756), has an unrivaled range of military memorabilia arranged through its halls and courtyard. With its 18th-century transfers from the Moscow Kremlin's Armory and Arsenal, the exhibits date back to the oldest known Russian firearm, a 14th-century harquebus. Other early pieces include the early cannon made by Andrey Chokhov, Tsar Peter's pike, a very advanced rapid-fire battery system invented by Andrey Nartov in 1754, and the Rastrelli-designed (1760) and tremendously ornate baroque "kettle drum" carriage that bore the First Artillery Regiment's standard on ceremonial occasions.

Displays dedicated to the Napoleonic War of 1812 feature numerous French trophies, medals, standards, and visual descriptions of the Battle of Borodino. The wars of the later 19th century and the civil war (and intervention) get similar treatment. The culmination is a vast record of the crucial Soviet effort in World War II.

One section reveals the changing fashion in uniforms; those of the Red Army seem particularly stylish. Communications displays cover a range of history, from Alexander Popov's first radio receiver (ca 1900) to a relatively modern satellite dish. A highlight of the museum is "The Enemy of Capital," the armored car in which Lenin rode (standing and proclaiming) across the city upon his return on April 3, 1917. And then, of course, there are the major weapons of the 20th century: the Katyusha multiple-rocket launcher; the world's first submachine gun; rockets; and a variety of tanks, mine layers, and antiaircraft weaponry.

Decembrists' monument

Within the Crown Work grounds, past a line of antique cannon, a granite obelisk rises above a lonely stretch of rampart by the moat. Here on July 25 (13), 1826, the five leaders of the Decembrists' uprising were hanged. The obelisk's plinth bears a bronze group comprising a bent sword, chain, and crushed epaulettes (by children's amusements. It contains a grotto café, restaurant, the city zoo, and some gentle sculptures from the 1970s.

Although Kamennoostrovsky Prospekt (see pp. 176–77) and the Gorkovskaya metro station intrude on (and add life to) its space, the park is really dominated by the central complex of the Nicholas II **People's House,** built

Alexander Ignatiev, 1975). The obelisk has a medallion featuring the heads of the five officers reformists in profile. Three of the officers died at the first attempt. The ropes broke for two of the men, so fresh ropes were found and they were hanged again.

ALEXANDER PARK

Alexander Park offers a semi-circular esplanade of gladed walks around the Kronverk, the former arsenal. Planned in the early 19th century by the Scottish architect Adam Menelaws, the park was laid out in the 1840s. In summer, it is partially turned over to chil-

at the turn of the 20th century to designs by Grigory Lyutsedarsky. Completed in 1911, the **Opera (now Music) Hall** reputedly then had the largest reinforced concrete dome in the world. Many packed postrevolutionary meetings, led by Lenin, took place under this dome. The eastern wing was rebuilt in the neoclassic style after a fire in the 1930s and now contains the **Baltic House Theater** (mainly children's programs), while a **planetarium** was added in 1959. In the 1990s the latter included St. Petersburg's first rave club, while nearby now is the trendy par.spb nightclub. ∎

The well-protected Artillery Museum, formerly the city arsenal, occupies the Crown Work.

Kamennoostrovsky Prospekt

Kamennoostrovsky Prospekt

Map p. 165

OF THE STREETS NORTH OF THE NEVA, KAMENNOOSTROVSKY Prospekt (Stone Island Avenue) is the most important. Unlike its rival Nevsky Prospekt, it actually goes somewhere and is more of a Petersburgers' street: Kamennoostrovsky is the main link between the northern suburbs and Gulf of Finland dacha resorts and the city center, and it is closer to everyday life than the show of Nevsky.

The mosque is a unique combination of northern and Islamic architectural features.

The development of Kamennoostrovsky really relates to the opening of the gracious, art nouveau **Trinity Bridge,** which extended the prospekt across the Neva River in 1903 and allowed Petrograd Island to flourish. Prior to then, the island's growth had been stunted. For although Peter initially had the heart of his new capital on its southwestern tip (and had even called the isle Town Island), after the center moved to Admiralty Island in the

1730s, for a century no stone buildings were allowed to the north of the Kronverk.

Kamennoostrovsky Prospekt is a little more than 2 miles (3.5 km) long and offers a range of shops, architectural styles, and a few monuments that give a good flavor of the island's modern, up-and-coming identity. Some of the side streets offer character as well: The Bolshoy Prospekt flourishes and the interesting Professor Popov Street leads to the less flourishing but fascinating Botanical Gardens. A walk along the prospekt's length to the romantic Lopukhin Garden and Kamenny Island in the north is worthwhile, but the main sights center around the prospekt's southern end.

The prospekt starts at **Trinity Square.** Here, safely tucked behind his new fortress, Peter established his new town: a wooden Trinity Cathedral (1709–1711), his first Senate and Colleges, a printing house, pub, and merchants' court. All have long since gone, though the cathedral survived until it was demolished in 1933. The Trinity Chapel here today was a gift from a Russian Orthodox millionaire in 2003.

Kuibyshev Street edges Trinity Square to the north. Turn east onto it to reach the **State Museum of Russian Political History** (*Kuibyshev Ulitsa 2–4, tel 233-7052, closed Thurs.*), formerly the Museum of the Great October Socialist Revolution. Its gift shop sells books and postcards dedicated to the diminutive Polish ballerina Matilda Kshesinskaya (1872–1971). This may seem odd, but she had been the lover of the last tsar and two grand dukes, and this may have enabled her to build the city's most high-profile art nouveau mansion (by Alexander von Hohen, 1904–06), in which the museum now resides.

Come the 1917 February Revolution, Kshesinskaya was out and Lenin moved straight in, making the ballerina's home the office of the Russian Social Democratic Labor Party. The house, and the neighboring mansion of the freemason Baron Brandt with which it was joined when the museum was set up in 1957, has lost its fine interiors, but there are some up-to-date political exhibitions (with English notes everywhere), including some strong examples of Soviet propaganda and decorative art.

Von Hohen, the architect of Kshesinskaya's mansion, was also responsible for the nearby **mosque** *(Kronverksky Prospekt 7)*. The building's unique combination of nordic and Central Asian qualities testify to its being the world's most northerly mosque and the origins of its major benefactor, the last Emir of Bukhara. Completed in 1920, its cladding is a mix of severe northern stone and ceramics decorated by Uzbek craftsmen. The interior, capable of holding 5,000 worshippers, is much less decorative. Among those it serves are Azeri, Tatar, and north Caucasian Muslims.

On the other side of Kamennoostrovsky, close to where it leaves Alexander Park, stands probably the best memorial erected during the reign of Nicholas II, the **Steregushchy monument.** It honors the 53

Russian sailors aboard the torpedo boat *Steregushchy*, which was captured after a battle near Port Arthur during the 1904–05 Russo-Japanese War. Two crewmen left alive heroically scuttled the ship and went down with it. Von Hohen was responsible for the architectural design of the

monument (1909–1911); Konstantin Izenberg cast the dramatic bronze sculpture that shows the sailors sinking the war-damaged ship.

Finally, be sure to take a close-up look at the stylish flora and fauna details of the apartment block at **Nos. 1–3** on Kamennoostrovsky just opposite Gorkovskaya metro station. This is a masterpiece of nordic art nouveau (1899–1904) by the Swedish architect Fredrik Lidvall. ∎

Konstantin Izenberg's 1911 cross-shaped bronze sculpture depicts the two sailors of the *Steregushchy* opening the Kingston valve to sink the ship.

An abundance of art nouveau

Travelers arriving in St. Petersburg a hundred years ago found themselves immersed in an art nouveau world. There was no escape. Love it or hate it, it challenged indifference. Its energy was everywhere: from station to spoon, hotel to hatpin, bank to bookbinding, vase to villa, doorknob to dress, poster to piano, tenement to table lamp. Nothing was left untouched by the art nouveau spirit. While exhibitions were full of it, this was no simple art style, but a lifestyle, a rage, the likes of which had never been seen before.

So let's imagine that you come to St. Petersburg in 1910, arriving as was quite likely, by train from the south or the west at what's now known as **Vitebsk Railway Station.** This was no industrial shed, this was a new kind of living gallery over which lay a whole layer of harmonious embellishment that cocooned you from the discomfort of travel. What you experienced here was enriching, smooth, cleansing, something you felt organically part of that gave you strength and helped you relax at the same time.

The station, designed by Stanislaw Brzozowski and completed in 1904, has restaurants, a clock tower, paintings, banisters, an elevator, stained-glass panels, railings, mirrors, and wall decorations that combine into a totally integrated piece of design. Their lines curve like slender unbreakable plant stems. The station's imperial pavilion served the tsar's family as they traveled to Tsarskoye Selo. There, in the Alexander Palace, they occupied a suite of art nouveau rooms.

The station set the Petersburg scene. From it you'd probably go to Nevsky Prospekt. You'd pass five-story art nouveau apartment houses on the way, distinguish-able by the finesse of their finish, an enjoyment of texture, attention to detail, and their departure from their regimented or fussy predecessors. Their decoration would not be slapped on the surface as some sculptural extra but would seem to grow from within, be it a beautiful female mask or some fragment of stylized nature.

You'd go down Nevsky toward the Neva. Perhaps you'd stop at the celebration of the possibilities of glass and metal that is **Yeliseev's delicatessen** *(No. 56)*, go upstairs to its theater, and then on to dine in the **Grand Hotel Europe's** *(Nevsky Prospekt 36)* new restaurant. Alternatively perhaps you had business at **Novitsky's little factory** *(Sadova Ulitsa 23)*, needed a new sewing machine from **Singer** *(Nevsky Prospekt 28)*, a fur coat from **Mertens** *(Nevsky Prospekt 21)*, some jewelry from **Fabergé** *(Bolshaya Morskaya 24)*, insurance from the **Rossiya Company** *(Bolshaya Morskaya Ulitsa 35)*, or something from the department store and photography shop on Bolshaya Konyushennaya. If you bought some perfume or beer, your bottles were either shaped or labeled in the art nouveau way, likewise your boxes of chocolates and cigarettes.

Finally, you'd head for somewhere to lay your head. Most likely over the art nouveau **Trinity Bridge** onto what's now Petrograd Island. As you went up Kamennoostrovsky Prospekt you'd have a choice of retreats, depending on your circumstances. If well-heeled, you'd stay in one of the refined apartment blocks by Fredrik Lidvall *(Nos. 1–3 or 61)*, likewise in one of the mansions on a side street (e.g., the **Chaev House** at No. 9 Rentgen Street) or up on Kamenny Island. The less fortunate might stay at the **Leuchtenberg House** *(Bolshaya Zelenina Ulitsa 28)*, but they'd be treated to the brilliant, apparently wall-defying decoration of its facade.

All of these buildings still stand, some you can even go inside. Many more exist; when your eye gets attuned, they start turning up in quite unexpected corners. ■

Interior of the Imperial Pavilion of the Vitebsk Railway Station

Peter the Great's cottage

Peter the Great's cottage

- Map p. 165
- Petrovskaya Naberezhnaya 6
- 232-4576
- Closed Tues. & last Mon. of month
- $
- Tram: 6 & 40; Metro: Gorkovskaya

VISITORS TO HISTORIC MONUMENTS OFTEN CONTEND with temporary scaffolding and wrapping spoiling views. But Peter's cottage has been permanently "wrapped" since 1723. The present brick-and-glass container (1844) is also a historic monument itself.

The cottage is hidden in its casing along the Peter Embankment, which for the first 20 years of the town's existence was the main port. Now the only reminder of that fact is the frigate *Blagodat*. Nearby are two indications of the rediscovery and potential of the island after the opening of the Trinity Bridge: Grand Duke Nicholas's neoclassic palace (1910–13) and the grand flight of

sures 40 by 18 by 9 feet (12 by 5.5 by 2.7 m) and various elements indicate Swedish craftsmanship.

The vestibule and each of the three rooms are furnished with Peter's belongings and fitting period items. His bedroom contains a 1707 iron cast of his hand. The dining room was turned into a chapel by his daughter Elizabeth in the 1740s; it used to contain his "Savior" icon (see p. 136). The

The chair in Peter's study was made by the pragmatic tsar himself.

embankment steps, flanked by a pair of Shih Tza (lion-frog) statues brought from Manchuria in 1907.

Early documents refer to Peter's cottage as the "Original Palace" and the "Red Mansion." Original and red are reasonable. For this pine-log hut is the oldest building in the city (May 1703) and was painted to look as though made of red brick. It mea-

galleries of the casing house a sailboat made by Peter and a model of how the cottage fitted into the area around the Trinity Cathedral in the early 18th century. Peter lived here just a few weeks before engaging in the Great Northern War. When he returned, he moved into his more convenient Winter Palace (see pp. 64–65). ■

The *Aurora*

THERE'S NO BIGGER SYMBOL OF RED LENINGRAD THAN THE cruiser *Aurora*, the ship that launched the revolution in 1917. A museum since 1957, it has consistently ranked among the top three tourist draws of the city. By 2006, some 30 million visitors from 154 countries had climbed its gangway, and do so at a rate of around 400,000 a year.

Moored permanently on Petrograd Embankment, the *Aurora* points its guns toward the heart of the old imperial capital.

The *Aurora*'s history has been anything but a cruise. Built 1897–1900 in St. Petersburg's New Admiralty wharf, it became one of the key players of Nicholas II's fleet in 1903. The ship headed off for action in the 1904–05 Russo-Japanese War. On board were a crew of 570, eight 152-mm guns, twenty 75-mm guns, and three torpedo firers. This armory helped save it during the calamitous (for Russia) engagement at Tsushima Bay in May 1905. The *Aurora* escaped and made it to Manila in the Philippines, where it was put under arrest by the United States until the war ended.

Exhibits on board relate the story of the *Aurora*, but you can prebook a guided tour that will take you around the less frequented, and less visitor-contrived, spaces below the wardrooms.

Back in St. Petersburg, in 1906 the *Aurora* was turned into a training ship, occasionally undertaking diplomatic missions, as in 1911 to the coronation of the king of Siam (Thailand). In 1917, its sailors mutinied, joined the February Revolution, killed their captain, M. I. Nikolsky, and were the first in the Baltic fleet to raise the red flag. On October 22, 1917, the crew refused to put to sea; two days later they were under the command of the Military-Revolutionary Committee of the Petrograd Soviet. On October 25 the *Aurora*'s radio broadcast Lenin's rousing speech, "To the Citizens of Russia!" At 9:40 that night, 20-year-old Seaman Evdokim Ognev fired the blank shot from the large bow gun that was the signal to storm the Winter Palace. ∎

The *Aurora*
www.aurora.org.ru
- Map p. 165
- Petrogradskaya Naberezhnaya
- 230-8440
- Closed Mon. & Fri.
- $$
- Tram: 6 & 40; Metro: Gorkovskaya

Vyborg Side

Vyborg Side

[A] Map p. 165

**St. Sampson
Cathedral**
www.cathedral.ru

[A] Map p. 165

[✉] Bolshoy
Sampsonievsky
Prospekt 41

[☎] 315-9732

[🕐] Closed Wed.

[$] $$

[🚇] Metro: Vyborgskaya

Note: St. Sampson's is
a branch museum of St.
Isaac's Cathedral, as is the
Smolny Cathedral. It is possible to buy a joint ticket
and, attractively, visit all
three by means of a boat
tour in summer (tickets
at St. Isaac's Cathedral, see
pp. 84–85).

VYBORG SIDE, WHICH LIES ACROSS THE BOLSHAYA NEVKA
east of Petrograd Side, was home to factories (notably Nobel's of
Nobel Prize fame) and early 20th-century workers' settlements. A
couple of interesting attractions lie hidden within its industrialized
sprawl. Although very different, they each are important memorials.

ST. SAMPSON CATHEDRAL

The tradition of building churches to commemorate military victories goes back a very long way
in Russia. The first such church in
St. Petersburg was dedicated to
the monk St. Sampson the Ho-
spitable. Peter commissioned it as
a memorial to his win in the Battle of Poltava against the Swedes.
The battle was won, according to
Old Style dating, on June 27,
1709, which is St. Sampson's Day
in the Russian Orthodox calendar.

Peter decided to build his victory church near the start of the
Vyborg Road—now known as
Great Sampson Avenue—the
highway to Sweden along which
his troops marched to face the
Scandinavian enemy.

The first wooden church was
replaced in 1728 to 1740 by the
stone one seen today; it is St.
Petersburg's third oldest church.
It's a lovely little five-cupola
building with open galleries to its
sides, an exceptional **bell-tower
entrance** (the only one in the city
to use the old Russian "tent" tower
capping), and an extended refec-
tory nave. It has three superb
baroque **iconostases** full of icons
from the early 18th century. There
is a serenity about St. Sampson's
that makes it a small treasure.

The grounds of the cathedral
contain a neobaroque **chapel,**
which was erected in 1909 on the
site of the original wooden
church. And nearby was St.
Petersburg's oldest **cemetery.**

The greats of the city's early years
were buried here, among them the
architects who created the core of
today's city: Trezzini, Schlüter, Le
Blond, Mattarnovi, Yeropkin, and
the sculptor Bartolomeo Carlo
Rastrelli. The gravestones haven't
survived, but near the church
entrance there's an 1885 memorial
to Pyotr Yeropkin, who was one of
the victims of the despotic regime
of Ernst-Johann Biron during
Anne's reign.

The park behind the cathedral
holds the vandalized remnants of
a Gothic window, a monument to
Petersburg's first builders (by
Mikhail Shemyakin, 1995). Don't
miss the famous **Peter I monument** facing the cathedral on the
other side of the road. Originally
cast in 1909 by Mark Antokolsky,
it was removed in 1929, recast in
2003, and then returned.

LENIN SQUARE & FINLAND STATION

For the most important monument to the second Russian leader
who gave his name to the city for
several years, head south a few
hundred yards from St. Sampson's
Cathedral to Lenin Square in
front of the Finland Station. Just
after the **Lenin statue** (by Sergey
Yevseev, Vladimir Shchuko, and
Vladimir Gelfreykh, 1926) went
up, the Peter in front of St.
Sampson's came down. Having
them both around now seems
reasonable, particularly in this
quarter, which they both knew as
a vital route across Finland.

When Lenin first arrived from his political exile on April 3, 1917, he was greeted by cheering crowds, jumped on the waiting armored car, and drove through the city proclaiming, "Long live the Socialist Revolution!" This monument, the first of many thousands that were to follow, was planned immediately after his death in January 1924. It shows him smartly dressed, cap in pocket, standing on a cubist-like interpretation of his armored car, and gesturing across the Neva River.

A series of fountains were installed in the square in 2005. At noon, 8, and 10 p.m., they shower Lenin with a rainbow of water, colored lights, and music. The distinguished yet modest late-1950s Finland Station has on display, under glass cover, **steam engine No. 293,** the famous little train that brought Lenin back to Petersburg in October 1917. ■

The emblematic Lenin outside the Finland Station is now surrounded by fountains.

Krestovsky Island
is fast turning into
the year-round
fun fair of St.
Petersburg.

Northern islands

THERE ARE THREE "GREEN" ISLANDS NORTH OF PETROGRAD
Island. Although all three are recreational islands and to some extent
garden suburbs, they each have a distinct identity, which means they
merit visiting for slightly different reasons.

Kamenny, Yelagin,
& Krestovsky
Islands

 Map p. 164–165

Metro: Chernaya
Rechka, Staraya
Derevnya, &
Krestovsky Ostrov

KAMENNY ISLAND

Despite *kamenny* meaning "stone,"
the isle is surprisingly green and
wooded. It essentially is a big park,
quiet rest park, sprinkled with elite
dachas from around the years
1820, 1900, and 2000. Motorized
transportation is very limited and
there are no shops.

The park lies to the west of
Kamennoostrovsky Prospekt,
which crosses a tip of the island.
Before heading there, quickly
glance at the striking little red
neo-Gothic **Church of the
Nativity of John the Baptist**
(by Yuri Felten). It ostensibly was
built in 1778 for the island's first
royal resident, the future tsar
Paul, but his mother, Catherine II,
considered it one of two memorial churches to her victory in the
Russo-Turkish War.

Catherine gave the island to
Paul in 1765 to keep him out of
her way. The style of the church,

with its pointed arches and windows, coincided with Paul's
predilection for things German,
medieval, masonic, and mystical.
At the same time, Catherine built
Paul the neoclassic summer
palace, which the church served;
it stands in the grounds to the
east (it's now a sanatorium).

Paul encouraged his favorite
nobles to live on the island, a policy that was continued by his sons
Alexander I and Nicholas I. Their
dachas and those of their successors (and the nouveau riche of
the early 20th and 21st centuries)
dot the park. At present, almost
all the houses are very private and
inaccessible to the public, but you
can admire them from afar.

The 1904 **Vollenweider
Mansion** *(Bolshaya Alleya 13),* an
outstanding example of northern
art nouveau designed by Roman
Meltser, is the Danish Consulate.
The graceful, simple **Stone Island**

Theater (*reki Krestovki Naberezhnaya 10*) was built in 40 days in 1827, and then rebuilt more slowly in 1844. Other houses reveal a range of styles, from grand interpretations of decorative Russian wooden cottages to the incredible **neoclassic mansion** (*reki Sredney Nevki Naberezhnaya 6*) built in 1913 by Ivan Fomin for the Polovtsov family.

YELAGIN ISLAND

A footbridge at the western end of Kamenny Island connects it to Yelagin Island, a landscaped wonderland of ponds and gladed walks. It is the most romantic of the three islands.

After Alexander I purchased the island for his mother, Maria Feodorovna, a palace was built and the whole isle turned into its picturesque park in the 1820s. Joseph Busch, the garden designer, introduced new varieties of trees and made the system of ponds ideal for rowing (today, you can rent paddleboats). In the 1930s, the island was turned into the **Central Park of Culture and Rest;** it acquired some sculptures, mainly pastoral, a few of which survive.

The **palace ensemble** owes its empire-style elegance to Carlo Rossi. Erected on a high base in a clearing at the eastern end of the island, the palace was Rossi's first major commission. He complemented it with separate service quarters, a greenhouse, stables, a pavilion by the jetty, a music pavilion, and a guardhouse. The palace's suite of immaculately decorated rooms, culminating in the Oval Hall and Mineral (Porcelain) Study, show Rossi at his best. Severely damaged during the Siege of Leningrad, they were restored in the 1950s and are open to visitors (*tel 430-1131, closed Mon.–Tues.*).

KRESTOVSKY ISLAND

The larger Krestovsky Island lies to the south of Yelagin and Kamenny Islands. It is part residential and part park. With its own metro station, Krestovsky is much more lively than its sedate neighbors. The life comes from its

amusement park, new luxury apartment blocks, restaurants, and sports clubs. The enormous **Seaside Victory Park** is a prime example of postwar Soviet park design. The famously large **Kirov Stadium** (1950) has deteriorated over recent years; it is to be replaced by a "flying saucer" arena in 2009 (by Kisho Kurokawa). Then, it will resume as the main home of the St. Petersburg Zenit FC soccer club. ∎

Petersburgers flock to the northern islands for sporting events and leisure.

The vast Piskarovskoye Cemetery is a somber reminder of the devastation of war.

More Places to visit north of Petrograd Side

STARAYA DEREVNYA

There are two good reasons to visit Staraya Derevnya, the Old Village, just north of Yelagin Island. The first is the **Buddhist Temple** *(Primorsky Prospekt 91, tel 430-1341)*, which fuses modern northern and ancient Eastern traditions. The city's Buddhist population grew steadily in the late 19th century, but Nicholas II only gave permission for a temple after the exiled Dalai Lama sought Russian protection in 1904.

Completed in 1915 in the style of a Tibetan *du khang*—assembly hall—the gray granite slanted walls are relieved by brightly colored trim. The skylit interior is a unique tribute to the Himalayan vision of Russia's most spiritual artist, Nicholas Roerich, who worked with Buryat lama craftsmen. After decades of misuse, the temple was returned to the Buddhists. Restoration was completed in 2004.

The other attraction in Staraya Derevnya is the newly opened **Hermitage Repository** *(Zausadebnaya Ulitsa 37a, tel 344-9226, guided tours only, closed Mon.–Tues., $$, metro: Staraya Derevnya)*. This vast (and growing) complex is full of paintings, sculptures, and applied art, as well as ceremonial carriages, Nicholas I's life-size wooden horse, and Sultan Selim III's luxurious tent. The viewing is an experience in itself—much is done from inside glass tunnels as if in an oceanarium.

Map p. 164

PISKAROVSKOYE CEMETERY

This reminder of the World War II 900-day Siege of Leningrad lies to the north of Vyborg Side. As the siege wore on, 470,000 unidentified bodies were tipped into pits blasted from the frozen ground. After the war, the cemetery was designed as a stark memorial. It was dedicated on May 9, 1960, the 15th anniversary of Victory Day.

The 186 burial mounds are marked by granite slabs that simply distinguish whether those interred were civilian or military. Funereal music plays all day. Exhibits showcase memorabilia dedicated to the dead. The cemetery culminates in a huge 19.7-foot-tall (6 m) sculpture of Mother Russia eloquently holding a garland of oak and laurel leaves. On the wall behind her sculpted reliefs depict the defenders of Leningrad and an inscription bears the words of the siege poet Olga Bergholts:

> *Here lie the Leningraders*
> *Here are the city dwellers—men, women*
>   *and children*
> *Beside them are the Red Army soldiers*
> *So many lie protected for ever by granite*
> *And for those honored by the stones*
> *Let no one forget and nothing be*
>   *forgotten*

Map p. 165 ✉ Prospekt Nepokorennykh 74 ☎ 247-5716 Metro: Muzhestva Ploshchad ∎

The spreading suburbs south of the Fontanka River offer some interesting alternatives to the well-worn routes. The areas inside the Obvodnyi Canal are Dostoyevsky territory; outside, they're Stalin's.

South of the Fontanka

The tsarist Moscow Triumphal Gate

The Cathedral of the Vladimir Mother of God Icon (1761–69) dominates Vladimir Square.

South of the Fontanka

ONCE THE LAND WITHIN THE FONTANKA ARC AND NORTH OF NEVSKY Prospekt had been developed, there was one obvious direction for the city to grow— south. The first land to be developed was that inside the Obvodnyi (Enclosing) Canal, which had been built as a first line of defense for the city between 1769 and 1833. Expansion beyond the canal began once St. Petersburg had been stripped of its capital status in 1918 and the direction toward Moscow seemed apposite.

Inevitably the new southern suburbs were poorer quarters, occupied by those on the fringes of Petersburg society. The area centered around Vladimir Cathedral attracted a rich mix of transient residents, from students to workers, traders to petty officials. It attracted Fyodor Dostoyevsky, who spent many of his years in the city moving between cheap apartments in this area. Other hard-up writers also migrated here and nowadays you can either sign up for the "Crime and Punishment" tour at the Dostoyevsky Museum, or go solo on signposted literary walking tramps through the district. Slightly more enticing might be a visit to some of the areas plentiful alternative music and art venues.

South of Obvodnyi Canal, the landmass between the Neva River and the coast starts to broaden. It is split right down the center by the Pulkovo Meridian, the line of which apparently starts from the Winter Palace and leads south to the observatory built 12 miles away on the Pulkovo heights in 1839. It also happens to be the straight line that took the royal family to their country palaces at Tsarksoye Selo. Since 1932, the meridian has also led from the city center to the airport (Pulkovo), as a result, much of its urban length was turned into an urban superhighway. At one point named Stalin Avenue, the meridian is now Moscow Avenue (Moskovsky Prospekt). In all likelihood, you'll flash along the avenue as you arrive or leave. But spare it a bit of time: The avenue holds many of the city's major Soviet monuments—Victory Square, the megasize House of Soviets, Victory Park, and considerable amounts of pompous

Stalinist housing blocks. It's skateboard and Rollerblade heaven.

For history buffs who wish to see some real socialist architecture of the 1920s, the place to head to is Stachek (Strike) Square in the west. There, not far from St. Petersburg's biggest factories, are some rare avant-garde buildings and community planning schemes; but beware, the area is a bit worse for wear. Other interesting things to do in addition to strolling around the area include climbing inside the Narva Gates, a triumphal arch built to honor the troops returning from defeating Napoleon. And you can also pass some time in the once beautiful Yekaterinhof, St. Petersburg's 19th-century amusement park. ■

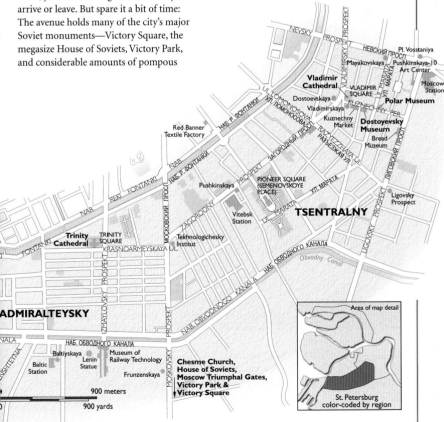

Vladimir Square & around

Vladimir Square

🗺 Map p. 189

🚇 Metro: Pushkinskaya, Vladimirskaya, Dostoevskaya, & Mayakovskaya

THE QUARTER IN WHICH FYODOR DOSTOYEVSKY SPENT his last days hides a few gems of interest. This area wasn't built for the wealthy. Lying beyond the Fontanka River, south of Nevsky, west of the disreputable Ligovsky Prospekt, and north of the industrial Obvodnyi Canal, it really only started to develop in the mid-19th century. Prior to that time, it had been very much a suburb housing soldiers and minor civil servants. Lacking a specific or noble character, the area usually only sees visitors going to the Dostoyevsky Museum or on their way to the Vitebsk Railway Station. Discerning visitors, however, stop for a while. To get a fair sense of the area take the metro from Vosstaniya Square to Pushkinskaya Street (where you can see the beautiful art nouveau Vitebsk station) and then walk back.

The pensive Alexander Griboedov (V. Lishev, 1950) rises above Pioneer Square.

ST. PETERSBURG'S FIRST METRO LINE

In the late 19th and late 20th centuries the Vladimir area, with its mixture of middle- and working-class residents, fostered the underground political and art movements. Coincidentally, the area stands above what was Leningrad's first subway line (1941–1955, now Line 1). It originally ran from Vosstaniya Square on Nevsky Prospekt to the workers' township of Avtovo in the west. Its eight stations were designed as neoclassic "underground palaces" and are worth a visit in their own right. Covered in various marbles and granite, the stations exemplify Stalinist triumphalism and pathos. They have distinguished overground pavilions while deep beneath the earth their platform halls contain colonnades and a wealth of monumental painting and sculpture. The two end stations are particularly striking: **Vosstaniya Square's** artistic decoration extols the revolution, **Avtovo's** the defense of the city and victory.

PIONEER SQUARE

On December 22, 1849, Dostoyevsky and 20 other young members of the reform-calling Petrashevsky Circle were led out onto Semenovskoye Place to be shot. Their sentences were commuted to long-term Siberian hard labor at the very last moment, but the square was the scene of execution of later radicals-revolutionaries, including 27-year-old Sofia Perovskaya and four other People's Will members involved in the assassination of Alexander II. Semenovskoye Place, one of St. Petersburg's largest squares, was earlier used for the drilling of the Semenovskoye Life Guards and other elite tsarist regiments. In a typical St. Petersburg–Leningrad twist, since 1959 it has been Pioneer Square, and home to the Theater of Young Spectators complete with large statue of the 19th-century playwright Alexander Griboedov.

AROUND VLADIMIR SQUARE

Northeast of Pioneer Square, toward Nevsky, there are several places worth visiting. The nicely pedestrianized **Pravda/Bolshaya Moskovskaya Street** is a new treat in this district. The marketing of Dostoyevsky begins at its northern end, with the unassuming **Dostoyevsky Monument** (1997), the **Dostoevsky Hotel** in a spruced-up art nouveau building on Vladimir Square, and, best of all, the **Dostoevskaya metro station** (1991).

During his last years, the writer occasionally attended services in the attractive, yellow **Cathedral of the Vladimir Mother of God Icon** (1761–69). With its five cupolas and separate bell tower (by Giacomo Quarenghi, 1783), it's a real mix of baroque, Russo-Byzantine, and classical traditions. It has an upper and lower church; the former is larger and contains a fine baroque iconostasis, transferred here from the Anichkov Palace in 1811. The church was named after Russia's most venerated, miracle-working icon, of which it had a 1763 reproduction (the original is in the Tretyakov Gallery, Moscow; the copy went missing

after 1917). Following decades as a factory and ambulance station, the cathedral was reconsecrated in 1990. Reconstruction is ongoing.

Head down nearby Kuznechny Lane to browse the overflowing aisles of **Kuznechny Market,** one of the best in town for everything from food to memorabilia. Continue down Kuznechny past

the Dostoyevsky Museum. At the junction with Marat Street, you'll encounter the **Polar Museum,** also known as the Museum of the Arctic and Antarctic. It has adapted endearingly to its location in an old neoclassic church (1838). Despite a lack of funds, the museum, under the directorship of a great present-day Arctic explorer, Viktor Boyarsky, contrives to show what a major, strategic part the ice caps have had, and continue to have, in Russian and world history.

Two other venues of interest located in the area are the large and generally lively complex of the **Pushkinskaya-10 Art Center,** which demonstrates all kinds of contemporary art and music, and the modern **Bread Museum,** which reveals the history of Russian bread and tempts you into trying some ultrafresh baking. ■

Polar Museum
www.polarmuseum.sp.ru
⬛ Map p. 189
✉ Marata Ulitsa 24a
☎ 717-2549
🕐 Closed Mon.–Tues.

Vladimirsky Prospekt 19 (A. K.V. Shulman, 1904), an example of nordic art nouveau

Pushkinskaya-10 Art Center
www.pushkinskaja-10.spb.ru
✉ Entrance at Ligovsky Prospekt 53
☎ 764-5371
🕐 Open 3 p.m.–7 p.m.; closed Mon.–Tues.

Bread Museum
✉ Ligovsky Prospekt 73
☎ 764-1110
💲 $
🕐 Closed Sun.–Mon.

Dostoyevsky preferred to live in corner apartments.

Dostoyevsky Museum

Dostoyevsky Literary–Memorial Museum

 Map p. 189

✉ Kuznechny Pereulok 5/2

☎ 571-4031

🕐 Closed Mon.

💲 $

🚇 Metro: Dostoevskaya & Vladimirskaya

RARELY CAN A NATIONALIST WRITER HAVE HAD SUCH AN international following as Fyodor Dostoyevsky (1821–1881). Yet this giant in the world literature, whose prose is so penetrating it can touch the most distant souls, is a principal reason why many non-Russians make the pilgrimage to St. Petersburg. They pay their respects graveside in the Tikhvin Cemetery (see p. 146), traipse around low-life venues on two-hour "Crime and Punishment" tours, and bow their heads at the door of the flat where he expired at 8:38 p.m., January 28, 1881.

Dostoyevsky's final apartment (where he spent 27 months and partly wrote his brilliant last novel, *Brothers Karamazov*) has been a museum since 1971. It caters well to foreign visitors, with audioguides and information in several languages. The apartment comprises the five-room second-floor memorial part of the Dostoyevsky Museum, with the adjoining **gallery** (in a separate apartment) dedicated to his life and literature. Downstairs, temporary exhibitions, literary performances, and meetings are held, and films of his novels are occasionally shown.

Despite the best efforts of his adoring wife, Anna, many of Dostoyevsky's personal effects were lost after his death, so the museum is very much an artificial re-creation. That limitation

The exhibition traces his moves around Russia (enforced Siberian exile, 1850–59), Germany (gambling addiction), and within St. Petersburg.

Dostoyevsky lived in St. Petersburg a total of 29 years at 22 known addresses, including eight months in the notorious Secret House prison of the SS Peter and Paul Fortress (see pp. 172–73). His neighborhood, however, is really the densely

Young Dostoyevsky

Born in Moscow, Dostoyevsky arrived in St. Petersburg in 1837 aged 16 to study at the Engineering College in Michael's Castle. Living at Vladimir Prospekt 11 from 1842–46, he dedicated himself to literature from 1844 and in 1846 published his first story, "Poor Folk." Due to his associations with the reformist Petrashevsky Circle, he was arrested in 1849 and spent the 1850s in forced Siberian exile. He returned to St. Petersburg in late 1859. For a short introduction to his early writing try, his "White Nights" (1848). ∎

notwithstanding, the museum does impart what kind of strict but committed family man he was, and how he dedicated himself obsessively to his writing. You also are given to understand how Anna kept him and the family together.

Dostoyevsky's apartment, and with it the writer's **study** (which you may look at but cannot enter), may seem surprisingly tame and unatmospheric. It lacks the heavy presence and psychological intensity that readers of Dostoyevsky may expect. For this, you need to go to the gallery next door. Here you can begin to comprehend the writer's struggle—in life and art. His own estrangement from the world, and that of his "heroes," is encapsulated through the theme of corners. Dostoyevsky lived in corner apartments and his characters were always cornered one way or another.

populated triangle between Nevsky and Voznezensky Prospekts. It is here that the plot of *Crime and Punishment* (1866), the first of Dostoyevsky's long novels, unfurls. This area becomes the setting for Dostoyevsky's most fundamental exploration of criminal consciousness, with the key protagonist, Rodion Raskolnikov, reckoned to have "lived" at No. 19 on Grazhdanskaya Street. The "Crime and Punishment" tour can be arranged at the museum. ∎

Stachek Square & around

Stachek Square

🅰 Map p. 188

**Narva Gates—
Branch of the
Museum of Urban
Sculpture**

www.avit-centre.spb.ru

www.gmgs.spb.ru

🅰 Map p. 188

✉ Stachek Ploshchad 1

☎ 786-9782

🕐 Closed Mon.–Tues. &
last Fri. of month

💲 $$

🚇 Metro: Narvskaya

ON JULY 30, 1814, THE TROOPS WHO HAD CHASED Napoleon out of Russia and taken Paris marched back into St. Petersburg through the new triumphal arch erected in their honor at the southwest border of the city on what is today Stachek (Strike) Square. On January 9, 1905, tsarist troops were again in action here, only on this occasion they were firing on the column of peaceful protesters heading from the nearby Putilov metal factory toward the Winter Palace. The killing and wounding of the workers who were calling for better working conditions marked the start of Bloody Sunday, and with it the first Russian Revolution.

Stachek Square and its vicinity has two faces: the imperial and the Soviet. This dichotomy is typical for much of St. Petersburg, but because of its particular situation and history, this area was the first to receive prototype socialist architecture. Previously known as the Narva Outpost, it was incorporated into the larger Kirov Region of Leningrad. It offers a different vision of the city from the center.

In the early 18th century, two main post roads headed south from St. Petersburg. One led southwest via Peterhof to Narva and Reval (Tallinn, Estonia); the other went due south to Novgorod and Moscow. The southwestern gates of the city lay just south of the Neva River's mouth. Beyond were a few villages and country estates. Everything changed when the main St. Petersburg iron foundry was established in the midst of these in 1801. By the mid-19th century the Narva Outpost had the Russian capital's worst workers' housing, which by the start of the 20th century was declared unfit for living.

NARVA GATES

Inspired by the triumphal arches in the Roman Forum, the Narva Gates were designed by the Italian classicist Giacomo Quarenghi.

The Gates also reveal a mocking aping of Napoleon's Parisian Arc du Carrousel. In its own turn, this one inspired the arch of the General Staff on Palace Square (see p. 62). Sticking with the same design, the original wooden gates were replaced by the present larger brick-and-metal structure in 1827 to 1834 (by Vasily Stasov). It is a resplendent vision, complete with Corinthian columns, sculptures of medieval Russian knights, and allegorical figures of Glory and Victory riding in her six-horse chariot. The space above the arch, accessible via a narrow iron spiral staircase (75 steps), holds a branch of the **Museum of Urban Sculpture.** This remarkable little venue showcases various temporary (mainly historical) exhibits.

YEKATERINHOF

A couple of hundred yards northwest of the gates, at the end of Perekopskaya Street, is one of St. Petersburg's largest and most historic parks—Yekaterinhof. Named after Peter's wife Catherine, it was founded as her summer estate in 1711. It was turned into a pleasure park in the 1820s and, although it has lost virtually all of its early pavilions, it is still picturesque. It offers attractions such as a small children's amusement park and activities such as horseback riding and tennis.

AVANT-GARDE ARCHITECTURE

Yekaterinhof has a younger cousin to its south along Prospekt Stachek—**January 9 Park.** Created in the early 1920s, it was named after Bloody Sunday 1905. Take a look at its amazing, swirling neobaroque railings (1899), which won Roman Meltser major prizes at the 1900 Paris World Exhibition. Initially installed around the Winter Palace's garden, separating it from the Admiralty, the railings were dismantled in 1920. Their installation here, four years later, around a factory workers' children's park, marked the emergence of the region as the site for Leningrad's experimental building projects.

Although Stachek Square is beginning to be littered with street furniture such as large kiosks and signs, you can still get an idea of the early Soviet architecture from No. 4, the **Gorky Palace of Culture** (by Alexander Gegello and David Krichevsky, 1925–27) with its House of Technical Studies (1932). The building belongs to Europe's foremost international style works: it is severely functionalist, devoid of ornament, and made of modern materials. The same can be said of No. 9 opposite, the USSR's original department store and municipal canteen (1929–1931).

More fetching but equally innovative is **Traktornaya Street** (Gegello and Alexander Nikolsky, 1925–27), a model workers' housing scheme with the houses joined by quarter-circular arches. But the masterpiece of constructivism may be the 1927 **10th Anniversary of October School**

(Stachek Prospekt 5), whose observatory and curved plan architect Alexander Nikolsky derived from the shape of the Soviet Hammer & Sickle emblem. Both of these architectural gems lie to the south of Stachek Square just before Kirov Square with its **Regional Soviet building** (by Noy Trotsky, 1930–35) and towering **Kirov monument** (by Nikolay Tomsky, 1938; see p. 196). Beyond this is January 9 Park, where you might want to take an avant-garde rest. ∎

The Narva Gates house an unusual and very small museum above the arch.

Stalinist Monuments

There is a lot less arm raising in the post-USSR monuments than there is in those created during St. Petersburg's 67 years as Leningrad (1924–1991). Statues have become more pensive. Arms hang loose, idly across laps or stiff behind backs. It wasn't like that before. Then the sculptures were more active, powerful, resolute. Even the most foppish of Pushkins could not be accused of limp wrists.

When Lenin set in motion his Plan for Monumental Propaganda after he seized power in 1917, he did not have in mind any monuments to himself. On the contrary, he forbade it, calling instead for monuments that embodied the socialist cause and took it to the people. Within months of his death in 1924, however, the city was renamed in his honor and a competition for the first Lenin statue took place. The statue spawned thousands of Lenin monuments across

the socialist world, many made by Winston Churchill's cousin Clare Sheridan. Leningrad got its fair share, with the thumbs-up statue in front of Finland Station (see pp. 182–83) setting the trend. Despite a post-Soviet purge of "offensive" Lenins and crew, a good amount survive, owing to their historic value.

So in this city where gesture is paramount, you can still look up to a good number of bronze raised arms. In the main, they've been produced to round off an architectural ensemble, usually a Soviet one. The biggest examples are monuments to Leningrad party boss **Sergey Kirov** (1886–1934), whose murder was arranged by Stalin as a pretext to start the mass repression of the 1930s. Two are outstanding: the one on Kirov Square (by Nikolay Tomsky, 1938) and the one in front of the great Kirov Stadium in the Seaside Victory Park on Krestovsky Island

Left: The Kirov Monument on Kirov Square, a giant of Stalinist monumental art, is surrounded by bas-reliefs dedicated to the Civil War and subsequent revival. Above: The vast House of Soviets on Moskovsky Prospekt has been fronted by fountains since 2006.

(by Vennamin Pinchuk, 1935–1950). Both show the flat-capped portly chief leading the crowd, paper projects in hand. The monument on Kirov Square has more flair, set as it is against the backdrop of a rather forceful modernist Regional Soviet building, planned by Kirov. In this proletarian area, Kirov faces and gestures toward the achievements of his eight years in charge of Leningrad: the city's first tractor factory, hospital, school, and the group of buildings around Stachek Square.

Kirov's death and his monuments proved a watershed. Before that time, Leningrad had been blessed with the modern **Red Banner Knitwear Factory** (*Pionerskaya Ulitsa 53*), designed by the world-renowned German architect Erich Mendelssohn in 1928. In addition, innovative communal blocks of apartments for the previous regime's political prisoners had been erected around **Trinity Square**

(1929–1933), as were fire stations and the Kuznechny Market (1925–27). The **secret police (future KGB) headquarters** (*Liteiny Prospekt 4*) was one of the highest-quality Leningrad buildings of the 1930s and was built on the site of the tsarist Regional Court. After Kirov's death, the Stalinist age brought the curtain down on art, architecture, and all kinds of freedoms. No. 4 Liteiny Prospekt became known as The Big House, and it was here that 47,000 death sentences were passed on Leningraders.

A new era began of essentially mega-pastiche, a so-called proletarian classicism, or Stalinist empire style, that grew increasingly pompous and decorative as the years went on. The style sprinkles the city (hint: look for oversize, often yellow and white, colonnades), but its most concentrated appearance is in the first line of the metro (see pp. 190–91) and the ensembles along Moskovsky Prospekt (see pp. 198–99). ■

The Victory Monument at the end of Moskovsky Prospekt sits on what was the front line during the Siege of Leningrad.

Moskovsky Prospekt

EVERY VISITOR FLYING INTO OR OUT OF ST. PETERSBURG goes down Moskovsky Prospekt (Moscow Avenue). Straight as a plumb line, it follows the line of the Pulkovo Meridian (by which Russian maps used to be drawn) for almost 7 miles (11 km). The prospekt encompasses at once a six-lane highway and a superscale ensemble of monuments that is, deliberately, awe-inspiring.

Moskovsky Prospekt

 Map p. 189

Metro: Sennaya Ploshchad to Moskovskaya (Line 2)

Note: To explore Moskovsky Prospekt, you'll need transportation of some kind. It is served by plenty of buses, trams for some sections, and seven metro stations.

The huge avenue started modestly. In the 18th century, it was simply a part of the post road linking St. Petersburg with Tsarskoye Selo, Novgorod, and Moscow. As the main route to the Russian heartland, its name was politically important. Serving various interests, it was once Trans-Balkan Avenue (so named in 1878 to honor the Russian soldiers who freed Bulgaria from the Ottomans), International Avenue (post–1917 Revolution), Stalin Avenue (1930s), and finally its present name (1956).

The prospekt begins at Sennaya Ploshchad (the old hay market) and heads south. Until it reaches the Obvodnyi Canal, it comprises fairly undistinguished pre-1917 buildings. From the canal on, it becomes an amalgam of Soviet giganticism speckled with historic monuments from earlier periods. The stretch between the Moscow Triumphal Gate and Victory Square holds the most interest.

The imperial pomp and style of the **Moscow Triumphal Gate** (by Vasily Stasov, 1834–38) fit too well with the Stalinist triumphalist vision, so they were dismantled in 1936. They were returned in 1959, six years after Stalin's death. Now essentially standing in the middle of the highway, Stasov's green Doric arch is a mightier version of the Brandenburg Gates in Berlin. It was made by the Scottish engineer Matthew Clark and completed with decorative sprays of arms by the sculptor Boris Orlovsky. The decoration and placement of the arch, at what was then the entrance to the city, celebrated Nicholas I's military prowess. The

Latin inscription on the entablature reads: "To the Victorious Russian Forces in commemoration of their great deeds in Persia and Turkey and in the pacification of Poland 1826, 27, 28, 29, 30, 31."

To mark the triumph of Soviet forces, Stalin's planners decided on **Victory Park** (1945–1950s), south of the gate and set on Moskovsky Prospekt's eastern side. A series of 1920–1930s buildings, including large residential blocks, the local Soviet, and the House of Culture stand between the park and the gate. Not surprisingly, the park is very big; it has some picturesque landscaping. Don't miss the sculptures of (mainly) Leningrad heroes, including six busts of Leningraders who were twice decorated as Heroes of the Soviet Union and two defiant young women Communists, Zoya Kosmodemyanskaya (1951) and Raimonda Diên (1953).

Continuing south from Victory Park, the prospekt is flanked with gigantic Stalinist blocks (1930–1950s) built in a grotesque form of classicism. The most important and monstrously large building is the **House of Soviets** (by Noy Trotsky, 1936–1941) on Moscow Square. It was meant to be the new seat of Leningrad, away from the tsarist heritage. In Nikolay Tomsky's great frieze, giants build the socialist utopia. The square in front of this white elephant (it never opened) has a colossal **Lenin monument** (by Mikhail Anikushin, 1970) and 11 fountains that perform to weekend sound-and-light shows.

The post-Stalin Victory Monument, or more formally the **Monument to the Heroic Defenders of Leningrad** (by Anikushin, 1957–1975), in the center of **Victory Square** marks the end of Moskovsky Prospekt. Its encircled lines of soldiers and workers around a 157-foot-tall (48 m) obelisk are perhaps over-characterized, but still they succeed in expressing a rhythmic combination of grief and celebration. Two very somber underground **memorial halls** (tel 371-2951, closed Wed.) chronicle the Siege of Leningrad. The monument marks the front line during the siege, and from its inception it became the new ceremonial southern gate of St. Petersburg. ■

More places to visit south of the Fontanka

CHESME CHURCH

Of all St. Petersburg's churches, possibly the most picturesque is the pink-and-white striped Chesme Church of the Nativity of St. John. The Yuri Felten–designed 1780 church sits in an area previously known to the Finns as Kekerekeksinen (frog swamp); it is now swamped by the Stalinist housing blocks on and around Moskovsky Prospekt.

Chesme Church was built as a memorial church, commemorating the major Russian naval victory in June 1770 against the Turks

The Chesme Church honors Catherine's military success against the Ottomans.

at Chesme Bay in the Aegean Sea. The battle, crucial for success in Catherine's crusading Turkish war, had started on the Orthodox day of the Nativity of St. John (June 24).

In a nod to political alliances, the church speaks with an interesting east-west, Orthodox-Catholic voice. It has a curved, four-leaf (quatrefoil) plan with five cupolas that come from Moscow baroque and yet it's finished with Gothic pinnacles, zigzag cornices, and lancet windows.

The church served Catherine's new **Chesme Palace**—she originally called it La Grenouillère (Frog Swamp)—which sits just across the road and is also a Felten creation. It provided court entertainment on the way from St. Petersburg to Tsarskoye Selo. You can admire its triangular, medieval castle appearance from the outside; it's now a campus for the State University of Aerospace Instrument-Making.

The church resumed services in 1990; in the 20 years prior, it had served as a branch of the Central Naval Museum. A sizable cemetery behind the church holds many unnamed graves of those who died in Russia's wars, dating from 1812 to 1944. Map p. 189   Lensovet Ulitsa 12
373-6114   Metro: Moskovskaya

TRINITY CATHEDRAL

There are few bigger contrasts in scale than that of the Chesme Church near the southern end of Moskovsky Prospekt and the Trinity Cathedral near its northern end. Yet both have centralized plans and five cupolas and both commemorate Russian action against the Ottoman Empire. Unlike the Chesme, however, the Trinity was built for the Izmailovsky Life-Guards Regiment, is typical empire-style classicism (by Vasily Stasov, 1835), reaches a height of 246 feet (75 m), and dominates its surroundings. Its blue, gold-star-speckled cupolas make it a distinctive landmark. While undergoing renovations, the cathedral suffered a disastrous fire in August 2006 that destroyed the main cupola and much more.

There are a few interesting sights in the vicinity of the cathedral. The nearby tall **Military Glory column** was made from Turkish cannon captured in the 1877–78 Balkan War; the Soviets removed it in 1936, but it was re-erected in 2003. The **Trinity Market** behind the cathedral is pretty good. And a few notable art nouveau tenement blocks line the 1 through 7 numbered series of Red Army (Krasnoarmeyskaya) Streets to the cathedral's immediate south. Map p. 189   Izmailovsky Prospekt 7a
Metro: Tekhnologichesky Institut ∎

The rural surroundings of St. Petersburg boast within a 40-mile (64 km) circumference of the city the "diamond necklace" of palatial country residences of the tsar aristocracy. Following tradition, today's Petersburgers also build their dachas (summer houses) here, enjoying the myriad bucolic offerings of the country.

Excursions

Tsar Peter's vision can be found all around the environs of St. Petersburg.

Excursions

THE METROPOLIS OF ST. PETERSBURG IS A WORLD APART FROM ITS RURAL surroundings. Leningrad Province stretches more than 200 miles (320 km) from east to west, with St. Petersburg, its capital, at its heart. The province, created in 1927, shares international borders with Finland and Estonia and, unlike its capital, did not change its name in the 1991 referendum. Nowadays reference to its old name of Izhora or Ingria is encountered with increasing frequency.

The 18th-century Shlisselburg fortress commands a key location on Lake Ladoga.

Distinctions are obvious between town and country, but in the case of St. Petersburg and its surroundings, one thing truly stands out: The environs were occupied during World War II; the city was not. The countryside was vandalized and destroyed; its settlements turned to rubble; its populations decimated; its forests, fields, and parks turned into firewood, trenches, and minefields; looting was wholesale. A dedicated reconstruction has been ongoing ever since.

Trips outside of St. Petersburg have a feeling of discovery and rediscovery. For instance, the estates of Strelna, Gatchina, and Oranienbaum, once closed to the public, are now newly, and in some cases still partially, restored, and welcome visitors en masse. It is not just a case of doors being opened: The investigation (and marketing) of heritage has suddenly, with the collapse of the Communist regime, been enlivened by a new incisive and multiangled relish for things of the past.

No matter which direction you choose to explore, you will discover that St. Petersburg is surrounded by forest and water. The first, and most popular, route is south and west. It takes you to the great string of imperial palace and park estates—among them Tsarskoye Selo and Peterhof—that fringe the southern shore of the Gulf of Finland and head inland

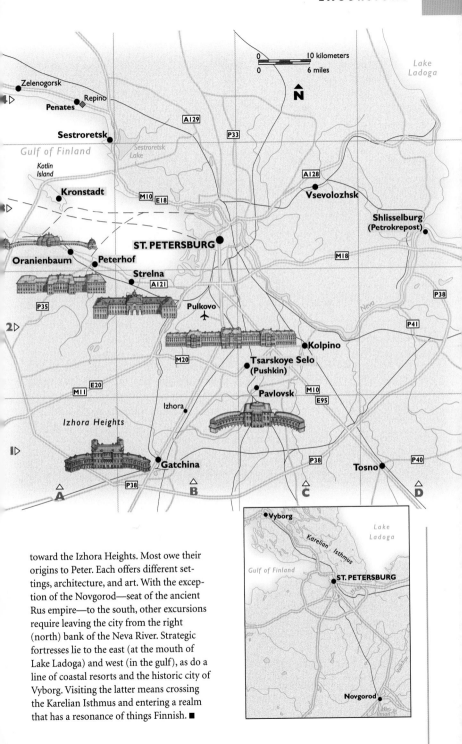

toward the Izhora Heights. Most owe their origins to Peter. Each offers different settings, architecture, and art. With the exception of the Novgorod—seat of the ancient Rus empire—to the south, other excursions require leaving the city from the right (north) bank of the Neva River. Strategic fortresses lie to the east (at the mouth of Lake Ladoga) and west (in the gulf), as do a line of coastal resorts and the historic city of Vyborg. Visiting the latter means crossing the Karelian Isthmus and entering a realm that has a resonance of things Finnish. ■

Strelna

THE IMPERIAL RESIDENCE AT STRELNA IS A REMARKABLE estate. The grand Konstantin Palace, newly restored and refurbished, feels fresh. Unlike other imperial palace restoration projects, the intention here was to loosely reminisce rather than strive for an accurate historical re-creation. As such, you feel like you're entering a brand-new place rather than a museum piece.

Strelna sits 12 miles (19 km) west of St. Petersburg along the Gulf of Finland. Its approach to the gulf first attracted Peter, and this aspect continues to make it attractive today. Taken with the grand idea of a palace that would rival King Louis XIV's of France, Peter decided to build a "Second Versailles," fountains and all. He chose Strelna as the location in 1708. A large wooden model was made on the grounds and a villa for the tsar was erected. Unlike the model, the latter survives as a rare example of timber architecture from the era. A few years into the project, Field Marshal Minich, Peter's engineer, recommended

that Peter's vision be built on a more convenient and less marshy site, 5 miles (8 km) to the west. Peter agreed and work on Peterhof (see pp. 206–213) began. Strelna was reduced to being a way station on trips to and from the fortress of Kronstadt on Kotlin Island. The change of plans, however, didn't stop Strelna from becoming a superb example of landscape design, nor a grand palace (for Elizabeth, Peter's daughter) in its own right, just not the Second Versailles.

Architects Francesco Bartolomeo Rastrelli, Jean-Baptiste Le Blond, and Niccolo Michetti began working on the estate in 1716. By 1722, canals had been dug, ponds and terraces formed, hothouses and avaries made, 83,000 trees planted, and a stone palace partially constructed. But somehow, the work at Strelna languished. The creation of Peterhof, the death of Peter, the reign of Anne, Elizabeth's focus on Tsarskoye Selo, Catherine's indifference (she used Strelna as a wine cellar for Peterhof)—these events stalled the palace's completion. No doubt the last factor spurred Catherine's son Paul to turn things around (contradicting the gaze of his mother was always a priority). After Paul became tsar, he gave Strelna to his own son Grand Duke Konstantin as his country residence and funneled funds to the estate. The palace then acquired its present shape and appearance (architects Andrey Voronikhin and Luigi Rusca), as well as a picturesque kind of park.

In 1848, the next Grand Duke Konstantin initiated another round of changes. The severe classicist interiors were brightened up with an array of more lively styles, especially rococo, by Andrey Stackenschneider, who also turned his hand to the gardens, improving the terracing and creating the grotto.

The palace suffered in the 20th century: It was a sanatorium following the 1917 Revolution; the Nazis occupied it then burned it; and then the Leningrad Arctic College took up residence for three decades until the new order of 1990s Russia devised other plans (see box below).

Since 2004 the Hermitage has organized exhibitions in the palace, which allow visitors to admire the recently refurbished halls. Permanent exhits are known as the **Museum of Heraldry** and the **Museum of Awards and Decorations.** The first details Russian coats-of-arms and has displays of medals, coins, banners, uniforms, and tableware as well as other emblems of imperial and aristocratic status. Also, be sure and take time to stroll through the park. ∎

Strelna Palace & Park Ensemble

⚠ 203 B2

✉ 12 miles (19 km) west of St. Petersburg

Visitor information

✉ Berezovaya Alleya 3, Strelna

☎ 438-5351; Konstantin Palace: 438-5440 or 438-5360

🕐 Closed Wed. & last Tues. of month; Konstantin Palace closed Mon.–Fri.

🚆 By train: Electric train from Baltic Station (Baltiskaya metro); By tram: 36 from Avtovo metro; By bus: 404-K or minibus T-224 from Avtovo metro & minibus T-103 from Leninsky Prospekt metro. Trip takes about 30 min.

A rebirth of purpose

As St. Petersburg headed toward its tricentennial in 2003, it put the imperial residence at Strelna back on the map. In 2001 President Putin decreed that Strelna should become the "State Palace of Congresses." Thus, rescuing this old estate of Peter's, which had been forever overshadowed by its neighbor Peterhof, from obscurity. It would be turned into the seaside residence of the president of Russia (a return of sorts to Peter's original intent). By 2003, after an investment of 280 million dollars, the job was done, and three years later, in July 2006,

world leaders arrived for a G-8 Summit. Strelna was back with a bang and with style. ∎

World leaders at the 2006 G–8 Summit in Strelna

The Great Cascade falls 52 feet (16 m) into the Marine Canal, which connected Peterhof with the Gulf of Finland.

Peterhof

THE "SECOND VERSAILLES" IS IN ITS SECOND INCARNATION. The first was built in a rush by a man in a hurry. Peter had the idea for the estate soon after he'd founded St. Petersburg, but in 1703 the war with Sweden had not yet been won. It took another 11 years before he felt safe to start work. Then, in the remaining decade of his life, during which time he actually visited Versailles, Peter created three palaces, a great park, and a system of fountains at Peterhof. It became the core of Russia's most celebrated imperial residences, the one most adored by his successors, and the grandest ray of triumphalist light in the world's northern climes. Nothing rivaled it. Until World War II intervened. Occupied and close to the front line during the Siege of Leningrad, Peterhof suffered more than the other estates in Petersburg's "diamond necklace" of imperial palaces. Its liberation in January 1944 revealed that it had been reduced to ruins. Its reincarnation has taken 60-plus years, and the job's still not quite done.

Petersburg that he kept taking risky boat rides to visit its outermost defense, his new forts on and around Kotlin Island in the gulf. Catherine suggested alleviating the strain by building a "wayside front room" near the shore from where the crossings were made. And so in 1705, the "front room" dwelling went up next to the tiny village of Kussoa in the vicinity of the later Marly Palace. It was surrounded by forest, marshes, and the occasional thatched-roof fisherman's hut or farmstead. This was the start of Peterhof. Nine years later, after victory at Poltava and Hangö, significant gains from the Swedes farther west, and declaring St. Petersburg the Russian capital in 1712, Peter felt safe. Work on Peterhof began.

No matter which way you approach Peterhof, be it by sea (which offers a majestic entry and fine panoramas) or by land, the impression will be that this place is much more than about victory over Sweden and the arrival of Russia as a topflight European empire. The artifice, the majesty, and the sheer scale of landscaping all make it clear that Peterhof is a statement about the triumph of human will over nature. It was this fact, not its tsarist heritage, that led Soviet authorities and thousands of workers to devote their resources to its restoration from the late 1940s on.

The world of Peter's Court (Peterhof), if not entirely as envisaged by Peter, very much adheres to the plans he sketched out in 1714. It was to be an international realm, given, like so many of his creations, a German name and designed and built by an array of architects, engineers, artists, and craftsmen from around Europe. Three rays would

If Peter was in a hurry, then the four million visitors who dash around Peterhof's five palaces and 2,500-acre (1,000 ha) parks every year are inevitably more so. Most people only devote half a day, but half a week wouldn't really suffice. Peterhof sits on the southern coast of the Gulf of Finland and from its westernmost palace, the Marly, to its easternmost, the Cottage, the distance across the parks is 2 miles (3.2 km). There's plenty of walking if you want to see it all.

A place at Peterhof wasn't Peter's idea. The honor belongs to his wife, Catherine. The tsar was so concerned with securing St.

Peterhof State Museum Reserve
www.peterhof.org
- 203 A3
- 18.5 miles (30 km) west of St. Petersburg

Visitor information
- Razvodnaya Ulitsa 2, Peterhof
- 420-0073 or 450-7425
- Closed Mon. & last Tues. of month May–Oct.; open (Sat.–Sun. Nov.–April
- $$$ (Park) $$$$ (Palace)
- By train: Baltic Station (Baltiskaya metro) to Novy Petergof, then bus 348, 350, 352, or 356; By minibus: T-404 from Baltic Station (Baltiskaya metro) or T-420 from Leninsky Prospekt metro; By hydrofoil (summer only): from near Hermitage, Bronze Horseman, or Aurora. Trip takes about 30–45 min.

Cottage Palace
- 420-0073, 427-7425, or 427-9953
- Closed Mon. & Wed.–Thurs.
- $$

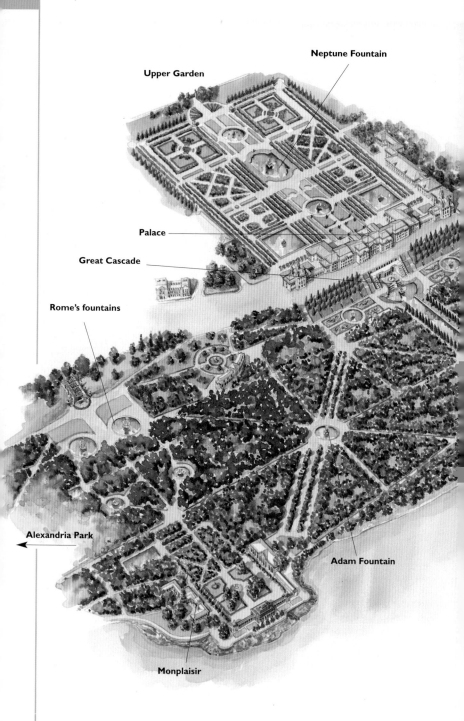

Neptune Fountain

Upper Garden

Palace

Great Cascade

Rome's fountains

Alexandria Park

Adam Fountain

Monplaisir

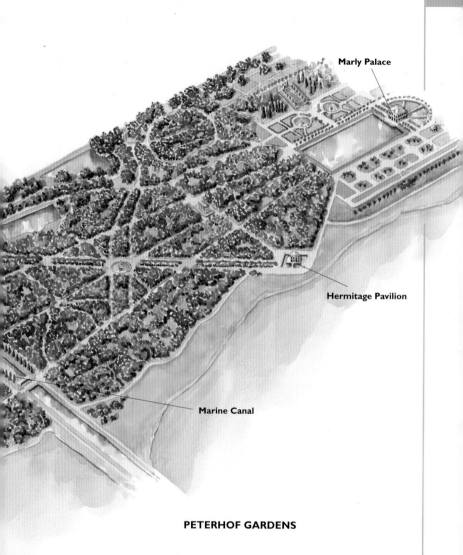

Marly Palace

Hermitage Pavilion

Marine Canal

PETERHOF GARDENS

The lavishly decorated Chinese Room is a small hall that Peter had Johann-Friedrich Braunstein design in the Monplaisir Palace for his Oriental porcelain.

fan out toward the shore from a central upper mansion. At the end of the two diagonal rays would be two buildings, while the central third ray would comprise a grand cascade and the marine canal. The ensemble would make use of the natural lay of the land and be adorned with fountains, sculptures, and pavilions.

GREAT PALACE

The original upper mansion, executed by Jean-Baptiste Le Blond in 1714–1721, was significantly altered when Peter's daughter, Empress Elizabeth, with the help of her favorite architect, Francesco Bartolomeo Rastrelli, turned the upper mansion into the Great Palace in the mid-18th century. Rastrelli's additions include the third story and the side wings that terminate in the church and "coat of arms" block, both of which are adorned with gilded cupolas.

Passing through the gates of the main entrance you enter the formal **Upper Garden.** Laid

out (1714–1724) to designs by Johann-Friedrich Braunstein and Le Blond, it was enlarged to match the extension of the palace by Rastrelli (1754–1760). Deprived of its well-established trees during World War II, it feels a bit barren, its avenues overbroad and lifeless. Still this parterre introduces visitors to the role that water is to play here through its five fountains and ponds. The central fountain, the **Neptune,** has twice traveled from Germany—first in 1799 when, as a piece of 17th-century German baroque sculpture, it was purchased from Nuremberg by Tsar Paul, and then in 1947 after its looting during the war. The Upper Garden brings you to the 984-foot-wide (300 m) rear facade of the Great Palace

Enter through the west wing and climb Rastrelli's ceremonial staircase, which effervesces with gold ornamentation, to the suite of state rooms on the second floor. Their decoration reveals the differences in taste between Russia's two empresses of the mid- to late 18th century: Elizabeth loved flamboyant baroque and Catherine preferred classic line. The first room is the **Chesme Hall,** designed in the 1770s around 12 canvases by Jacob Philipp Hackert that celebrate Catherine's naval victory over the Ottoman fleet in the Aegean in 1770. Off to the right is Elizabeth's large **ballroom** with its gilded lacing of stuccowork. Next comes the **Throne Hall,** where the decor again is subservient to a painting—an emblematic equestrian portrait of Catherine. Other interesting rooms include the **Western Chinese Study,** which is filled with 1760s chinoiserie; the large central **Picture Hall,** which contains 368 portraits of female grace and style; a suite of less formal rooms; and finally, the modest, wood-paneled study of Peter.

LOWER PARK

The immaculate, almost sacred, re-creation of the magnificent palace is not the highlight of most people's experience at Peterhof. Most find the Lower Park much more wondrous and enjoyable.

From the terrace in front of the palace, take in the commanding view of the Baltic. Then immerse yourself in the celebration of water that Peter, the maritime emperor, planned for this place. The majestic **Great Cascade** rolls down like a great double staircase from the center of the palace. Completed by 75 fountains, it was the 18th century's largest fountain ensemble. It's adorned with gilded statues of mythological heroes and gods. The centerpiece is the 65-foot-high (20 m) jet in the cascade's bottom basin that spouts from a group depicting Samson tearing open the jaws

of a lion, symbolizing Russia's victory over Sweden in the Battle of Poltava. Myriad other fountains, in a profusion of styles—there's even some trick ones—dot the Lower Park. Wander to your heart's content; there is no best way to explore.

MARLY PALACE & HERMITAGE PAVILION

To the west of the Grand Palace lies Peter's interpretation of the Marly-le-Rois park outside Paris (destroyed in the French Revolution): fruit gardens, fish-ponds, the Golden Hill cascade, the miniature Marly Palace, and the Hermitage Pavilion. There's an air of restraint and pragmatism in this quiet corner. The 16-room palace features Peter's collection of 17th-century Dutch genre paintings. The waterside

Peter's bedroom at Monplaisir. The painted ceiling by Philippe Pillement depicts carnival figures and has rococo ornamentation.

Hermitage was designed to serve as a servant-free dining area: Food was delivered to the upstairs dining room by means of a "magic table" mechanical device.

MONPLAISIR

Crossing the Lower Park to the east brings you to Monplaisir (My Pleasure), Peter's version of an amusement park. It has six themed gardens, a maze, aviary, and fountains galore (watch out for fir trees that spray and an umbrella that drips). Completed at the top by the Dragon (or Checkerboard) Cascade and at sea level by a one-story palace, Monplaisir also features a bay-shaped greenhouse, which now serves as the park's café.

The palace, not its adjoined (later) Catherine Block, is the real gem. Peter's favorite and the first to be built (1714–1723), it is a simple Dutch-style house surrounded on two sides by low galleries. It is the country equivalent to the Summer Palace in St. Petersburg (see pp. 56–57). Here you can best sense Peter's personal, domestic taste.

The palace hugs the coastline, is small (seven rooms), made of brick, and faced in oak panels and Dutch tiles. Of particular interest are **Peter's Maritime Study,** from which he could view both Kronstadt and Petersburg with his telescope, and the **central hall.** The latter is decorated at ceiling level with allegorical consoles (by Bartolomeo Carlo Rastrelli) that depict the seasons and a rococo painted interpretation (by Philippe Pillement) of the sun god Apollo in control of the elements. For Apollo read Peter. This palace was the venue for Peter's great drinking bouts and his tempestuous interrogation of his son Alexey.

ALEXANDRIA PARK

The most romantic part of Peterhof, Alexandria Park usually gets ignored. Part of the difficulty is that although it borders the eastern part of the Lower Park, it's currently sealed off by a wall. It's worth a separate trip, perhaps combined with a visit to neighboring Strelna (see pp. 204–205). The crowds are fewer and the immense park appears wild due to its undulating, picturesque landscaping with numerous varieties of well-established trees and shrubs.

Alexandria was initially Alexander Menshikov's Moncourage estate and later Empress Anne's hunting grounds. In the 1820s and '30s, Nicholas I and his consort Alexandra Feodorovna converted it into their summer dacha. Scotsman Adam Menelaws's Gothic Revival designs represent a dramatic departure from the proclamatory pomp and ceremony of the park's neighboring estates. The two palaces were named "cottage" and "farm." A striking neo-Gothic **chapel** in the west of the park, built to designs of the great Prussian architect Karl Friedrich Schinkel, complements the palaces. The intimate **Cottage Palace** was Nicholas and Alexandra's favored home. It is basically a two-story house with a garret for the tsar's naval study. It contains Oriental references to Nicholas's 1828–29 war with the Ottomans and a small suite of rooms that were converted around 1900 into a rather French art nouveau style. ■

Johann-Friedrich Braunstein designed the square Marly Palace to be in harmony with its waterside setting.

Antonio Rinaldi's Sliding Hill Pavilion is one of Oranienbaum's most delightful features.

Oranienbaum

THE MOST AUTHENTIC IMPERIAL RESIDENCE IN THE ENvirons of St. Petersburg is Oranienbaum (Orange Tree). While the other palace estates were occupied and devastated during World War II, it survived—not unscathed, but still largely intact. The estate, the farthest west from the city, was surrounded by German-held territory, but it lay in a pocket of land covered by the Soviet batteries from Kronstadt fort on Kotlin Island. Furthermore, a good proportion of that which survived had also avoided the fever of stylistic change that gripped the Russian court continuously from the late 18th century on. This wasn't luck: An orange tree in Russia is a rare thing, and worth preserving.

Peter gave his right-hand man, Alexander Menshikov, the land and villages around present-day Oranienbaum to turn into his country residence, one befitting the governor of the province of Ingermanland (Ingria/Izhora). This post made Menshikov the most powerful man in Russia after the tsar. Gossip has it that their relationship was more than friendly. Menshikov loved the place, determined that it would become his paradise (with orange trees), gave Peter a suite of rooms in his new palace, and turned it into the center of out-of-town court parties. For 30 months following the death of Peter, during the short reigns of Peter's widow and then his teenage grandson Peter II (1715–1730), the lowborn Menshikov ran the country from Oranienbaum and his city palace. It led to his undoing. Situated too far away from St. Petersburg, and with the tsar's residence at Peterhof in between, highborn intriguers isolated him at Oranienbaum and staged a coup. Menshikov was arrested, stripped of all his possessions, and sent with his family to Siberia. A worse fate awaited Peter's other grandson, Peter III (1728–1762), who received the estate as heir to the throne in 1743, made it his main residence, and then was forced out (and killed) in the plot that turned his wife into Empress Catherine II (the Great).

Oranienbaum has several treats. Menshikov's **Great Palace** (by Giovanni Fontana and Johann Gottfried Schedel, 1710–1721) overlooks the Lower Garden and the sea. It's a pleasant U-shaped two-story building, but there is not much to see. Where the two wings meet the central block, large domed pavilions housed the Church of St. Pantelymon and the Japanese Hall. The rococo latter displays some Oriental art (ironically, mainly Chinese vases). The parks and the estate's other buildings hold more interest for visitors.

To the east of the Great Palace lies the **Lower Pond** where Karl

Oranienbaum State Museum-Reserve

203 A3

25 miles (41 km) west of St. Petersburg.

Visitor information

Dvortsovy Prospekt 48, Lomonosov

422-3756, 422-8016, 422-3753, or 422-1636

Closed Tues. & last Fri. of month; Chinese Palace closed Oct.–mid-May

$$

By train: Electric train from Baltic Station (Baltiskaya metro) to Oranienbaum;
By bus: K, T-300, or T-343 from Prospekt Veteranov metro; minibus T-300 or T-424a from Avtovo metro.
Trip takes about 1 hr.

The Great Hall of Oranienbaum Palace features "Day Conquering Night," an allegorical ceiling painting by Stefano Torelli.

Peter, the future Tsar Peter III, practiced naval war games with his model fleet (two frigates and two galleys with bronze cannon) and pretended he was King Frederick II of Prussia. On its shores he built a little wood-and-earth fortress called Peterstadt, where he played tactics with invited officers and troops from his native north German principality of Holstein-Gottorp.

The spired ceremonial gate and **Peter III Palace,** are gems designed by Antonio Rinaldi (1758–1762). The ceiling of the palace boudoir is a masterpiece of plaster reliefwork that depicts the history of Peterstadt. But pride of place goes to the lacquer decoration of the Picture Hall, a unique example of mid-18th-century Chinese-style decorative painting in Russia, with lots of little scenes depicting Chinese life. It frames walls covered in a tapestry of 58 paintings in the style of West European old masters (some are genuine). Peter III may have lived in a fantasy world but he had some taste.

The picturesque **Peter Park** surrounds Peter's palace; the little Karost River runs through the valley. To the delight of many visitors, Siberian deer occasionally graze in the park. Across the river and up Walnut Avenue lies the Upper Park. At either end of this park stand Oranienbaum's two main attractions, both of which owe their existence to Catherine II.

The seemingly ordinary park pavilion at the park's southern end is the **Chinese Palace** (by Rinaldi, 1762–68). It was built as an entertainment centerpiece for Catherine II as she juxtaposed her dead husband's playground with her own. It is *the* Russian rococo monument. Color and line run riot in a suite of highly decorated rooms. The ornamentation is all about pleasure, in plentiful measure and variety. Surfaces from floor to curved ceiling writhe in an orgy of kaleidoscopic art. From the gilded intricacies of the Buglework Study to the marquetry wonderland that is the Large Chinese Study, from Catherine's seemingly luminescent study to the artistic triumph of the Hall of Muses and the kitsch vaulting of the Damask Bedroom, there's no keeping still. Movement is paramount in the decoration and the eye doesn't know where to turn next. Take a deep breath before entering.

The second treasure of Oranienbaum is the **Sliding Hill Pavilion** (by Rinaldi, 1762–64). It lies to the north of the Chinese Pavilion, marking the other end of the park territory that Catherine called her "own dacha." It's the surviving element of a great artificial sliding hill. This galleried slope (now just a meadow) ran south for 382 yards (530 m) from the exquisite pavilion. The slope was the largest of its kind in Russia, where they were created as a popular form of entertainment. The tall pavilion is tiered and bell-domed. Designed in the shape of a three-pinned cog, the pavilion was used to pull up the sleds and for relaxation. It's a rococo haven, complete with 40 mythological and allegorical Meissen porcelain groups bracketed onto the walls of the study. The statues tell Catherine's interpretation of Russia's dominance as a maritime power. Forever grasping the nettle of politics together with the cloak of culture in one hand, Catherine ensured that here, above appropriately slippery slopes, foreign ministers and Gustav III of Sweden were regularly entertained. ■

Gatchina

EMPRESS CATHERINE II GAVE GATCHINA, THE MOST distant of the estates in St. Petersburg's "diamond necklace" of royal palace-park ensembles, to her detested son Paul in 1783 to keep him out of the way. Over the next two decades, the future tsar and grand master of the Knights Hospitaller, or Order of St. John, turned the estate into a mini-state within a state. It appeared that Paul was developing the make-believe orderly realm his father Peter III had constructed at Oranienbaum when he was a boy. Gatchina became known as the Gatchina Empire; it got its own coat of arms, town status, and border control (sentry boxes, barracks, and fortifications). It also acquired the Gatchina Fleet, the maneuvers of which (on the lakes in the park) Paul personally supervised.

Gatchina Museum-Reserve

203 B1

28 miles (45 km) southwest of St. Petersburg

Deep in the forested countryside, 30 miles (48 km) from the coast, the former manor at Gatchina had been turned into a romantic retreat by Catherine's favorite Count Grigory Orlov. Catherine had granted him the estate in 1765, in part as payment for his leading the coup that brought about the demise of Peter III and her own elevation to the throne.

An externally rather severe-looking castle was designed by Antonio Rinaldi (1766–1781) and a picturesque park laid out. After Orlov's death and Paul's acquisition of the estate, the heir to the throne set about removing from it the imprint of the man responsible for his father's murder. The 600-room Great Palace was redecorated and wings,

Tsar Paul's Throne Room contains a reproduction of a 1731 throne made in England.

The monument of Tsar Paul (by Ivan Vitali, 1850) surveys his "Gatchina Empire."

towers, and a church were added. A parade ground with a moat and drawbridge replaced the green meadow that had been in front of building. Gates, terraces, stairs, bridges, pavilions, and the remarkable clay *(pisé)* **Priory Palace** (by Nikolay Lvov, 1798–99) were built in the park. The latter was designed as a refuge for the Knights of St. John who had been forced out of Malta by Napoleon. This lakeside palace, with its Gothic features and tall spired tower, looks like it was transplanted from a West European village. What's more, it

has stood the test of time— unlike so much of the estate that was reproduced following the devastation of World War II, the Priory Palace is original.

When Paul and his family took over Gatchina as their main residence, Paul radically altered the interiors of the **Great Palace;** his descendants also made changes through the mid- to late 19th century. Hitler's forces fire-gutted the building after their two-year occupation, so a lot on view is a reconstruction. One noteworthy change among Paul's alterations was

reflections, light, and shade (it was always loved by painters). Start at the palace's terrace and walk along the long island in the center of White Lake, crossing over the Hunchback Bridge to the Eagle Pavilion. To the south you can see the Chesme Column. To

Made of clay, the Priory Palace was intended as a refuge for the Maltese Knights of St. John.

Vincenzo Brenna's transformation of Orlov's small study into the **Throne Room** (note the reproduction throne, the 1731 English original of which is in the Winter Palace). Ever fearful (rightly as it turned out) of assassination plots, Paul did not get rid of the palace's secret underground passages. You can stoop through the one leading to Silver Lake.

A walk around the **park** is a definite must. The German occupation took its toll here as well, but the park has revived and is a place of remarkable colors,

the west lies the **Silvia Park** with its earth amphitheater designed for jousting tournaments in 1798.

To the north lies the **Island of Love** with its Venus Pavilion, which is a copy of a similar pavilion that Paul and his wife Maria Feodorovna had seen when they toured Europe incognito as Comte and Comtesse du Nord just before moving to Gatchina. The island, like the Silvia, was inspired by Prince de Condé's park at Chantilly near Paris. Just beyond the island is the reproduction of the log cabin **Birch Cottage,** which is "masked" by a large stone neoclassic portal and gate. This folly was Maria's retreat. East of here is White Lake's water labyrinth, an archipelago of mini-islands, and then Paul's wooden **Admiralty,** which although a simple boat store, comes replete with a triumphal arch. ■

Visitor information

✉ Krasnoarmeysky Prospekt 1, Gatchina

☎ (8 813-71) 215-09 or (8 813-71) 134-92

🕐 Closed Mon. & first Tues. of month

💲 $$

🚆 By train: Electric train from Baltic Station (Baltiskaya metro) or Kupchino to Gatchina; By bus: K-18 from Pobedy Ploshchad (Moskvovskaya metro) or Sredney Rogatki. Trip takes about 1 hr.

The sumptuous courtyard facade of Francesco Bartolomeo Rastrelli's Catherine Palace

Tsarskoye Selo

BEFORE THE 1720s, TSARSKOYE SELO, WHICH MEANS "ROYAL village," was known to Russians as Sarskaya Myza, which derives from the Finnish for "raised farming place." The change from Sarskaya to Tsarskoye was far more than a play on words: The isolated, impoverished farmstead became the well-connected country realm of Russia's 18th-century empresses.

Peterhof with its fountains was Peter's idea of a Russian Versailles on the coast; Tsarskoye Selo was his daughter Elizabeth's (and after her, Catherine II's) inland version on the same theme. It was the grandest, most luxurious, and "ideal" ensemble of palaces, parks, and model town. When Hitler's troops left after their 28-month uninvited stay, it was a 1,500-acre wasteland of empty ruins. Restoration on this magnificent jewel started immediately in January 1944. It continues today.

CATHERINE PALACE
Lauded as one of the 18th century's most glorious works of art and architecture, the Catherine Palace you see today is, in many respects, the highest achievement of mid 20th-century Stalinist empire style.

Elizabeth's contribution

The Catherine Palace was built by Elizabeth in memory of her mother Catherine I, to whom the modest estate had belonged from 1710. It, perhaps more than the Winter Palace, Smolny Cathedral, or Peterhof Palace, is *the* symbol of the Elizabethan epoch, the epitome of exuberant baroque gesture. If it seems like self-indulgence, it is also a daughter's homage to the grand schemes started but left unfinished by her parents.

Elizabeth's Tsarskoye Selo did not spring from nothing. She inherited the estate from her mother who, by 1724, had created there a small Dutch-style mansion (16 rooms) with a park, orchard, greenhouses, and menagerie. Elizabeth loved it and once she

became empress in 1741, she set about transforming it into a majestic palace whose facades added up to more than a half mile (1 km) in length and whose surfaces were covered in more than 220 pounds (100 kg) of gold leaf. Elizabeth's favorite architect, Francesco Bartolomeo Rastrelli, completed the stunning changes with his usual flourish of columns, pilasters, and caryatids. Viewed from the exterior, what was essentially a long straight block was transformed into a rippling melody of blue, white, and gold. The decoration was capped by the five ribboned gilded onion domes of the palace church over its northern corner.

Inside, the neorococo finesse of the blanched state staircase does not quite prepare you for the suite of golden state rooms that extend along the second floor. South of the staircase, the Cavaliers' Dining Room adjoins the **Great Hall,** one of the most exquisite ballrooms in the world. It covers a floorspace of about 9,000 square feet (830 sq m) and is lit by large, typically Rastrellian windows in two tiers, between which were placed mirrors. In the 18th century, this room was known as the Gallery of Light. The carved, golden decoration took 130 master craftsmen to complete. The whole is surmounted by a monumental, three-part, allegorical ceiling painting, the "Triumph of Russia" (the original was painted by the Venetian Guiseppe Valeriani, 1752–54). For Elizabeth's grand balls and masquerades, an 80-musician orchestra would play and the hall would be lit by 1,200 candles. Glass doors at the ballroom's southern end lead to three similarly decorated but smaller antechambers.

Tsarskoye Selo Museum-Reserve
www.tzar.ru

🗺 203 C2

✉ 15 miles (24 km) south of St. Petersburg

Visitor information
www.tzar.ru

✉ Sadovaya Ulitsa 7, Pushkin

☎ 465-2024, 466-5831, or 451-7281; Imperial Lycée: 476-6411

🕐 Closed Tues. & last Mon. of month; Cold Baths & Agate Rooms closed Mon.–Tues.; Imperial Lycée closed Tues.

💲 $$$$

🚊 By train: Electric train from Vitebsk Station (Pushkinskaya metro) or Kupchino to Detskoye Selo; By minibus: T-287 from Moskovskaya metro. Trip takes about 25 min.

The Amber Room: the "eighth wonder of the world"

On the other side of the staircase, the golden suite continues. The portraits of Russia's 18th-century rulers that hang in the **Portrait Hall** serve as a prelude for the next room, the "eighth wonder of the world," the **Amber Room.**

Amber, fossilized conifer resin, has always been cherished by man. Its mysterious transparency, resonant colors, and alternative medicinal uses have stimulated its transformation not least into works of art. Deposits of amber lie on the southern Baltic coast around Kaliningrad (previously Königsberg). In 1717, as part of an exchange of gifts marking their new alliance, King Frederick William I of Prussia presented to Tsar Peter a set of amber panels that had been made for his father

before his death. Elizabeth brought the panels to Tsarskoye in 1755 and commissioned Rastrelli to design a room around them. He did so magnificently. The panels were complemented by new Florentine mosaics representing the five senses, rocaille cartouches and painted ceiling, gilded friezes, mirror pilasters, and a display of 60 articles of luxury amberware. When the Third Reich's Kunstkommission (Art Committee) arrived in 1941, the panels were packed up and repatriated to Königsberg, where they disappeared. The re-creation of the room began in 1979 and was completed in 2003. Note the intricate craftsmanship. Feel the honeycomb ooze.

After the Amber Room the rest of the palace apartments appear relatively restrained. There are more Rastrelli rooms—first the **Picture Hall** with its walls made up of a jigsaw of various canvases by 17th- and 18th-century masters and then what became **Alexander I's drawing room.** Beyond these lie the private apartments Catherine's son Paul and his wife, which bear the 1780s neoclassic imprint of Scottish architect Charles Cameron.

Catherine II's contributions

Elizabeth's changes to Tsarskoye Selo can be considered the florid climax of the artistic trends begun by her father, yet when Catherine II laid her hands on the estate, she sought to override and expunge what she perceived as Elizabeth's excessive, vulgar frolics. They were to be replaced by an ideal reflection of her Greek Project, a return to Orthodox Constantinople. Part of this plan meant an invocation of the ideal values and forms of antiquity. In her own words the estate was to become a "Greco-Roman rhapsody." Cameron captured this sense of eternal idyll in the wing of the palace containing the Pompeiian **Cold Baths,** their **Agate Rooms,** the neighboring **Cameron Gallery,** and the **Hanging Garden** (1779–1795). They all speak of refinement and perfection, cleansing acts in which communication with the elements and cosmos was pure, harmonic, and unencumbered. The immaculate play of external-internal space in the colonnaded gallery was completed by busts of ancient military leaders, emperors, writers, philosophers, and honored contemporaries. Catherine viewed herself as the Russian Minerva (as Peter had done before her), the protective deity of civilization and much more.

CATHERINE PARK

The garden in front of the Catherine Palace was planned in the 1720s as a French-style formal garden with a regular layout of avenues, mirror ponds, and parterres. In the mid-18th century, Elizabeth extended the garden and had Rastrelli enhance it with the **Grotto** and **Hermitage Pavilions** in a style similar to the

Map labels:
- Lamskie Ponds
- St. Theodore (Feodorovsky) Townstead
- AKADEMICHESKY PROSPECT
- DVORTSOVAYA UL
- 0   500 meters
- 0   500 yards
- Arsenal
- Heirs' (White) Tower
- ALEXANDER PARK
- N
- Alexander Palace
- Menagerie
- Chapel
- Chinese Theater
- Kitchen Pond
- DVORTSOVAYA UL
- Chinese Village
- PODKAPRIZOVAYA DOROGA
- CATHERINE PARK
- Squeaking (Chinese) Summer House
- Chinese Bridge
- Catherine Palace
- Agate Rooms
- Lycée
- Cameron Gallery & Hanging Gardens
- Pompeiian Cold Baths
- Milkmaid Fountain
- SADOVAYA UL
- Tower-Ruin
- Palladian (Marble) Bridge
- Great Pond
- Grotto Pavilion
- Hermitage Pavilion
- Turkish Baths
- Chesme Column
- Admiralty
- Cascade Ponds
- PARKOVAYA UL

The partly ruined St. Theodore Townstead was built in a neo-Russian style as a barracks for Nicholas II's guards.

palace. At the same time, she relocated more than 60 baroque sculptures here from the Summer Garden in St. Petersburg.

As you walk around the southern, picturesque part of the Catherine Park you'll notice a great variety of monuments and pavilions. Many of these were erected in Catherine's time to commemorate Russian successes in the wars against the Ottomans. They include the picturesque Tower-Ruin, the rostral Chesme Column in the **Great Pond,** the mosque-like Turkish Baths, the Turkish Cascade, and the Kagul Obelisk. Also worth a look are the Squeaking (or Chinese) Summer House (by Yuri Felten, 1778–1786), the sublime Palladian (Marble) Bridge, and the neo-Gothic Admiralty (both by Vasily Neelov, 1777). The latter holds temporary exhibitions.

Be sure to spend some time admiring the melancholy **Milkmaid fountain** (1816, Pavel Sokolov), which takes water from Tsarskoye Selo's only natural spring. Also known as Girl with a Pitcher, it was immortalized by Alexander Pushkin in his 1830 poem "Tsarskoye Selo Statue" and was inspired by a 17th-century "don't build castles in the air" fable by Jean de La Fontaine: Peretta the milkmaid breaks her jug on the way to market just as she dreams of what riches the sale of its milk may bring her.

ALEXANDER PARK

The Alexander Park, northwest of the Catherine Palace, appears the most untamed, forested part of the estate. But it, too, has two faces. The first, closest to the palace, was laid out by Elizabeth as four large rectangular gardens surrounded by mini-canals. Catherine, however, then put an Eastern stamp on the grounds: Chinese bridges, a Chinese Theater, and a miniature Chinese Village. Beyond lies the wilder part and the early 19th-century realm of Catherine's grandchildren, future tsars Alexander I and Nicholas I. This enchanting and still partly ruinous place used to be called the Menagerie. Gothic-style pavilions, stables, and a farm were built for the royal llamas, elephants, retired horses, and cows. Some symbolic buildings were erected among the trees, including the extant neo-Gothic chapel, the six-story Heirs' (White) Tower, and the castle-like Arsenal (by Adam Menelaws, 1819–1834); the latter was designed to house the Tsars' 5,000-piece collection of arms.

Bordering the park to its north is a noteworthy, curious, late addition: **St. Theodore (Feodorovsky) Townstead.** It was built in 1912 in the neo-Russian style to resemble an ancient kremlin, but it actually served as a barracks for Tsar Nicholas II's guards.

The creation of the townstead coincided with Nicholas's adoption of Tsarskoye Selo as his young family's permanent residence. They chose to live in the giant neoclassic **Alexander Palace** (by Giacomo Quarenghi, 1792–96), which Catherine had built for her grandson the future Alexander I. They made it their nest and turned their living quarters into an elegant ensemble of art nouveau, commissioning Roman Meltser to craft the designs. Fearful of the revolutionary movements, Nicholas and Alexandra installed themselves here from 1905. It was here that Rasputin came calling, here that the royals were confined after the February Revolution of 1917, and from here that they were taken away on their last journey to Siberia. After recent restoration, it is possible to visit their wing once again.

OTHER SIGHTS

If you've got any energy left after visiting the palaces and parks of Tsarskoye Selo, then turn your attention to the **Imperial Lycée,** which stands at the northern end of the Catherine Palace. Pushkin was in the first cohort of students educated here. You can get acquainted with the boarding school as it was during the none-too-diligent Pushkin's six hard years within its walls (1811–17). The garden embraces a pleasant

monument to the poet (by Robert Bach, 1900), who sits nonchalantly yet earnestly on a park bench. From here, venture through the gridiron plan of the early 19th-century model town of Pushkin to that of **Sofiya** at the southern edge of the Catherine Park, where you can enter the just restored, impressive, and highly symbolic Palladianist **St. Sophia's Cathedral** (by Cameron, 1782–88). Catherine II planned Sofiya (named for herself and the Greek for "wisdom") as the cornerstone of her new classically-inspired Russian Empire. Hard to believe when you see the undeveloped and remote corner it has become. ■

Alexander Pushkin reflects in the gardens near the Imperial Lycée, where he went to school in the early 19th century.

As at Gatchina, a statue of Tsar Paul, by Ivan Vitali, surveys the estate at Pavlovsk.

Pavlovsk State Museum-Reserve
www.pavlovsk.org

 203 C2

 17 miles (27 km) south of St. Petersburg

Pavlovsk

TRADITIONALLY, WEALTHY RUSSIAN PARENTS GAVE THEIR children a gift of land on the arrival of their first grandchild. And so, for all her misgivings about her son Paul, upon the birth of his son Alexander, in 1777 Catherine II gave Paul 2 sq. miles (540 ha) of gently undulating land around the meandering Slavyanka River, 3 miles (4.8 km) southeast of Tsarskoye Selo. Paul turned these former hunting grounds into Russia's primary picturesque park.

The heart of the park is a relatively small neo-Palladian palace that became the role model for country palaces on other estates of the Russian nobility. Its pedigree was the Venetian Renaissance filtered through the experience of 18th-century British classicism.

Pavlovsk was named after Paul (Pavel), but his wife, Maria Feodorovna, the former German princess Sophia-Dorothea of Württemberg, had the most impact on its appearance. It reflects her taste and lifestyle. At the same time, it also embodies the architect Charles Cameron's spiritual vision: Every element is integrated like poetry. Here art approaches nature as never before in Russia. During the Nazi occupation, all-destructive human nature reduced the art to ruins and ashes, felling 70,000 trees, dynamiting pavilions and bridges, and burning the palace. Restoration of the palace took 26 years, that of the park continues.

GREAT PALACE

The palace crowns a small hill. It has a central ceremonial block flanked by two long, low wings that curve around to form the courtyard. It appears severe, simple, dignified, light, and harmonized with its surroundings. Its central dome, the symbol of Beauty inspired by Reason, is flat, surrounded by an incredible 64 columns, and surprisingly visible. Cameron's attention to ideal proportions and symmetrical forms draws upon the 16th-century Italian villa designs of Andrea Palladio.

The present interiors are an interpretation of those created after Cameron had been dismissed in 1787 for not bending to Maria Feodorovna's changing stylistic demands. They showcase the richer, more ornate, and mannered creations of Vincenzo Brenna, and then the more reserved qualities introduced by Andrey Voronokhin, Giacomo Quarenghi, and Carlo Rossi originally made after Pavlovsk became an imperial residence in 1796, and then after a fire in 1803.

The stairs from the Egyptian Vestibule lead to the small suite of rooms designed around the central **Italian Hall.** This round space, with its symmetrically placed four doors and niches, and its lighting from the dome, reflected Cameron's idea of an Olympian temple. Beyond this hall lies the **Grecian Hall,** a luxurious ballroom with green Corinthian columns and French tapestries. Small state rooms to either side of these halls basically divide between Paul's preferred martial style and Maria's more intricate, domestic taste. Still on the second floor, the **Picture Gallery,** stocked with 17th- and 18th-century European paintings, stretches along the curve of the southern wing. It leads to the **Throne (Dining) Room,** highlighted by the trompe l'oeil ceiling painted to look like an uncovered dome. Then comes the **Hall of Knights,** a museum of classical-style sculpture designed for the rituals of the Maltese Order of the Knights of St. John after Paul became their grand master.

You'll get a greater sense of Cameron's intended austerity downstairs in the less ornate living apartments.

PAVLOVSK PARK

The romance of Pavlovsk Park centers around Cameron's concept that the park should be morally uplifting and inspirational. (Unless noted, all the elements in the park are the creation of Cameron.) In keeping with the style of the day, various areas were designed to emulate gardens in other parts of Europe.

The park's variety of lines, which actually mark distinct areas, converge on the palace near the southern border with the town of Pavlovsk. First, the formal Dutch-style **Private Garden** was regarded as a "continuation of the palace hall," its axes extending from the spatial arrangement of the palace, with its main avenue leading from Maria's boudoir. It was completed by the little Greek temple-like **Three Graces Pavilion** (1801), in the center of which is a marble group of Joy, Flowering, and Brilliance (by Paolo Triscorni) reaching up to a vase.

Around the back of the palace, cross the beautiful little Centaurs' Bridge, pass the Cold Baths, and wander through the upper garden to the **Apollo Colonnade** (1780–83), a double semicircle of

Visitor information

- ✉ Sadovaya Ulitsa 20, Pavlovsk
- ☎ 452-2155/2156 or 470-6536
- 🕐 Closed Fri. in winter & sometimes in summer
- 💲 $$$
- 🚆 By train: Electric train from Vitebsk Station (Pushkinskaya metro) or Kupchino to Pavlovsk; By bus: 479 from Zvezdnaya metro to Pavlovsk or T-286 or T-299 from Moskovskaya metro. Trip takes about 40 min.

Graceful allegorical statues adorn Pavlovsk Park, especially in the Old Silvia woods landscaped by Vincenzo Brenna.

Doric columns surrounding a copy of the Vatican's Apollo Belvedere. This image of the god of light (and poetry) marked the start of an Apollo cult at Pavlovsk (he also adorns the Three Graces Pavilion, for instance). Here, unlike at the Tsarskoye Selo of Minerva, Paul's mother's place down the road, light and poetry rule.

Cameron gave the hilly vale of the Slavyanka River some meandering paths, select groups of trees, and intermittent sights. The **Temple of Friendship** (1780), one of the most alluring visions in the park, resembles an ancient temple-rotunda with no windows. It was intended as a Temple of Gratitude to celebrate the empress's gift of Pavlovsk to her son, but when Emperor Joseph II of Austria made a state visit in 1780, Catherine decreed that the temple be a symbol of political accord. Joseph laid its foundation stone with much more ceremony than had greeted that of the palace itself. A statue of Catherine II as Minerva once stood inside; Paul ensured it was in darkness.

Heading north from here along the Slavyanka, there are more picturesque bridges and the round **Pil Tower** with its illusionistic windows (by Brenna, 1797). On the other side of the river is the **Old Silvia** (Woods), in which 12 paths radiate like a spiderweb from an Apollo statue near Maria's Monument to **My Parents** (1786). The latter, basically an outdoor niche, acts as a cenotaph to the Duke and Duchess of Württemberg. Within is a sculpture of mourning.

The more remote Red (Beautiful) Valley and White Birch parts of Pavlovsk Park both contain a few monuments (for example, the End of the World Column, Paul Mausoleum). But many people at this point turn back toward the palace. Leaving Old Silvia, the path brings you to the rustic **Dairy** (1782). It was designed to look like a coarse cottage with thatched roof, akin to the kind found on the estates of Frederick Eugene of Württemberg. But the interior, after the Pavlovsk farm was moved farther away, was luxuriously appointed as the setting for Maria's breakfasts during her morning walks.

Beyond the Dairy you reach the **Triple Lime Avenue** that led straight out of the front of the palace to a parade ground, where Paul loved to drill his small guard. Note the small arched **monument to Maria** (by Rossi, 1816, erected 1914) and the elegant three-halled **Aviary** (1781). It was in this area that Cameron created a leisure garden complete with maze, antique sculptures, rose garden, groves, bowling green, and swings. These elements offered some relief to Paul's large family from his obsessive and oppressive soldier games.

In the distance to the south, past the Pavlovsk foundation Obelisk, you might be able to make out the ruins of Paul's toy castle, **Bip** (by Brenna, 1795). It stands at the confluence of the Tyza and Slavyanka Rivers, on ramparts built by the Swedes and on the site of an earlier house called Marienthal in honor of Maria. Paul took his protection seriously and as such the fortress castle had its own artillery brigade, its cannon were fired at noon, its drawbridges were raised at night, and its garrison activities were strictly controlled. None of which helped save Paul from the assassination he so feared. ■

Opposite: One of the most pleasant architectural accents in the park, the rustic belvedere known as the Pil Tower was painted with fake windows and half-timbering by Pietro Gonzago.

Novgorod

LONG BEFORE ST. PETERSBURG EXISTED, THE TERRITORY IT occupies was a domain of the principality of Novgorod (New Town). This city lies 120 miles (192 km) to the south, just above the northern shores of Lake Ilmen. Reputedly founded in the ninth century by the Viking prince Rurik, Novgorod linked to the Neva Delta via the long Volkhov River, which empties into the Neva's source, Lake Ladoga. By the 14th century, the town was known as Great Novgorod, and by the following century as Lord Novgorod the Great. Its realms and contacts were extensive, its culture high and trendsetting. It was no mere "window on the West," but a conduit of values and art in all directions. With its unique beauty and history, Novgorod is a perfect, contrasting and yet anticipatory, partner to St. Petersburg.

Novgorod and St. Sophia are among the holiest and most spiritual ancient Russian cities.

In 1478, Novgorod and its northern Izhora lands came (reluctantly) under the control of a new, centralized Russian state whose capital was Moscow. Its golden days were past. With Peter's reassertion of Russian control over Izhora in the early 18th century, not least through the establishment of such strongholds as Narva in the west and St. Petersburg in the north, Novgorod lost its military significance as well. Its fortress was abandoned in 1720. Thereafter it existed as a provincial center. During World War II it kept changing hands and was almost entirely destroyed. Largely rebuilt in the 1950s and 60s, Novgorod is now a city of 240,000 people. It has also returned to being Great Novgorod.

The wealth of Novgorodian culture was unsurpassed. By the early 12th century it had several remarkable cathedrals and a school of icon painters and it was producing beautifully illustrated manuscripts. Its populace was literate, its merchants well organized, and its government democratized. In addition, making use of the natural lay of the land, the city was rationally planned on either side of the Volkhov River and was served by water mains and wooden sidewalks. All this, made it old Rus's New Town.

Prince Yaroslav the Wise (978–1054) and his son Vladimir

(1020–1052) shepherded Novgorod to its great heights. Yaroslav handed the Novgorod reins to Vladimir in 1036 when he devoted himself to ruling Kiev and its territories. He himself was the great-great-grandson of Rurik and the son of another Vladimir, the 10th-century Christianizer of Russia. He was married to a Swedish princess; had his sons marry Scandinavian, Polish, and Byzantine princesses; and married his daughters to kings of France, Norway, and Hungary. Yaroslav gave Novgorod its charter, through which a general town meeting *(veche)* decided things; he cemented the town's conversion to Christianity; and he assembled the talents of builders, artists, and scribes.

KREMLIN

The centerpiece of Novgorod—the fortified citadel known as the Detinets or Kremlin—sits on the Volkhov's left bank, the western Sophia's Side. Construction of the Kremlin began in 1044; its present size was reached in 1116. By 1420 it was completely stone-built and 70 years later, as Moscow imposed its authority on Novgorod, defensive brick-and-stone walls were erected. Kidney-bean in shape, the crenellated walls are guarded by nine distinct towers.

St. Sophia Cathedral

The gem of the Novgorod's Kremlin, St. Sophia's Cathedral, begun by Yaroslav's father as a wooden church in 991, was completed in stone by his son in 1050. It is the oldest stone church in Russia and a simplified version of the St. Sophia's Cathedral Yaroslav built in Kiev in the 1030s. Most likely, since it is essentially Byzantine and is named after Constantinople's all-important

Hagia Sophia (Church of the Holy Wisdom), it was built by Greek masters. But it took into account the north Russian climate with its feel of verticality, small windows, and bulbous onion domes. Its stone exterior was plastered in 1151. It became the burial place of local dignitaries as well as the Novgorod treasury, library, and archive.

The **bronze doors** of the western facade may be the oldest work of Christian sculpture in Russia and have been the subject of great intrigue. They were made in the German Catholic city of Magdeburg in the mid-12th century and comprise 24 panels with Romanesque reliefs of predominately Old and New Testament scenes, topped by two larger panels depicting the Ascension and theophany. Portraits of the artists Riquin, Weissmut, and Avraam adorn the lower left corner. Elsewhere are images of donor-bishops, including Alexander of Plock (Blucich) in Poland, as well as Cyrillic inscriptions.

Originally the doors were intended for Plock Cathedral; however, Jogaila, the pagan Grand Duke of Lithuania who became the Catholic king of Poland in 1386, gave them instead to his brother Simeon, who in 1389 had been selected as prince of Novgorod. They were Russified for the local population and subsequently various legends were born about their transference, the most popular being their seizure as a war trophy in Sweden in 1187. We can only speculate about Jogaila's intentions in sending these Catholic images to Orthodox Rus.

The restored cathedral interior is dominated by massive piers. Although fragments of 11th- and 12th-century frescoes survive—

Novgorod

🅰 203 inset

✉ 120 miles (192 km) southeast of St. Petersburg

🚆 By train: 905A from Vitebsk Station then bus 7 from Novgorod station. Trip takes 4.75 hr. By bus: Regular buses leave from kanala Obvodnogo Naberzhnaya 36 (Ligovsky Prospekt metro), call 766-5777 or 577-0255 (group bookings) for information. Trip takes 3.5 hr.

Novgorod State Museum-Preserve

✉ Novgorod Kremlin 11, Novgorod

☎ (8 816) 227-3770

💲 $$ (guided tours of Kremlin, St. Sophia's Cathedral)

The artistry of the medieval treasures in Novgorod's Faceted Chamber impresses visitors.

notably the images of Emperor Constantine and his mother Helen, in the southern Martirius apse—many of the murals date from around 1900. The five-tiered **main iconostasis** is mostly from the 16th century. The great, four-ton **chandelier** was a gift from Tsar Boris Godunov around 1600.

Archbishop's court

The northern part of the Kremlin encloses the archbishop's court. A dominating 155-foot-tall (44 m) **clock and bell tower** (1671–73) stands on the site of Archbishop Yefimy's earlier clock tower (1436).

The court also contains Yefimy's relatively unassuming **Faceted Chamber** (ca 1433), the only surviving example of Gothic architecture in Novgorod and the oldest example of civic architecture in Russia. Built by foreign and local masters, it has a marvellous rib-vaulted hall, which was designed for noble receptions. It is now a museum of Novgorodian ecclesiastical treasures, from jeweled crosses to silver vessels, gold embroidery to illuminated manuscripts. The large **belfry** (15th–19th centuries) sits on the opposite side of the cathedral.

Millennial Monument & farther south

In the center of the Kremlin stands a 52-foot-tall (15.7 m) encyclopedia of Russian history. The Millennial Monument (by Mikhail Mikeshin et al, 1862) celebrates Rurik's founding of Russian political order in Novgorod in 862. This 65-ton giant is *the* monument to Russia. It was cast by the English foundry of Nicholls and Plinck. The bell-shaped monument is crowned by an imperial orb on which Russia kneels before her cross-bearing guardian angel. Six groups of figures, dominated by Russian monarchs from Rurik to Peter, surround the orb while an 89-foot (27 m) bronze frieze depicting 109 historical figures wraps around the orb's pedestal. The figures are divided into four groups: statesmen, military heroes, writers and artists, and "enlighteners." An **Eternal Flame** burns next to the monument.

The provincial government building (1817–1822), which houses the **Novgorod Museum,** lies to the south of the monument. It has historical and art exhibitions, including some superb icons dating back to the 11th century.

YAROSLAV'S COURT

The merchants' quarter of Novgorod grew up on the right bank of the Volkhov, opposite the Kremlin. Yaroslav built his residence, Yaroslav's Court, here, and while that palace no longer exists, it lends its name to the dense cluster of surviving medieval buildings, predominantly marked by a long fragment of the market arcade and several churches.

The oldest building is the **Cathedral of St. Nicholas** (1113–1136), whose restrained Byzantine exterior shelters a flamboyant 18th-century baroque iconostasis. The "overseas merchant's" **Church of St. Parasceva Pyatnitsa** dates from 1207 and five other single-dome churches date from the 12th to

The bell-shaped Millennial Monument commemorates a thousand years of Novgorod's existence and summarizes Russian history.

Picturesque Vitoslavitsy (above & below) preserves Russian, and in particular Novgorodian, folk culture.

16th centuries. The **Church of the Holy Women** (1510) and the **Church of St. Procopius** (1529), with their refectories and decoration, reflect the arrival of Moscow fashions.

Just a little farther east, outside the court, lies the

Vitoslavitsy— Museum of Wooden Architecture
☎ (8 816) 233-5519
💲 $$$ (guided tour)

picturesque and most venerated **Church of the Transfiguration on Elijah Street** (1374). It still has its original, very refined, and expressive frescoes (1378) by the painter Theophanes the Greek. In the neighborhood is the five-domed **Cathedral of the Virgin of the Sign** (1682–88), which appears really

Muscovite. To the north is the **Church of St. Theodore Stratilates** (1360), a cube marked by graceful trefoil curves.

SIGHTS OUTSIDE TOWN

Many monasteries surrounded Novgorod. **St. George's (Yuryev),** 2 miles (3.2 km) south of Novgorod, near the shores of Lake Ilmen, was first mentioned in 1119. It was the largest Novogorodian monastery; it owned 4,500 serfs in the mid-18th century. Its great white walls hide a majestic, 12th-century Novgorod-style cathedral. It seems to surge powerfully from the ground. The multitiered bell tower (1841) marks a rare excursion into Russian Orthodox design by the Petersburg empire-style architect Carlo Rossi.

Just before St. George's, on the banks of the Myachino Lake, is **Vitoslavlitsy.** This site of a former 12th-century village was turned into Russia's main **Museum of Wooden Architecture** in 1964. It is a treasure trove of timber buildings from the 17th to early 20th centuries—cottages, a windmill, farmsteads, and churches, all from the Novgorod region. Wood was the most common building material in Russia; what you see here represents how most folk lived. The churches come in a variety of cross, ship, and octagonal forms, but they are invariably topped by beautiful little onion domes and Orthodox crosses. The geometric openwork carving around the gables is characteristically Russian. The permanent exhibitions "Folk Art of the Novgorod Area" and "Holidays and Festivities of the Novgorod Peasantry" show various domestic utensils and handicrafts. ■

More places to visit outside St. Petersburg

GULF OF FINLAND COASTAL TOWNS, KARELIAN ISTHMUS

Peter established Russian rule over the Karelian Isthmus in the early 18th century, but the area was regarded as "Finland" to St. Petersburg artists, writers, and nouveau riche who built their wooden dachas (summer houses) in seaside resorts here prior to the 1917 Revolution. Between 1917 and 1944 most of the resorts actually were in independent Finland. Having felt obliged to join Hitler's side rather than Stalin's, the Finnish territories became Soviet after the war. Today they are Russian again.

The dacha resorts strung along the gulf coast of the Karelian Isthmus between St. Petersburg and Zelenogorsk provide a welcome respite from the bustle of the city. Petersburgers descend en masse on weekends and in summer. **Sestroretsk** offers the **Razliv Reservoir,** where you can swim or picnic on its shores then visit the nearby *shalash* (fisherman's straw hut) where Lenin hid in July 1917. Just north of Sestroretsk lies **Solnechnoye,** which possesses one of the best beaches and an extensive forest park.

The next stop is **Repino,** so named in 1948 after its most famous resident: the foremost painter of the late tsarist period, Ilya Repin (1844–1930). Before you reach the settlement, stop in at **Penaty** *(Primorskoye Shosse 411, Repino, tel 432-0828, closed Mon.–Tues., $$)* on its eastern outskirts. This large, wooden house and glazed studio belonged to the artist; he lived here from 1899 until his death. While living here with his wife, the photographer Natalya Nordman (1863–1914), the house was a gathering place for many of the pre-revolutionary cultural elite. In accordance with Repin's wishes as stated in his will, the estate was turned into a memorial museum. Penaty burned down in World War II, but it was faithfully restored and opened in 1962. It captures the essence of this prolific realist artist who championed the new and progressive while still young, was always a liberal of sorts, but who later fell out irreconcilably with the more radical avant-garde after he moved here. Repin's grave

Penaty, the studio-home of Ilya Repin, Russia's most famous late 19th-century artist, sits on the edge of a resort that bears his name—Repino.

can be found on the fairly extensive and beautiful silver-birch-filled grounds.

The popular dacha resorts of **Komarovo** and the adjoining **Zelenogorsk** lie farther west along the coast.

Continue to follow the coastline around to **Vyborg.** This historic town, 80 miles (130 km) from St. Petersburg and a mere 18.5 miles (30 km) from Finland, is returning to its Finnicized past, even reclaiming its Finnish name—Viipuri. The town has four main, very different attractions. **Vyborg Castle** (now a museum) dates back to 1293, when the Swedes ousted the Novgorodians as the local governors. The highly romantic **Mon Repos** park estate of Baron Paul von Nicolai was designed in the Scottish, "wild" landscape style in the early 19th century. There are some fine, if dilapidated, **new town buildings from around 1900,** among them some art nouveau apartment houses and banks. And lastly, don't miss the **Library,** an iconic modernist building whose white cubic forms stand out in the park. Designed by world-renowned Finnish architect Alvar Aalto, it was regarded as "the most advanced town library in the world" when it was completed in 1935.

 Map p. 203 🚆 By train: Electric train from Finland Station to Repino (Krugovoy line) or to Vyborg; By bus: Minibuses to Zelenogorsk leave from Staraya Derevnya metro (buses may not stop at all coastal towns; ask before boarding).

KRONSTADT

Up until a few years ago, Kronstadt was a closed military base, the home of the Soviet Fleet in the Baltic. It's still a naval center, but nowadays it is also a commercial port and has opened for tourism. Situated on Kotlin Island in the middle of the Gulf of Finland, Kronstadt is actually a town of some 50,000

inhabitants. Kotlin's name derives from a legendary cooking pot *(kotel)* left behind by the Swedes retreating before Alexander Menshikov in the autumn of 1703. The pot features on the island's coat of arms. Since the late 20th century, this small, thin island has been linked to the mainland by a drivable, unfinished barrage. From May 1704, the island and its offshore forts served as Peter's main defense against seaborne attack. The island later became the main northern port of the tsarist fleet and a vital means of protection for Leningrad during World War II.

This history lends it a very special atmosphere. In some ways it's a simpler, miniature Petersburg—with its canals, harbors, regular plan, neoclassic architecture, and characteristic churches and monuments. But it's also slightly more severe, generally cleaner, and contains more red brick. Kronstadt's own version of the Hagia Sophia in Istanbul, the 1913 **St. Nicholas Naval Cathedral** *(Yakornaya Ploshchad 1)*, is the island's most striking building. Incredibly ornate, it houses a **museum** *(tel 311-4713, closed Mon.–Tues., $$$)* dedicated to the history of the port. Kronstadt's sea views can be spectacular, especially the one toward Petersburg from the yacht club at the eastern edge of the island.

Kronstadt is a quiet place, which made it all the more attractive as the setting for the first Petersburg raves in 1997. They still occur each summer and are known as the Forts, since they also take place on some of the artificial fortified islands around Kotlin. Map p. 203 ✉ 16 miles (26 km) from St. Petersburg By bus: 101 or 510 from Staraya Derevnya metro or 405 and K-510 from Chernaya Rechka metro; By ferry (summer only): from Tuchkov Bridge and Oranienbaum.

SHLISSELBURG FORTRESS

A 400-yard (367 m) ferry ride from the southern shores of Lake Ladoga takes you to the island fortress known as Shlisselburg. Or is it Schlüsselburg? Or Oreshek. Or Nöteborg. Or Petrokrepost. The changing names of the fortress amply reflect its turbulent history, and the fact that it was the "key" to the control of the Neva Delta, which served as the gateway to the trade route to the Russian and east European interior. The tiny island stands right at the source point of the Neva River. Its fort was founded as Oreshek (Little Nut) by the Novgorodians in 1323. Conquering Swedes renamed it Nöteborg in 1612. And in 1702, Peter I's seizing of it was crucial to the

A statue of Vice Adm. Stepan Makarov, the commander of Kronstadt port and the Baltic and Pacific fleets, gestures before the cathedral whose construction he ordered.

Above: The strategically crucial Schlüsselburg island fortress became a prison and place of execution. Below: The nearby Sailors' Memorial

founding of St. Petersburg, 40 miles (64 km) away; hence Peter changed the fort's name to Schlüsselburg (Key Town). (Shlisselburg is the Russified version of this name.)

Almost immediately, the fort became a political prison. Throughout numerous Russian regime changes, many big-name "undesirables" were held here, including Peter's first wife, Evdokiya Lopukhina, Ernst-Johann Biron, various members of the Decembrists, the anarchist Mikhail Bakunin, and Lenin's brother Alexander Ulyanov. Many were also executed on the island. The island is a grim, windswept place and the fort was partly ruined during World War II. Several towers have been restored and you can see both the **Old and New Prisons;** the latter was built in 1884 to house the Populists and Nihilists. It's a fascinating, different world.

The small town of **Shlisselburg,** from where most people catch the ferry to the island fortress, has two early churches and four picturesque canals. It makes for a pleasant stroll while you wait for the ferry. 🗺 Map p. 203 ☎ (8-813) 627-4104, 238-0679, or 238-0511 🕐 Closed Nov.–April 🚆 By train: Electric train from Finland Station to town of Morozovka or Petrokrepost, then ferry to island; By road: bus 575 or minibus or taxi from Ulitsa Dybenko metro, then ferry (jetty is within walking distance of Shlisselburg bus station) to island. ■

Travelwise

One of the best ways to explore St. Petersburg is by boat.

TRAVELWISE INFORMATION

PLANNING YOUR TRIP

Despite its relative youthfulness as a city, St. Petersburg is rich in fascinating history, with a broad cultural heritage that's second to none. As you immerse yourself in its vibrant present, the dramatic past is never far away.

Over the past couple of decades this former Russian capital has transformed into a bustling, modern international metropolis. Yet traditions run deep here. Seventy years of communism and two centuries of tsarist imperialism have left an indelible mark. This dichotomy fosters a remarkable, and sometimes surprising, blend of attitudes and approaches.

Most visitors fall in love with these disparate worlds that comprise St. Petersburg. They are also mesmerized by its unparalleled beauty—so much so they discover one trip is not enough.

WHEN TO GO

A top tourist destination, St. Petersburg is besieged by domestic and foreign visitors alike and throbs with activity year-round. Of course, there are times when the streets literally overflow with tourists—for example, during the peak summer stretch from early May to late July, as well as Christmas and New Year's Eve. That said, in midsummer many Petersburgers themselves leave for their dachas (country homes) on a three-month break that coincides with school holidays.

Despite the heat, the pace is quick and your choices myriad, particularly with regard to restaurants, cafés, bars, clubs, galleries, museums, shops, and events and sights. Beware though—seasonal hotel tariffs vary widely. Summer peak rates are much higher than winter low-season rates.

Festivals and public and national holidays are an integral part of city life. Russians revel in every opportunity to enjoy themselves, and every event is celebrated with considerable show and exuberance. Among the best known events are the **White Nights** festivals, which stretch from late May to mid-July. As it lies so far north, St. Petersburg experiences an enchanting period when the sun doesn't quite fully set and a beautiful luminescence permeates the city round the clock. During this time of much light, tourists arrive by the thousands to enjoy the cultural feast on offer, as stars of classical music, ballet, and opera offer scheduled performances in the city's concert and theatrical venues, as well as impromptu sets in the city squares and along its embankments.

For many the best time to visit is between May and August, when the weather is warmest and the days longer. For a quieter experience, visit in fall or winter.

Winters are long, generally beginning in November and blowing through by mid-April. Temperatures fall below zero, freezing the rivers and ponds into popular ice rinks. The coldest months are January and February, while snow lingers through early spring. Though these are certainly lighter travel months, many still come in search of a magical Russian white Christmas and New Year.

CLIMATE

St. Petersburg's climate is best described as maritime, remaining humid year-round. Summer can be particularly oppressive, with days of intense heat punctuated by heavy rainfall. August is both the rainiest and hottest month. Sea breezes help to mitigate the heat and humidity. While temperatures average 68°F (20°C) in summer and 48°F (9°C) in winter, they can climb as high as 82°F (28°C) in midsummer and drop as low as -4°F (-20°C) in the dead of winter. Recent years have witnessed a trend toward milder winters and hotter summers. The weather is subject to unpredictable change, so it's advisable to bring a range of suitable clothing. A raincoat and umbrella are essential in summer. Also bring light, loose-fitting garments to help cope with the heat.

From September on, the city cools off considerably. Be sure to pack warm, layered clothing. When the snow starts falling around November, you'll need better protection against the low temperatures and frigid winds. Proper headgear is a must. Those not averse to fur would benefit most from its insulating properties. Russians harbor no such objections—just about anyone who can afford fur wears it.

WHAT TO BRING

Many of the younger set of Petersburgers are image conscious and thus make a big effort to look their best at all times. You'll likely notice young women wearing what could be deemed over-the-top outfits—miniskirts, high heels, and lots of makeup are the norm. With regard to one's own appearance, however, it's best to dress comfortably. You needn't feel pressure to conform to local styles.

If you plan to attend a concert or theater performance, be sure to pack a set of evening clothes. Likewise, those intending to do any exploring should bring appropriate footwear.

As in any other large city, tourists in St. Petersburg are targets for pickpockets, so it's in your best interest to keep any money or documents safely tucked away in a beneath-the-clothes wallet.

TRAVEL INSURANCE

Visitors bound for Russia are required to carry travel insurance, and officials will check for it when you apply for a visa. Regardless of your destination, however, travel insurance is a good idea, as it will cover such contingencies as theft, illness, loss of possessions, and delayed or canceled travel.

PASSPORTS & VISA

You'll need not only a valid passport to enter Russia but also a visa.

The visa application process can be tiresome, and it's advisable to apply as early as possible, which is more than one month in advance of your intended travel. If you're visiting on a vacation package, or tour, the operator will typically assist you in making the necessary arrangements.

Independent travelers face a bit more bureaucratic difficulty, as they must first obtain **an invitation** from a Russian individual or organization, then apply for a visa from a Russian consulate. A more common, less tedious process is to provide proof of prebooked accommodations in St. Petersburg. Known as "visa support," such paperwork is available through various tourist agencies or hotels for a fee of around $45 to $50. You could purchase visa support on the Internet, but it's better to have a tourist agency do all the paperwork for you.

For the exact requirements, contact:

United States
Embassy of the Russian Fed.
2650 Wisconsin Ave., NW
Washington, DC 20007
Tel 202/298-5700
Fax 202/298-7535
www. russianembassy.org

Canada
Russian Embassy
285 Charlotte St.
Ottawa, ON, K1N 8L5
Canada
Tel 613/235-4341 or 236-1413
Fax 613/236-6342
http://ottawa.rusembassy.org

VISA REGISTRATION

Upon arrival in St. Petersburg, you'll need to complete an immigration form. Customs will check this form and return part of it to you—don't lose it. Additionally, within three working days of your arrival, you must register your visa and immigration forms. Agencies throughout the city can complete this paperwork for you. (Check on the Internet for a list of such agencies and be prepared to pay an additional fee of $20 to $40.) If you're staying at a hotel, management will handle this formality. Be sure to carry proof of your registration with you at all times.

TRAVELING TO ST. PETERSBURG

American and Canadian travelers will most likely reach St. Petersburg by air.

It's also possible to visit by taking the train from Helsinki, the Baltic States, and Moscow (that is, if you choose to fly to Moscow from another destination).

Another popular means of travel is by boat. Many luxury cruise ships sail from European cities and dock on the Neva Embankments, where coach tours meet the passengers. A passenger ferry service also operates between St. Petersburg and Germany.

BY PLANE

St. Petersburg has two major airports: Pulkovo 1 (domestic flights, about 11 miles/18 km south of the city center) and Pulkovo 2 (international flights, 10 miles/17 km south of the city). **Pulkovo 1** (tel 704-3822). If you wish to fly to other parts of Russia (or arrive from them), this is the airport you'll likely use. Flights connect to 40 cities in Russia and 11 in the CIS. The airport also offers a charter service for flights abroad.

You can reach the city from Pulkovo in a number of ways. The 39 bus (6 a.m.–midnight) and express taxi 213 (7 am to 10 pm) will take you as far as Sennaya Ploshchad.

Pulkovo 2 (tel 704-3444). No airlines offer direct flights between St. Petersburg and North America. Instead, you'll have to take a connecting flight from one of 30 European or Asian cities. Whichever route you choose, this is no cheap affair. Budget airlines don't offer cheap seats to the city.

The 13 bus (6 a.m.–midnight) and express taxi T-13 (7 a.m.–10 p.m.) travel to town along the route to the Moskovskaya metro station. Express taxi T-213 (7 a.m. –10 p.m.) will take you into town.

Alternatively, you could hire a taxi, which should cost about $20. Beware of rogue drivers who charge unwary passengers anywhere between $30 and $50.

Those staying at such top hotels as the Astoria or Grand Hotel Europe will probably be taken to and from the airport by the hotels' own minibuses.

AIRLINES
Aeroflot,
 5 Kazanskaya Ulitsa,
 tel 327-3872
British Airways,
 1/3a Malaya Konyushennaya,
 tel 380-0626, or Pulkovo 2,
 tel 346-8146
CSA,
 36 Bolshaya Morskaya Ulitsa,
 tel 315-5259
Delta,
 36 Bolshaya Morskaya Ulitsa,
 tel 311-5820
Finnair,
 1/3a Malaya Konyushennaya
 Ulitsa,
 tel 303-9898, or Pulkovo 2,
 tel 324-3249
Lufthansa,
 32 Nevsky Prospekt,
 tel 320-1000, or Pulkovo 2,
 tel 325-9140
Rossiya,
 18 Pilotov Ulitsa,
 tel 704-3738

BY BOAT

The sea passenger terminal at Vasilyevsky Island is a fairly busy complex that welcomes up to four ships at a time. Ferry services take passengers to and from Stockholm and ports in Germany. Tickets are available at the terminal (1 Morskoy Slavy Ploshchad, Metro: Primorskaya; tel 322-1616).

A second passenger terminal on the Neva provides cruises and ferry services to and from Moscow and Valaam and Kizhi Islands. Tickets are available at the terminal (195 Obukhovskoi Oborony Prospekt) or by phone (262-2474).

BY BUS

St. Petersburg's central **Bus Station No. 2** (36 kanala Obvodnogo Naberezhnaya, tel 766-5777; Ligovskiy Prospekt metro or bus stop N2) offers service to other Russian cities and abroad. A number of other companies serve various European and Scandinavian cities.

Long-distance coach service is available between Helsinki and St. Petersburg. Two operators, **Finnord** (37 Italyanskaya Ulitsa, 314-8951) and **Saimaan Liikenne** (53 Sadovaya Ulitsa, 310-2920), offer an eight-hour route that stops in the heart of the city at Hotel Astoria and terminates at Hotel Pulkovskaya.

BY CAR

The most direct route to St. Petersburg from continental Europe is via Germany, Poland, Lithuania, Latvia, and Estonia. While you can drive from Helsinki (about 215 miles/350 km), this relatively short hop can take many hours, as the border crossing often bogs down. A word of caution: These long, empty stretches of road have a reputation for robberies, so be careful where you stop and where and how you leave the car.

BY TRAIN

St. Petersburg's central railway stations are conveniently located near metro stations.

Those traveling from Moscow can catch a popular overnight train to the heart of the city at **Moscow Station** (85 Nevsky Prospekt, tel 055). You'll emerge near the Vosstaniya Ploshchad metro station.

Helsinki is another popular gateway to St. Petersburg. This route offers a peaceful seven-hour prelude to busy times ahead and easy-to-clear immigration and customs. The train terminates at **Ladozhsky Station** (73 Zanevsky Prospekt, tel 436-5310), near the Ladozhskaya metro. (Expect to pay $20 for a taxi to city center.)

Trains from western, central, southern and eastern Europe, e.g., Kiev, Minsk, Praga, Warsaw, Tallinn, Riga, Berlin, Budapest, Dnepropetrovsk, Vilnius, now arrive at **Vitebsk Station** (52 Zagorodny Prospekt, Metro: Pushkinskaya; tel 055 or 168-5807).

Tickets for long-distance trains can be purchased at the Central Railway Ticket Office, 24 kanal Griboedova Naberezhnaya (Metro: Nevsky Prospekt) 8 a.m.–8 p.m. (–4 p.m. Sun.) tel 762-4455 or just 201. Elsewhere, care is needed if buying tickets from non-official ticket offices.

GETTING AROUND

BY CAR

A car is only necessary if you intend to travel beyond the city limits. St. Petersburg's extensive public transportation system accesses just about any point of interest and is much easier and cheaper than renting a car. One option is to rent a car with a driver, which costs only a bit more than car rental alone but could save you a lot of hassle. Traffic in many parts of the city

is very busy, particularly the city center during rush hour—a true driver's nightmare.

CAR RENTALS
Hertz,
Pulkovo 1 & 2 or
23 Malaya Morskaya Ulitsa,
tel 326-4505, www.hertz.spb.ru

Prokat,
162 Nevsky Prospekt, Office 26,
tel 322-5800,
www.auto-prokat.ru

Pulkovo Rent-A-Car,
5 Startovaya Ulitsa, tel 331-7779,
www.pulkoworent.ru

DRIVING REGULATIONS & CONVENTIONS
If you do intend to drive in St. Petersburg, you'll need to carry an international driver's license, your domestic driver's license, and insurance documents from both your insurer and a Russian insurance company. You must also carry documents showing you're legally allowed to drive the car, as well as copies of your visa and passport.

Car theft is fairly common, so carry with you any valuables such as travel documents.

Traffic in St. Petersburg is often frantic and dangerous. Only those with experience and confidence should take up the challenge. Perhaps it is best to observe the streets before renting an automobile.

Be forewarned that local drivers are not known for their courteousness to others or respect for pedestrians. Many routinely flout traffic lights and other warning signals. When on foot, always use underpasses and crossings where provided and even then exercise caution.

Traffic police (the GAI) may pull you over and check your documents. Should they attempt to fine you, their reputation suggests they may be open to negotiation (unless you are stopped by a particularly scrupulous officer).

Speed limits are 37 mph (60 kmph) within the city and up to

50 mph (80 kmph) out on the highway. Driving is on the right side of the road, and left turns are prohibited unless a sign indicates you can do so. Consumption of alcohol while driving is forbidden, and although Russians themselves rarely wear seatbelts, it's an important precaution, given other drivers' fairly erratic nature.

If your rental car breaks down, call the appropriate emergency contact number provided by your rental agency. If you're driving a private car, call the number provided by your Russian insurance company. Local emergency services include **Spas** (tel 327-7001 or 234-9885) and **Veber-Auto** (tel 321-0000 or 987-0111). That said, help is not always readily available. In the event of a breakdown, your best bet is to notify the St. Petersburg **GAI**: tel 234-2646.

BY PUBLIC TRANSPORATION

St. Petersburg has a far-reaching transportation system. Using the metro, buses, trolleybuses, trams, and minibuses, you can access virtually any point in the city cheaply and quickly. Vehicles are either operated by municipal or private companies. Fares are fixed regardless of distance. Tickets for single trip are available on board (excluding the metro and minibuses) from the conductor. Fares average around 50 cents. Monthly tickets (either all-inclusive or for one mode of transportation) are a worthwhile investment for anyone on a long-term stay (note that such tickets can only be used on city-operated vehicles). Plainclothes ticket inspectors are regularly aboard to ensure everyone has paid their fare.

BUS OR TROLLEYBUS

Operating roughly from 6 a.m. to midnight (some services start earlier and end later), St. Petersburg's broad network of bus and trolleybus routes was until recently plied mainly by rusting, run-down vehicles. These are being replaced by newer, more comfortable models.

MINIBUS

Operating from 6 a.m. to 10 or 11 p.m., minibuses are a handy and increasingly popular means of getting across town. Known locally as *marshrutki* (slang for "fixed-route taxis"), minibuses follow a set route, often the same as buses and trolleybuses that share the same number. Would-be passengers simply flag down the vehicle, much like a taxi, and pay the driver directly in cash. Fares usually run around 50 cents, regardless of the distance, although these are subject to fairly frequent change. Passengers signal when they wish to get off, and the driver will pull over as close as possible to the desired spot. Transportation minibuses are often yellow, gray, or white.

METRO

Operating from 5:45 a.m. to midnight, the metro runs four numbered and color-coded lines. Users pay only for access to a platform via turnstiles—there is no fixed distance or time limit, and the fare is relatively nominal. Tokens are available from service windows upstairs at each station. Given a daily passenger count that exceeds 2.5 million, be prepared for crowded conditions.

The world's deepest underground railway, the metro is also renowned for the architectural beauty of some stations and is well worth a visit for its own sake. Especially spectacular are the central sections of the Kirovsko-Vyborgskaya line (aka Line 1 or the red line).

TRAM

Operating from 6 a.m. to midnight, trams are a vital means of transport in some areas. First put into service in 1907, few serve central St. Petersburg anymore.

SIGNS

Bus stops—yellow with an A for "avtobus"

Minibuses—picture of a bus (usually black on white within blue)
Trams stops—a red T on white background
Trolleybuses—a red T surrounded by white within blue or a blue squared-off M (i.e., what looks like an E turned 90 degrees right—which is also a Cyrillic T) on white.

BY TAXI

There's no shortage of taxis zipping around St. Petersburg at all hours, so you should have no trouble flagging one down. However, an abundance of taxi companies lacking any defined corporate image results in a rather confused situation. Old-style taxis still feature trademark black-and-yellow checkered logos on (mainly) Volgas with roof-mounted plastic lights (lighted means the taxi is vacant).

Operating around the clock, **City Taxi Service** (tel 068) or **Taxi Blues** (tel 321-8888 www.taxiblues.ru) are the most reliable. They lack a corporate image and use all sorts of models. About 20 minutes prior to your prebooked pickup, a dispatcher will phone to tell you the model, color, and registration number of the car. You can reach other taxi companies by calling 312-0022 or 700-0000.

After telling the dispatcher your destination, be sure to confirm the fare. If you flag down a taxi on the street, drivers may try to charge more if they notice you're a foreigner. Agree on a fare before getting in the cab.

BY TOURS & ORGANIZED SIGHTSEEING

BOAT TOURS

As St. Petersburg is crisscrossed by 85 scenic rivers and canals, visitors should try to take at least one boat tour. Landings dot the embankments. Many excursions along the inner-city waterways depart from near the Anichkov Bridge on the Fontanka Canal. Other tours depart from spots along the Neva River and the Griboedov Canal. The landings are hard to miss, as agents appeal to customers via loudspeaker. Providing a unique and relaxing way to see the city, tours cover several different circuits and typically last between one and two hours. Other tours take in sights beyond the city. The "Romantic Nights" and "Past & Present" tours are particularly recommended. Contact **AstraMarine** (tel 320-7786 or 320 0877). For cruises to Valaam and Kizhi on Lake Ladoga, call 325-6120 or 914-0100.

Due to weather conditions, boat tours are only offered between May and September. While many companies use Russian-speaking guides, it's often possible to reserve a tour with an English-speaking guide.

BUS TOURS

A comprehensive range of tours access the splendid imperial palaces beyond the city. A popular starting point is on **Nevsky** outside the Gostiny Dvor department store (35 Nevsky Prospekt). The tours here are offered in many languages.

You'll also find a bus tour kiosk on **Dvortsovy Prospekt** by the east end of the Admiralty and Alexander Garden. Passengers can reserve trips in advance or just turn up on the day of travel. Trips run regularly, and seats are frequently available.

Note that foreign tourists pay higher rates than locals, and the price—which includes your return fare and access to the palaces—may seem high. But the advantage is that you'll avoid the often long palace admission lines.

HELICOPTER TOURS

This is a superb way to see the city, especially in good weather. **Baltic Air** (tel 104-1676 or 311-0084) operates chopper tours from the SS Peter and Paul

Fortress. Trips last 15 minutes and cost around $25 per person. Another company offering air tours is **Exima** (tel 314-4183 or 702-2585, www.airtours.spb.ru).

INDEPENDENT TOURS

Seasoned travelers will tell you the best way to tour a city is to stroll it independently. Before setting out, jot down a rough plan of what you want to see and the general route you'll follow. Certainly take advantage of St. Petersburg's extensive public transportation system, as distances are often longer than they appear on a city map.

WALKING TOURS

Walking tours of St. Petersburg are available through the **City Tourist Information Center** (14/52 Sadovaya Ulitsa, tel 310-2822, www.saintpetersburgvisit.ru; metro: Nevsky Prospekt, Gostiny Dvor), **Eclectica Guide** (tel 710-5529) or **Petersburg Holidays** (tel 388-2845).

WATER TAXIS

One of the best—if somewhat pricey—ways to experience St. Petersburg is by water taxi. These crewed boats follow a route tailored to your choosing. Although more expensive (roughly $100 per hour) than an ordinary boat tour, when split between parties of up to 20 passengers, the price can be fairly reasonable. For a bit more, some boats offer catering options, though you're always welcome to bring along your own drinks and nibbles to add to the fun of the occasion. Water taxis are available at landings along the embankments.

PRACTICAL ADVICE

COMMUNICATIONS

POST OFFICES

Open 24/7, the **main post office** (tel 312-8302) is at 9 Pochtamtskaya Ulitsa, accessible

via the 22 bus. Hours vary at local branches.

Although there have been improvements in recent years, the postal service still has a long way to go in terms of reliability. Postcards and letters should reach your addressees, but it's best to send more important things via registered mail or private shipping companies.

If you wish to send a parcel abroad, you must first have it inspected at the main post office. Following this inspection, you can send the package from any post office. You'll find hundreds of branch post offices and blue mailboxes scattered throughout St. Petersburg, particularly near the city center. Be sure you've affixed proper postage before depositing a letter or postcard in a mailbox.

The Grand Hotel Europe and Corinthia Nevskij Palace Hotel each offer express shipping services for letters directed to Europe or North America for reasonable rates (usually around $1.50–$2.00 per letter). These typically arrive within four or five days.

Another option is to make use of an international firm specializing in fast delivery and worldwide courier services. The higher costs are certainly worth avoiding the risks with important documents. These include:

DHL
10 Nevsky Prospekt or
4 Izmailovsky Prospekt
tel 326-6400

FedEx
30 Nevsky Prospekt
tel 449-1878 or
6 Grivtsova Pereulok
tel 571-5930

Garantpost,
109 Moskovsky Prospekt
tel 325-7525

TNT
14 Sofiyskaya Ulitsa
tel 718-3330

UP
6 Voroshilova Ulitsa
tel 703-3939

Westpost
86 Nevsky Prospekt
tel 327-3211 or 327-3092.

TELEPHONE

Russian phone numbers have seven digits, but when making a call to another state, you'll need to enter its three-digit code before the number. St. Petersburg's code is 812. Cell phone numbers begin with 8. In general, numbers beginning with 0 are free.

To call St. Petersburg from the United States, dial 011 7 812 (international code, followed by the Russian country code and St. Petersburg city code), then the seven-digit number.

To make a call to somewhere else in Russia from a public phone, you'll need a phone card, as hardly any public phones accept coins. Cards are available at metro stations, post offices, newsstands, and tobacco kiosks. There's a wide selection, so be sure to pick the card best suited to your needs. New cards regularly appear on the market, offering cheap rates for international calls. Card instructions are often printed in several languages. Follow these instructions carefully, as the dialing process varies widely. Typically they involve free dial-in numbers and PIN codes.

If you bring your cell phone with you, consider obtaining a SIM card from one of the cell phone companies throughout St. Petersburg. The cards themselves are available at very low prices (sometimes free) and often include prepaid minutes. The call time stretches far here and is especially useful if you're visiting with someone who also has a cell phone. At the end of your stay, simply remove the SIM card and reinsert yours.

To make an international call from Russia, dial 8 and wait for the dial tone to change, then dial 10, the country code (1 for the United States and Canada), the area code, and the number.

ELECTRICITY

Russian circuits use 220 volts. You'll need an adapter to use American appliances; those that operate on 110 volts also require a transformer. It's best to bring these with you.

ETIQUETTE & LOCAL CUSTOMS

As when visiting any foreign country, you should come prepared with a smattering of basic "please" and "thank you" phrases in the local language—for example, *pozhaluysta* means both "please" and "you're welcome." (See pp. 264–265.)

Although many Russians can speak English, it's often basic, and you may experience difficulties in communicating. Only the younger generation can claim proficiency beyond basic English—if you expect the majority to understand, expect to be disappointed. Any effort you make to communicate in Russian will be well received, as it will be clear you're not just relying on the worldwide misconception that everyone speaks English.

Another piece of etiquette involves the summoning of an employee in a shop or café. Almost all shop and café workers are female, thus you would use *devushka* (which means "girl") to get their attention. This may seem odd (especially when young girls summon older women this way), but it's the norm.

HOLIDAYS

The following holidays are either specific to St. Petersburg itself or celebrated nationwide:
Jan. 1 New Year's Day
Jan. 6–7 Russian Orthodox Christmas
Jan. 19 Epiphany
Feb. 23 Defenders' Day
March 8 International Women's Day
Good Friday, Easter,
May 9 Victory Day
May 27 City Day
June 12 Russian Independence Day

July (last Sunday) Navy Day
Dec. 12 Constitution Day

MEDIA

NEWSPAPERS

Foreign edition newspapers are not that easy to come by in St. Petersburg. They are normally only available at bigger hotels for much higher prices than they would be back home.

That said, a number of local English-language publications are distributed on a regular basis. The *St. Petersburg Times* is a pretty solid and very useful newspaper. Published twice a week, it covers local, international, and sporting news and provides listings and reviews for clubs, restaurants, films, galleries, exhibitions, etc. Copies are available at just about any of the city's restaurants, cafés, hotels, and museums.

Where is an indispensable monthly that covers upcoming events and various items of cultural interest, providing restaurant, shopping, and entertainment listings and information on local services and businesses. Pick up a copy at various restaurants and museums, and it's more informative than rival *Pulse*.

RADIO

The airwaves throb with a medley of FM music stations peddling pop and rock music. The most popular ones are Radio Rox (102 FM) and Europa Plus (100.5 FM). If you're curious about Russian music, tune to Russkoe Radio (105.2 FM). Shortwave radio listeners can pick up Voice of America (6866 MHz).

TELEVISION

A wide range of channels are broadcast in St. Petersburg, including the national ORT, Rossiya, and Kultura channels, as well as local Channel 5.

MONEY MATTERS

Russia's official currency is the ruble. Each ruble is divided into 100 kopecks. Kopecks come in coins of 1, 5, 10, and 50, while there are also 1, 2, and 5 ruble coins. Bills are denominated in 10, 50, 100, 500, and 1,000 rubles.

Most St. Petersburg banks and hundreds of exchange offices (particularly along Nevsky Prospekt) can change your money into rubles. Boards outside the exchange offices detail the exchange rates. Commissions vary widely, so choose carefully for the best deal. Remember to bring your passport, as you won't be able to change currency without identification. Offices can be fussy about the quality of notes and may not accept torn or marked ones.

The best sources of currency are ATMs, which you'll find outside many banks and inside the main post office. While ATMs accept most major credit cards (Visa, MasterCard, etc.), you should check with your bank or credit card company that your PIN is valid overseas beforehand. ATMs typically conduct transactions in multiple languages. Cash advances, whether obtained in person or through an ATM, will incur a transaction charge. Another source is **American Express,** at 23 Malaya Morskaya Ulitsa, tel 326-4500, or at the Nevsky Prospekt and Gostiny Dvor metro stations.

BUSINESS HOURS

Banking hours stretch from 10 a.m. to 5 p.m., with a lunch break between 1 and 2 p.m. **Stores** do business from 10 a.m. to 8 p.m., with a lunch break between 2 and 3 p.m. Many stores, however, forgo lunch breaks and stay open weekends, instead granting employees time off on Mondays. **Food** shops generally operate from 8 or 9 a.m. to 10 p.m., though a number remain open 24/7. **Restaurants** are generally open from noon till midnight or until the last customer leaves. Cafés and bars vary their hours depending on their clientele, but most stay open late.

TIME DIFFERENCE

The time difference is something you should bear in mind, as it can be quite considerable. Russia is three hours ahead of Greenwich Mean Time. If it's noon in New York, it's 8 p.m. in St. Petersburg.

TIPPING

While tipping is not ingrained into the Russian service culture, it is acceptable to leave a little cash at whatever café, bar, or restaurant you visit.

TRAVELERS WITH DISABILITIES

It has to be said that people with disabilities will not find St. Petersburg an easy city in which to get around. Most tourist destinations offer no facilities for the disabled, and wheelchair access is extremely limited. While wheelchair access is available at the majority of international hotels, it's still not universal. Those offering the best access include the Grand Hotel Europe and Corinthia Nevskij Palace Hotel. It's virtually impossible for wheelchair users to access any mode of public transportation. Disabled riders are not required to wait in line.

VISITOR INFORMATION

St. Petersburg is fast earning a reputation as a tourist-friendly destination. The municipal administration considers the hospitality industry strategically important for local development and is making an attempt to raise service standards. The newly opened **City Tourist Infor-mation Center** (14/52 Sadovaya Ulitsa, tel 310-2822, www.saintpetersburgvisit.ru; metro: Nevsky Prospect or Gostiny Dvor) or the branch visitor center at 12 Dvortsovaya Ploshchad is a sign of the times, offering a range of visitor information.

A number of local guides detail in English upcoming cultural events and provide timely information about museums and galleries. Look for the handy pocket-size *Visitor,* as well as *St. Petersburg: The Official City Guide.* The first costs a few rubles, while the second is free. Both offer the latest information on just about every aspect of city life. Copies are available at visitor kiosks, museums, hotels, cafés, and bars.

A relatively new feature of the tourist-friendly drive is the corps of so-called City Angels. Strategically positioned at key locations around St. Petersburg, these are usually young people trained to give free advice and help to tourists. All speak English and are recognizable by their uniforms. The city has also installed new visitor information boards in English and Russian with local maps.

EMERGENCIES

CONSULATES

British Consulate
5 Proletarskoy Diktatury Ploshchad
tel 320-3200
bus 46, 74; trolleybus 5, metro Chernyshevskaya

Canadian Consulate
32 Molodetskoselsky Prospekt
tel 325-8448
trolleybus 15, 17; metro Frunzenskaya

United States Consulate
15 Furshtatskaya Ulitsa
tel 331-2600
bus 46; trolleybus 15, 49; metro Chernyshevskaya

CRIME & POLICE

Scare stories about a crime-ridden city belong to the past. These days St. Petersburg is no more dangerous than any other big city. Just be aware of your surroundings and keep track of valuables. Carry all documents, credit cards, and extra money in either a money belt or another secure place, preferably beneath your clothes. Strap bags, cameras, and the like securely across your body and keep a hand on them in crowded places.

Tourists should be on guard for two particular criminal elements. First, pickpockets. They operate in the city center, especially on crowded public transportation, often using children to distract tourists' attention. Second, gypsy gangs, which require firm handling. It's hard to ignore a mother begging with her baby, but you have to remember that the plan is to identify where your money is, then follow you and choose the right moment to rob you.

If you are robbed or lose valuables, report your loss to the police and obtain a report for insurance purposes. City Angels can come in very handy in these situations, as they can direct you to the nearest police station. The police also operate a 24-hour phone service (tel 764 9787 or 578 3014) staffed with attendants who speak foreign languages.

MEDICAL EMERGENCIES

Dialing 03 from any telephone connects you to the free state medical emergency service.

Free information about medical centers and hospitals (how to find a doctor) is available 9 a.m.–9 p.m. at tel 718-6575 or 24/7 at www.healthnet.ru.

For information on emergency medical services, phone the **Public Health Committee** at the St. Petersburg

Administration: tel 571-0906.

Private medical care is obtainable 24/7 at the **American Medical Clinic** (Naberezhnaya reki Moiki 78, tel 740-2090); **Medem Clinic & Hospital** (ulitsa Marata 6, tel 336-3333, www.medem.ru); or **Coris Assistance St. Petersburg,** (Chugunnaya ulitsa 46, tel 327-1313).

Free information about the availability of medicines at the pharmacies and medical services can be obtained by calling 325-0900 or 712-0903.

You'll find several 24-hour pharmacies in St. Petersburg, including ones at:
22 Nevsky Prospekt
tel 314-5401
19 Vosstaniya Ulitsa
tel 579-0831
32 Moskovsky Prospekt
tel 316-5507
4/1 Sennaya Ploshchad
tel 319-4532.

USEFUL NUMBERS

The state-run **Ministry of Emergencies** (tel 01 or 07) offers assistance in general emergencies and fires.

The **Rescue Service** (tel 380-9119 or 545-4745) also extends help in emergencies, in addition to carrying out rescues.

Other useful numbers include:
Police, tel 02
Ambulance, tel 03

LOST PROPERTY

Stol Nakhodok, state-run lost-property service (19 Zakharyevskaya Ulitsa, 578-3690; metro: Chernyshevskaya).

City Center for Lost Documents & Communication Devices (16 Bolshaya Monetnaya, tel 336-5109; metro: Gorkovskaya).

Airport lost-and-found
Pulkovo 1, tel 723-8361
Pulkovo 2, tel 324-3787

Lost credit/debit cards:
American Express
23 Malaya Morskaya Ulitsa,
tel 326-4500
metro: Nevsky Prospekt or Gostiny Dvor

For other lost cards, phone **UCS**, tel 718-6858

To obtain a **police report,** phone the 24-hour police hot line for foreigners, tel 764-9787 or 578-3014).

FURTHER READING

An impressive introduction to the cultural history of the city is offered in Simon Volkov's *St. Petersburg: A Cultural History (1995)*. This scholastic yet readable book contains a comprehensive overview of the evolution of the city's architecture, art, music, and philosophy.

Robert Massie's *Peter the Great* (many editions since 1980) provides an engrossing account of Peter's life and legacy. Invaluable source of Petersburg's early history. Likewise Lindsey Hughes's informative *Russia in the Age of Peter the Great* (1998).

For a broad survey of Russia's arts, see George Heard Hamilton's *The Art and Architecture of Russia* (several editions since 1954) and for a study of how St. Petersburg fits into the European and world art scene, see Jeremy Howard's *East European Art* (2006).

If you want to find out about the origins of most of the preconceptions and myths about Russia and its people, read *Empire of the Czar by Marquis de Custine* (1990 English edition). The French diplomat, who visited Russia in the 1830s, produced a very western critique of the Russian society, which survives to this day due to its general witticism and keen observation.

HOTELS & RESTAURANTS

Until recently the number of accommodations in St. Petersburg was surprisingly small. Foreign tourists on package tours were channeled into very few, predictable places. The drive to transform the city into a world-class tourist destination has been reflected in the rapid rise of lodgings in all price ranges. While leading five-star hotels remain the preserve of the rich and elite, they inspire smaller, cheaper places to also raise their standards.

Exploring the restaurant milieu of St. Petersburg is a rewarding experience. You'll find a broad range of cuisine and styles, most of which can be accessed at relatively modest prices.

HOTELS

Generally speaking, the recent hotel building boom has given rise to two types of lodgings—those that are at the top end of the market and those that aren't. The latter category has seen a trend toward mini-hotels, which for the most part meet the needs of the traveling public.

At the heart of St. Petersburg are those few luxury hotels with a rich past and fairly prohibitive prices. Newer luxuries spare no expense in competition with these grand doyens of the trade and remain in continual search for innovative ideas to draw customers. Seemingly oblivious to the high-end power struggle, mini-hotels have moved into the neighborhood to claim equally prestigious addresses. Often these are just converted apartments in multifunctional buildings, though all provide secure entry systems. Apart from a few exceptions, however, the decor in these places is disappointing and can be best described as functional and predictable. The following listings include only those mini-hotels with something special to offer or in unbeatable locations.

Demand accelerates as midsummer high season approaches, thus finding deals can be a challenge. If you know what you want, it's best to reserve in advance. Many hotels will accept a fax confirmation, while some require credit card information to process your reservation. Most accept all major cards, although cheaper mini-hotels may decline American Express, citing high transaction fees.

Street parking has become increasingly difficult throughout St. Petersburg and virtually impossible in the center. Even some high-end hotels can no longer guarantee parking spaces. Mini-hotels have an unexpected advantage here, as they often own or have access to secure courtyards where guests may park. If you plan to drive, be sure to ask about parking when making your reservations.

Rating system

St. Petersburg's homegrown hotel rating system is a gray area. At the high end of the spectrum, the star rating system serves as a fairly reliable quality indicator. That said, many hotels, particularly recent constructions, lack a rating. When asked why, many managers pointed to the expense of getting a star rating and the irrelevance of it to the quality of service they provide.

The vast majority of mini-hotels also lack a star rating. Instead, quality assurance is provided by stringent rules city authorities impose on the hotel industry. All mini-hotels are strictly regulated for fire safety and cleanliness standards.

Rooms in all of the following listed hotels include either private baths or shower stalls.

RESTAURANTS

The foremost feature of St. Petersburg's restaurants is the incredible imagination their creators applied when choosing themes to impress patrons—with both their menus and interior design. Some designers have created truly impressive settings to reflect their chosen name and focus.

International cuisine was welcomed from the very outset of the recent restaurant revolution. Indeed, it's hard to find a style not represented among the myriad menus. In this respect St. Petersburg can compete with any major city in the world.

Some restaurants proudly devote their gastronomical endeavors to Russian cuisine. Typically a Russian menu will start with salad or a soup as the first course, with meat or fish as the second. Vegetables are usually included with the dish. But there are no set rules, and you can choose any course you like or just stop in for a drink and light snack. Prices tend to remain steady regardless of the mealtime.

Except in a few instances, seating availability is rarely an issue. Only on busy weekends should you consider making reservations. Unfortunately, smoking is permitted in almost all restaurants. St. Petersburg claims only a few nonsmoking establishments.

PRICES

HOTELS

An indication of the cost of a double room without breakfast is given by $ signs.

$$$$$	Over $300
$$$$	$225–$300
$$$	$150–$225
$$	$100–$150
$	Under $100

RESTAURANTS

An indication of the cost of a three-course dinner without drinks is given by $ signs.

$$$$$	Over $80
$$$$	$50–$80
$$$	$35–$50
$$	$20–$35
$	Under $20

Dining hours

Adjusting to the local restaurant timetable shouldn't be a problem, as it generally follows a northern European pattern.

Lunch (or dinner, as Russians refer to it) is served from noon to 2 p.m., and many places won't serve you any earlier—this despite the fact that restaurants are often quite empty around midday. If you do seek company, choose a more intimate café, which can be just as satisfying.

Dinner (or supper, as Russians prefer to call it) starts around 6 p.m. Most restaurants stay open until midnight, or as the waitstaff may say proudly, "Until the last guest leaves."

Closure & holidays

While some restaurants close on Mondays, there are no hard-and-fast rules. Many remain open seven days a week, and rare is the day they close for public holidays. If anything, they hope for brisk business at these times.

Tipping

Service charges are occasionally, but not always, included in the bill. While tipping isn't customary, a bit of small change is always welcome. If service hasn't been included, and you feel a tip is in order, about 5 percent is more than sufficient.

CREDIT CARDS

The majority of hotels and restaurants accept all major credit cards. Smaller ones may accept some or none, as shown in their entry. Abbreviations used are: AE (American Express), DC (Diners Club), MC (MasterCard), and V (Visa).

ORGANIZATION

Hotels and restaurants are listed first by chapter area, then by price category, then alphabetically.

In the hotel entries, on-site restaurants of note are indicated by a restaurant icon beneath the hotel icon (if unusually special, they're described in a separate entry in the restaurant section).

NEVA TO GRIBOEDOV CANAL

HOTELS

HOTEL ANGLETERRE
$$$$$

ST. ISAAC'S SQUARE
24 MALAYA MORSKAYA ULITSA
TEL 494-5666
FAX 494-5125
www.angleterrehotel.com
The Angleterre shares a similar sense of grandiose pride but doesn't quite reach the same level as its sister hotel, the Astoria (see below). It preserves an ambience of refined modernism blended with classical features. At present, it's the only five-star hotel in the city to have a swimming pool. The wonderful gallery is a choice place to sit for tea or coffee while enjoying rotating art exhibitions and splendid views of St. Isaac's Cathedral.
🛈 193 🅿 🚇 Nevsky Prospekt; bus 22, 27; trolleybus 5, 22 🚌 🅰 🚤 🚻 🅰 All major cards

SOMETHING SPECIAL

HOTEL ASTORIA

Part of the Rocco Forte group, this hotel on St. Isaac's Square easily ranks among the city's most prestigious. Opened in 1912 and renovated in 2002, it retains its traditional elegance, exuding an air of genuine glamour not found in most modern hotels. Its interior design is sublime. A feeling of comfortable luxury is achieved throughout in the furnishings, works of art, parquet flooring, marble bathrooms, and otherwise fine decor. Some rooms have unsurpassed views of St. Isaac's, while the suites are simply divine.
$$$$$
ST. ISAAC'S SQUARE
39 BOLSHAYA MORSKAYA ULITSA

TEL 494-5757
FAX 494-5059
www.astoria.spb.ru
🛈 223 🅿 🚇 Nevsky Prospekt; bus 22, 27; trolleybus 5, 22 🚌 🅰 🚻 🅰 All major cards

KEMPINSKI HOTEL
$$$$$

22 REKI MOIKI NABEREZHNAYA
TEL 335-9111
FAX 335-9190
www.kempinski.com
Fronting Palace Square, the Kempinski is convenient to most major attractions. The exterior was recently renovated to preserve its 19th-century architectural beauty. Inside, a tasteful blend of modern and antique furnishings creates a sense of contemporary opulence. Rooms have a nautical theme, and the top-floor bar and restaurant (often fully booked) is reminiscent of a cruise ship.
🛈 197 🅿 🚇 Nevsky Prospekt; bus 3, 7; trolleybus 1, 7, 10 🚌 🅰 🚻 🅰 All major cards

RENAISSANCE
ST. PETERSBURG BALTIC HOTEL
$$$$$

4 POCHTAMTSKAYA ULITSA
TEL 380-4000
FAX 380-4001
www.renaissancehotels.com/ledbr
Opened in 2004 as part of the Marriott chain, this is one of the newest and most modern hotels in the city center. The glass roof is a prominent feature on the skyline, and the sixth-floor Terrace Bar commands superb city views. Rooms are spacious and luxuriously furnished, yet there's a perceptible corporate ambience throughout the hotel. The **Canvas** restaurant serves a creative and innovative menu.
🛈 102 🚇 Nevsky Prospekt; bus 3, 22, 27; trolleybus 5, 22

HOTELS & RESTAURANTS

🔁 🚭 Nonsmoking in some rooms 🛗 📺
🃏 All major cards

🏨 CASA LETO
$$$$
34 BOLSHAYA MORSKAYA ULITSA
TEL 600-1096 OR 314-6622
FAX 314-6639
www.casaleto.com
Those looking for intimate glamour have a perfect choice in this small family-run hotel in the heart of St. Petersburg. All rooms are spacious and lavishly furnished. Breakfast, refreshments, local phone calls, and Internet access are included in the comparatively affordable prices.
ⓘ 5 P 🚇 Nevsky Prospekt; bus 3, 22, 27; trolleybus 5, 22 🚭 🛗 📺
🃏 All major cards

🏨 ERMITAGE HOTEL
$$$
11 MILLIONNAYA ULITSA
TEL 571-5497
www.ermitage.spb.ru
This tiny hotel boasts an interesting history and one of the best locations in the city (right beside the Hermitage). Comfortable, stylish interior. Can be booked in its entirety.
ⓘ 4 🚇 Nevsky Prospekt; bus 7; trolleybus 1, 7, 10
🃏 All major cards

🏨 PUSHKA INN HOTEL
🍴 **$$$**
14 REKI MOIKI NABEREZHNAYA
TEL 312-0913
FAX 571-9557
www.pushkainn.ru
Pushka Inn offers a desirable spot in the city center—just a stone's throw from the Hermitage. Though modern, the hotel retains some charming original features. The decor is simple and elegant. Some rooms overlook the Moika River, while affordable, spacious family rooms are a rare, attractive feature.

ⓘ 31 P 🚇 Nevsky Prospekt 🔁 🛗 🚇 MC, V

🏨 ASTER
$$
25 BOLSHAYA KONYUSHENNAYA ULITSA
TEL 336-6585
www.hon.ru
This small private hotel in a period building belongs to a chain of hotels and apartments in the city center. The premises have been fully modernized, offering guests a comfortable stay. Its prime location makes up for the somewhat bland decor.
ⓘ 26 P 🚇 Nevsky Prospekt; bus 7, 22; trolleybus 1, 7, 10, 5 🛗 🃏 All major cards

🏨 COMFORT HOTEL
🍴 **$$**
25 BOLSHAYA MORSKAYA ULITSA.
TEL 314-6523 OR 570-6700
FAX 571-6724
www.comfort-hotel.spb.ru
Opened in 2003, this hotel is at the very heart of the city, within easy walking distance of Nevsky, St. Isaac's, and the Hermitage. Although rooms feature standard hotel decor, they are acceptably spacious and comfortable.
ⓘ 14 P 🚇 Nevsky Prospekt; bus 3, 22, 27; trolleybus 5, 22 🛗 🃏 All major cards

🏨 HERZEN HOTEL
$$
25 BOLSHAYA MORSKAYA ULITSA
TEL 571-5098
FAX 314-6406
www.herzen-hotel.spb.ru
In the same building as the Comfort Hotel, the Herzen shares aspects of its character and ambience in spite of its distinct appearance. The atmosphere is homey, and its proximity to the city's countless cultural treasures make this an attractive option. It's named for radical writer and philosopher Alexander

Herzen, who's said to have lived here in the early 1840s.
ⓘ 20 P 🚇 Nevsky Prospekt; bus 3, 22, 27; trolleybus 5, 22 🔁 🛗
🃏 All major cards

🏨 MATISOV DOMIK
🍴 **$$**
3/1 PRYAZHKA NABEREZHNAYA
TEL 495-1439
FAX 495-2419
www.matisov.com
A rather standard mid-range hotel in an unusual location (on small Matisov Island near the mouth of the Neva), the Matisov Domik offers simple, comfortable rooms. Decor is nothing out of the ordinary, but the place is decent and clean. Suites and apartments are available.
ⓘ 46 P 🚇 Sennaya; bus 22 🃏 All major cards

RESTAURANTS

🍴 DVORYANSKOE GNEZDO
$$$$$
21 DEKABRISTOV ULITSA
TEL 312-3205
An exclusive restaurant, the "Nobles' Nest" occupies

a tea pavilion adjacent to the Yusupov Palace garden. It was a particular mark of distinction to eat here ten years ago, and the service alone is still enough to leave you feeling like royalty. Live grand piano from 8 p.m. adds to the highbrow ambience.
🛏 60 🚇 Sennaya; bus 3, 10, 22, 27; trolleybus 5, 22 🗝 All major cards

🍴 PRINCE KOCHUBEY
$$$$
7 KONNOGVARDEYSKY BULVAR
TEL 312-8934
On the lower floors of the Kochubey Palace (later turned into a beauty parlor), this restaurant prepares traditional Russian recipes, including a good selection of fish dishes—try the pike perch in potato scales with wood mushrooms and quail eggs.
🛏 110 🚇 Nevsky Prospekt; bus 3, 22, 27; trolleybus 5, 22 🗝 All major cards

🍴 BACKSTAGE
$$$
18/10 TEATRALNAYA PLOSHCHAD
TEL 327-0521
Owned by the Mariinsky Theater, this restaurant draws true ballet and opera lovers. The interior design brings together various theater artifacts, including the original stage floorboards and prop statues from *Aida*. Lucky patrons may catch some of the Mariinsky stars rehearsing on the ballet rail.
🛏 50 🚇 Sennaya; bus 3, 22, 27; trolleybus 5, 22 🗝 All major cards

🍴 SILK
$$$
4/2 MALAYA KONYUSHENNAYA ULITSA
TEL 571-5078
Stylishly bare, with large square tables and inviting sofas, this trendy restaurant offers an exotic menu of Japanese and Italian dishes.

Upbeat, funky music and a live DJ attract the younger set, while wine tasting and cigar nights are more popular with the older generation.
🛏 70 🅿 🚇 Nevsky Prospekt; bus 3, 7, 22; trolleybus 1, 7, 10 🗝 All major cards

🍴 PARIS
$$$
63 BOLSHAYA MORSKAYA ULITSA
TEL 571-9545
This quiet place is one of St. Petersburg's first haute cuisine restaurants. The mainly French menu includes some unexpectedly simple dishes, complemented by a very expensive wine list. The perfect place for a pre- or post-ballet meal, as the Mariinsky is a ten-minute walk from here.
🛏 80 🚇 Nevsky Prospekt or Sennaya Ploshchad; bus 3, 10, 22, 27; trolleybus 5, 22 🗝 All major cards

🍴 THE IDIOT
$$
82 REKI MOIKI NABEREZHNAYA
TEL 315-1675
Named for the Dostoevsky novel, this is perhaps the most famous café-bar in the city. The vegetarian menu has won high acclaim, and the cozy, informal interior attracts a mixed crowd of local intellectuals and curious foreigners. Try one of the delicious mushroom dishes.
🛏 100 🚇 Nevsky Prospekt; bus 3, 22; trolleybus 5, 22 🗝 All major cards

🍴 SADKO
$$
2 GLINKI ULITSA
TEL 920-8228
A stylish new restaurant and wine bar just minutes from the Mariinsky, Sadko makes a perfect option for pretheater meals. The menu centers on Russian cuisine, though you'll also find some European dishes. Try the Herring in a Fur Coat or specialty pancakes.

🛏 150 🚇 Sennaya Ploshchad 🗝 All major cards

🍴 NEP
$
37 REKI MOIKI NABEREZHNAYA
TEL 571-7591
This cozy sublevel restaurant is low lit, with couches that run the lengths of the walls. While the cuisine is Russian, a specialty awaits those with a more adventurous palate: marinated ostrich fillet in kiwi. Cabaret and jazz singers perform twice weekly.
🛏 60 🚇 Nevsky Prospekt; bus 7, 22, 27; trolleybus 1, 5, 7, 10 🗝 All major cards

🍴 OLIVA
$
31 BOLSHAYA MORSKAYA ULITSA
TEL 314-6563
This jolly Greek taverna promises both an authentic feel and marvelous food. Much of the produce is delivered from Greece, and the salad bar is laden with tantalizing options.
🛏 230 🚇 Nevsky Prospekt; bus 3, 22, 27; trolleybus 5, 22 🗝 MC, V

EAST OF GRIBOEDOV CANAL

HOTELS

🏨 CORINTHIA NEVSKIJ
🍴 PALACE HOTEL
$$$$$
57 NEVSKY PROSPEKT
TEL 380-2001
FAX 380-1937
www.corinthiahotels.com
Upon entering the Corinthia, you'd be forgiven for assuming it to be a business center. Visible through the curved glass foyer, its towers do look rather corporate. However, the rooms are more than comfortable, and its restaurants offer an array of international cuisines. In contrast to its commercial character, a corner of the hotel houses the Samoilov

HOTELS & RESTAURANTS

Memorial Museum.
📍 282 🅿 🚇 Nevsky Prospekt; bus 7, 22, 27; trolleybus 1, 5, 7, 10 🛗 🚇 🚪 📇 All major cards

🏨 GRAND HOTEL 🍴 EMERALD
$$$$$
18 SUVOROVSKY PROSPEKT
TEL 740-5000
FAX 740-5006
www.grandhotelemerald.com
Just a few years old, this hotel's youth is tangible. While the exterior reflects glazed modern sensibilities, the interior is sumptuous, with classical furnishings and a large, glitzy gold chandelier in the lobby. Rooms are ample, with fine furniture. Some overlook the beautiful atrium, where drinks and refreshments are available at surprisingly low prices.
📍 90 🚇 Vosstaniya Ploshchad; bus 22, 27; trolleybus 5, 22 🛗 🚪 📇 📇 All major cards

🏨 GRAND HOTEL 🍴 EUROPE
$$$$$
NEVSKY PROSPEKT
1/7 MIKHAILOVSKAYA ULITSA
TEL 329-6000
FAX 329 6001
www.grandhoteleurope.com
At 130 years old, this is St. Petersburg's oldest hotel. Recently refurbished, it still oozes an air of opulent luxury, with fabulous original features that subtly combine with barely noticeable modern conveniences. The palatial lobby features a red carpet on the main staircase, large chandeliers, and flamboyant pillars. The rooms are most pleasing, with antique furniture and fittings preserved by the city administration. Soundproof windows ensure that its central location on Nevsky doesn't disturb guests. The hotel houses seven bars and restaurants, including Chinese and Italian. The

gem of them all is **L'Europe** (see p. 253), which in 2006 won a prestigious award as the city's best restaurant.
📍 301 🅿 🚇 Gostiny Dvor; bus 3, 7, 22, 27; trolleybus 1, 5, 7, 10, 22 🛗 🚪 🚇 📇 All major cards

🏨 NOVOTEL 🍴 $$$$$
NEVSKY PROSPEKT
3A MAYAKOVSKOGO ULITSA
TEL 335-1188
FAX 335-9153
www.novotel.com
French designers finished this smart, chic hotel, which is staffed by friendly, helpful young graduates. Spacious and peaceful, the rooms include large semicircular windows with distinctive beds. The award-winning restaurant features rotating monthly themes to promote its distinguished cuisine.
📍 233 🅿 🚇 Mayakovskaya; bus 7; trolleybus 1, 5, 7, 10, 22 🛗 🚭 Nonsmoking rooms available 🚪 📇 All major cards

🏨 RADISSON SAS ROYAL 🍴 HOTEL
$$$$$
49/2 NEVSKY PROSPEKT
TEL 322-5000
FAX 322-5002
www.radissonsas.com
Although housed in a beautiful 18th-century building, the Radisson's somewhat dull, uninspiring lobby doesn't quite meet expectations. Regardless, the rooms are spacious and comfortable with an overall business sensibility and elegant design touches. As expected, all are fully equipped with modern conveniences.
📍 164 🚇 Mayakovskaya; bus 3, 7, 22, 27; trolleybus 1, 5, 7, 22 🛗 🚪 📇 🚪 All major cards

🏨 AMBASSADOR 🍴 $$$$
5–7 RIMSKOGO-KORSAKOVA PROSPEKT
TEL 331-8844
FAX 331-9300
www.ambassador-hotel.ru
This new hotel with friendly service and an obvious sense of class is rapidly gaining popularity. Guests will find everything they expect from a hotel of this category. Don't miss stunning views from the rooftop restaurant, **Le Vernissage** (see p. 253).
📍 255 🚇 Sennaya Ploshchad, Sadovaya; bus 3, 22, 27; trolleybus 3, 14, 29 🛗 🚪 📇 All major cards

🏨 ARBAT NORD HOTEL 🍴 $$$$
4 ARTILLERYSKAYA ULITSA
TEL 703-1899
FAX 703-1898
www.arbat-nord.ru
In a quiet area only a few minutes from Nevsky, this well-furnished hotel boasts a classy design. Rooms offer a pleasant character, albeit simple, standard decor. Smoking is prohibited on the second floor. Business and transportation services are available.

KEY   🏨 Hotel   🍴 Restaurant   📍 No. of bedrooms   🪑 No. of seats   🅿 Parking   🚪 Closed   🚇 Metro   🛗 Elevator

ⓘ 38 🅿 🚇 Chernyshevskaya; bus 22, 46, 105; trolleybus 3, 8, 15, 49 🔁 🚭 🚬 🔑 All major cards

MARSHAL HOTEL
⑪ $$$
41 SHPALERNAYA ULITSA
TEL 579-9995
www.marshal-hotel.spb.ru
This small hotel provides a comfortable stay in an area not yet explored by big hotel companies. The building boasts interesting historical connections and houses a small museum to honor the fact. Adjacent to the extensive Tauride Gardens and the Neva Embankment, it offers guests distinct, beautiful surroundings.
ⓘ 25 🚇 Chernyshevskaya, bus 46, 136 🚬 🔑 All major cards

OKTIABRSKAYA
⑪ $$$
10 LIGOVSKY PROSPEKT
TEL 578-1144 OR 578-1515
FAX 315-7501
www.oktober-hotel.spb.ru
Aside from its convenient location, this massive edifice has little to offer, with a dull interior that verges on depressing.
ⓘ 373 🅿 🚇 Vosstaniya Ploshchad; bus 5, 7, 22, 27; trolleybus 1, 5, 7, 10, 22 🔁 🚬 🔑 All major cards

PRESTIGE HOTEL CENTER
$$$
5 GOROKHOVAYA ULITSA
TEL 312-0405 OR 315-9397
FAX 315-9357
www.prestigehotel.spb.ru
Opened in 2005, this Prestige location is much nicer than its older sister on Vasilevsky Island (see p. 255). The interior is modern, and some rooms feature an Asian theme. Palace Square and the Hermitage are a five-minute walk.
ⓘ 27 🚇 Nevsky Prospekt; bus 22, 27; trolleybus 5, 22 🚬 🔑 All major cards

🚇 ANABEL
⑪ $$
74 NEVSKY PROSPEKT
TEL 717-0255 OR 717-0800
www.anabel.ru
The Anabel is one of a string of mini-hotels on located on Nevsky Prospekt. (Other properties include 88 and 147/33.) The friendly staff delivers excellent service.
ⓘ 79 🚇 Mayakovskaya, Aleksandra Nevskogo Ploshchad; bus 7; trolleybus 1, 7, 10 🔑 All major cards

🚇 BASKOV MINI-HOTEL
$$
23/6 MAYAKOVSKOGO
APT. 2
TEL 272-6493
FAX 272-3470
Typical of the many private mini-hotels scattered across the city, this small place offers a cheaper, perfectly satisfactory option for those seeking to remain close to the action on Nevsky Prospekt.
ⓘ 13 🚇 Mayakovskaya; bus 7; trolleybus 1, 7, 10 🔁 🔑 All major cards

RESTAURANTS

⑪ L'EUROPE
A mong the city's most prominent restaurants, this award-winning gourmet wonderland serves up French and European specialties. Popular choices include the *pot-au-feu de la mer* and the fried goose liver with orange brioche. The art nouveau interior with trademark stained-glass window is in itself a wonder to behold, but even more delightful during a live harp performance.
$$$$$
GRAND HOTEL EUROPE
NEVSKY PROSPEKT
1/7 MIKHAILOVSKAYA ULITSA
TEL 329-6630
🍴 55 🚇 Gostiny Dvor; bus 3, 7, 22, 27; trolleybus 1,

5, 7, 10, 22 🔑 All major cards

⑪ LE VERNISSAGE
$$$$$
AMBASSADOR HOTEL
5–7 RIMSKOGO-KORSAKOVA PROSPEKT
TEL 331-8844
This ninth-floor restaurant with panoramic views serves European and traditional Russian dishes. The split-level layout and obviously expensive decor lend the space a relaxing bourgeois atmosphere. Friendly service complements the delicious gourmet menu.
🍴 200 🚇 Sennaya Ploshchad or Sadovaya; bus 3, 22, 27; trolleybus 3, 14, 29 🔑 All major cards

⑪ PALKIN
$$$$$
47 NEVSKY PROSPEKT
TEL 703 5371
Since 1785 this prestigious establishment has wowed even the most worldly connoisseurs with its aristocratic Russian menu. With new life breathed into it recently, Palkin is doing so again. Despite a conspicuous level of security, the atmosphere is warm and the service very pleasant.
🍴 65 🚇 Mayakovskaya; bus 5, 7, 22, 27; trolleybus 1, 5, 7, 10, 22 🔑 All major cards

⑪ DEMIDOV
$$$
14 FONTANKA NABEREZHNAYA
TEL 272-9181
This popular place attracts diners with cuisine based on classic Russian recipes. Foreigners are particularly charmed by the live gypsy music—and possibly the overdone decor.
🚇 Gostiny Dvor; bus 46, tram 3 🔑 All major cards

🍴 BAGRATIONI

$$

5/19 LITEYNY PROSPEKT

TEL 272-7448

$$

A tribute to Georgia and the eponymous hero of the Napoleonic Wars, this establishment serves Georgian haute cuisine. When political relations allow, the staff imports all ingredients from Georgia.
🚇 Chernyshevskaya; bus 28, 37; trolleybus 3, 8, 15; tram 14
💳 All major cards

🍴 BISTRO GARÇON

$$

95 NEVSKY PROSPEKT

TEL 277-2467

Boasting authentic French cuisine and decor, this is the place to reminisce about your last visit to Paris. Better known for its breakfasts than its dinners.
🚇 Vosstaniya Ploshchad; bus 5, 7; trolleybus 1, 5, 7, 10, 22 💳 All major cards

🍴 DOLYA ANGELA

$$

16/19 ITALYANSKAYA ULITSA

TEL 571-7716

"Angel's Share" serves mainly Italian food, including a good selection of fish dishes. Also worth a look at breakfast.
🍽 40 🚇 Gostiny Dvor; bus 7, 22; trolleybus 1, 5, 7, 10
💳 All major cards

🍴 PORTO MALTESE

$$

174 NEVSKY PROSPEKT

TEL 271-7677

On the less frequented end of Nevsky Prospekt, this restaurant sticks to theme, with walls lined by Maltese flags. Customers pick their fish from an icy stall and instruct the chef how they'd like it cooked. Very good wine list.
🚇 Aleksandra Nevskogo Ploshchad; bus 27, 46; trolleybus 1, 6, 22 💳 All major cards

🍴 YOLKI-PALKI

$$

88 NEVSKY PROSPEKT

TEL 273-1594

This family-geared restaurant chain serves up traditional Russian fare, including an all-you-can-eat "hay-cart" smorgasbord. The interior is designed to resemble a peasant's hut, the novelty of which lures locals and visitors alike—as a result it's often rather crowded and noisy.
🍽 150 🚇 Mayakovskaya; bus 5, 7; trolleybus 1, 5, 7, 10, 22 💳 MC, V

🍴 CAFÉ ART DECO

$

64 KANALA GRIBOEDOVA NABEREZHNAYA & 47 SADOVAYA

TEL 310-6454

This delightful, casual corner restaurant overlooks the canal. Its funky art deco interior, coupled with upbeat lounge and deep house music, makes it a popular hangout among locals and tourists. Relax and enjoy simple, hearty meals at reasonable prices.
🍽 70 🚇 Sadovaya or Sennaya Ploshchad; bus 10; tram 3, 14, 29 💳 MC, V

🍴 LAIMA

$

16 KANALA GRIBOEDOVA NABEREZHNAYA

TEL 449-4153

The cheapest and quickest place to eat on Nevsky, Laima has a surprisingly broad menu for a bistro. Housed inside a tastefully restored 19th-century building visited by Pushkin, it's immensely popular among budget-conscious gourmets.
🍽 80 🚇 Nevsky Prospekt; bus 7; trolleybus 1, 7, 10
💳 MC, V

🍴 RAZGULYAY

$

14 KARAVANNAYA ULITSA

TEL 571-1115

The serious, attentive staff

---

at Razgulyay serves a variety of traditional Russian cuisine amid rustic surroundings. Each day of the week features a different specialty.
🍽 80 🚇 Gostiny Dvor; bus 3, 7, 22, 27; trolleybus 1, 5, 7, 10, 22 💳 All major cards

VASILEVSKY ISLAND

HOTELS

🏨 NASHOTEL

🍴 $$$

50 11TH LINE

TEL-323 2231

FAX-328 3546

www.nashotel.ru

Easily the best hotel on the island, NashOtel offers a refreshing contrast to Petersburgian aristocratic grandeur. Its funky, playful decor features glass tables, orange leather couches, and a simply astounding atrium. The large rooms include big windows that let in plenty of light. Certainly worth a visit, if only for a coffee break at the lobby bar while on a sightseeing excursion.
🛏 58 🅿 🚇 Vasileostrovskaya; bus 1, 6, 7, 41, 42, 128,

152; trolleybus 10 🔁 📶 📶 Smoking only on the second floor 📶 All major cards

PRESTIGE HOTEL BASIL
$$$
52 3RD LINE
TEL 328-5338 OR 328-4228
FAX 328-5011
www.prestigehotel.spb.ru
Although this Prestige location opened in 2001, the somewhat crass decor in certain rooms already seems dated. Two rooms include large Jacuzzis. Views take in either a quiet street or surrounding buildings and garden features.
ℹ️ 10 🅿️ 📶 Vasileostrov-skaya; bus 1, 6, 7, 41, 42, 128, 152; trolleybus 10 📶 Air-conditioning in some rooms 📶 All major cards

PRIBALTIYSKAYA
$$$
14 KORABLESTROITELEY ULITSA
TEL 356-3001
www.pribaltiyskaya.ru
In the Soviet era this vast, remote, imposing building possessed a certain grandeur and was considered the city's best hotel. Permeated with standard hotel decor, the place now just comes across as functional, though it offers everything required by its four-star status. Rooms span a wide range of rates.
ℹ️ 840 🅿️ 📶 Primorskaya; bus 7, 128, 151, 152 🔁 📶 📶 All major cards

SHELFORT
$$$
26 3RD LINE
TEL 328-0555 OR 323-5154
FAX 327-0984 OR 323-3626
www.shelfort.ru
A slightly dilapidated entrance (perked up with some fairy lights) welcomes you to this hotel. Opened in 2001, it's fairly homely and modest, and perfectly satisfactory, with spacious rooms and pleasant

enough decor. As with many local hotels, this one provides such additional services as laundry and ironing, business support, ticket arrangements, and transfers. The location is safe and quiet.
ℹ️ 15 📶 Vasileostrovskaya; bus 1, 6, 7, 41, 42, 128, 152; trolleybus 10 📶 All major cards

RESTAURANTS

BELLINI
$$$$
13 UNIVERSITETSKAYA NABEREZHNAYA
TEL 331-1001
On the second floor of an 18th-century building, this restaurant is a paragon of restrained opulence. Having tasted the exquisite French cuisine, enjoy an after-dinner coffee on the balcony. Try to reserve a table near one of the windows, as the splendid views of the Neva, St. Isaac's, and the Winter Palace alone are worth the expense.
🍴 52 📶 Vasileostrovskaya; bus 7, 47; trolleybus 1, 10 📶 All major cards

STARAYA TAMOZHNYA
$$$$
1 TAMOZHENNY PEREULOK
TEL 327-8990
Although this dimly lit basement restaurant is somewhat claustrophobic, it boasts famous diners and a well-earned reputation for its extensive wine list and generous portions of excellent French cuisine.
🍴 150 📶 Vasileostrovskaya; bus 7, 47; trolleybus 1, 10 📶 All major cards

RESTORAN
$$
2 TAMOZHENNY PEREULOK
TEL 327-8979
Designed like a peasant's hut, this roomy restaurant offers excellent traditional Russian cuisine. University professors often entertain foreign guests here, though the broad space

can inhibit intimate gatherings.
🍴 350 📶 Vasileostrovskaya; bus 7; trolleybus 1, 10 📶 All major cards

RUSSIAN KITSCH
$
25 UNIVERSITETSKAYA NABEREZHNAYA
TEL 325-1122
For several years running this unique grand café has been celebrating all things kitsch in a stylish way. Its glass-fronted gallery and sushi bar command superb views of the Neva—perhaps the primary reason for its steady popularity. Others come for its delectable menu and fun setting, with six different rooms and a dance hall.
🍴 320 📶 Vasileostrovskaya; bus 7; trolleybus 1, 10 📶 All major cards

PETROGRAD SIDE & BEYOND

HOTELS

GUYOT HOTEL
$$$
23 PROFESSORA POPOVA ULITSA
TEL 347-5628
FAX 703-1245
In the Guyot Business Center, this quirky hotel includes an Oriental Room (with hookah available) for loung-ing, as well as a private dining space dubbed the Old Room, which showcases genuine antique curiosities (e.g., a wooden fridge). One section of the restaurant is designed like an old English gentlemen's club, with a fireplace, billiard table, and leather armchairs. Rooms are rather bland but adequate.
ℹ️ 46 🅿️ 📶 Petrogradskaya; bus 10, 25 🔁 📶 📶 📶 📶 All major cards

AMULET
$$
12 BOLSHOY PROSPEKT
APT. 5
TEL 235-8232

FAX 232-9245
www.amulet-hotels.ru
Tucked out of sight and lacking a conspicuous sign, this is not the easiest hotel to find. While the entrance has been somewhat restored, shabbiness remains. Rooms have just enough space and are furnished modestly.

🛏 8 🚇 Sportivnaya; trolleybus 7 🚭

🏨 KRONVERK
🍴 **$$**
9 BLOKHINA ULITSA
TEL 703-3663
FAX 449-6701
www.kronverk.com
Opened in 2004 in a quiet area, this hotel flaunts a sleek black facade with an ultramodern, almost futuristic feel to it. The interior is spacious, with minimal furnishings and decoration, while the fashionably minimalist rooms feature large windows.

🛏 26 🅿 🚇 Sportivnaya; trolleybus 7 🛗 🚭 🚭 MC, V

🏨 SAINT-PETERSBURG
🍴 **$$**
5/2 PIROGOVSKAYA NABEREZHNAYA
TEL 380-1909/1911/1919
FAX 380-1906/1920
www.hotel-spb.ru
This very Soviet hotel is "guarded" by the famous cruiser *Aurora*—the ship whose guns signaled the start of the October Revolution in 1917. Lacking in style and offering a rather standard list of guest services, it wouldn't make a short list of most inviting hotels. The only thing going for it are fine views across the Neva from rooms that come at a premium.

🛏 400 🅿 🚇 Lenina Ploshchad; tram 3 🛗 🚭 🚭 All major cards

RESTAURANTS

🍴 LETUCHY GOLLANDETS
$$$$$
MYTNINSKAYA NABEREZHNAYA (NEAR BIRZEVOY BRIDGE)
TEL 336-3737
A replica of the *Flying Dutchman*, this floating restaurant features three sections, each serving different cuisine (e.g., Zebra offers original Russian dishes and drinks). Created by a Belgian chef, desserts are a taste of heaven. If you overindulge, there's even an onboard fitness club.

🍽 70 🚇 Sportivnaya; trolleybus 7 🚭 DC, MC

🍴 LESNOY
$$$$
47 LESNOY PROSPEKT
TEL 596-3932
Everything about Lesnoy is big. The place itself is vast, and the menu exhaustive, featuring mouthwatering European, Russian, Caucasian, and Uzbek dishes. Fans of kebabs, or *shashliks,* are spoiled for choice.

🍽 600 🚇 Lesnaya; bus 86; tram 20 🚭 All major cards

🍴 RUSSKAYA RYBALKA
Fish aficionados will love this place. Not only is the menu mainly fish focused, but diners have the satisfaction of literally catching their dinner from the adjacent stocked lake. Outdoor seating with breathtaking views of the Gulf of Finland make this a very popular spot (politicians often dine here, hence the special President's Menu). Reservations are strongly recommended.

$$$$
KRESTOVSKY OSTROV
11 YUZHNAYA DOROGA
TEL 323-9813
🍽 270 🚇 Krestovsky

PRICES

HOTELS
An indication of the cost of a double room without breakfast is given by $ signs.

$$$$$	Over $300
$$$$	$225–$300
$$$	$150–$225
$$	$100–$150
$	Under $100

RESTAURANTS
An indication of the cost of a three-course dinner without drinks is given by $ signs.

$$$$$	Over $80
$$$$	$50–$80
$$$	$35–$50
$$	$20–$35
$	Under $20

Ostrov; tram 17, 40 🚭 DC, MC

🍴 VOLNA
$$$
4 PETROVSKAYA NABEREZHNAYA
TEL 322-5383
Fusion menus are fast becoming popular here, and Volna (Wave) perfectly executes the style, blending Asian and Italian ingredients to create enticing new tastes—lobster with spaghetti is a choice option. Service isn't quite as polished—staff can come across as arrogant.

🍽 60 🚇 Gorkovskaya; tram 3, 40 🚭 All major cards

🍴 PUBLIKA
$$
2 GATCHINSKAYA ULITSA
TEL 232-9981
This restaurant's tasteful interior has a club feel about it. The chef has an excellent reputation. A rather modest wine list accompanies the mainly European menu.

🚇 Chkalovskaya bus 10, 128, 492; trolleybus 1, 9, 31 🚭 All major cards

SOUTH OF THE FONTANKA

HOTELS

🏨 GOLDEN GARDEN
🍴 CLUB
$$$$$
9 VLADIMIRSKY PROSPEKT
TEL 572-2233
FAX 572-2248
www.goldengardenclub.com
This exquisite boutique hotel close to the center of Nevsky may not be as big or imposing as the other grand hotels, but it's every bit as luxurious. Its smaller size affords a more exclusive feeling and private atmosphere. It boasts two fine restaurants and a Monte Carlo casino. The Golden Garden Courtyard houses boutiques selling such high-end goods as Swiss watches and Persian carpets.
🛈 24 🚇 Vladimirskaya, Dostoevskaya; trolleybus 3, 18, 15 🔄 🆒 🗝 All major cards

🏨 DOSTOEVSKY
🍴 $$$$
19 VLADIMIRSKY PROSPEKT
TEL 331-3200
FAX 331-3201
www.dostoevsky-hotel.ru
Occupying a spruced-up and quite beautiful art nouveau building in a very busy area, this hotel seems out of place. Inside you'll find a lively if lackluster hotel atmosphere.
🛈 208 🚇 Vladimirskaya, Dostoevskaya; trolleybus 3, 8, 15 🔄 🆒 🗝 All major cards

🏨 HELVETIA
🍴 $$$$
11 MARATA ULITSA
TEL 326-5353 OR 712-3076
www.helvetia-suites.ru
This Swiss-owned hotel combines St. Petersburg grandeur and Swiss quality. Rooms are tastefully decorated and include all possible comforts. Secured in a private courtyard, it's well-protected from the hustle of the busy street.
🛈 59 🚇 Mayakovskaya; bus 3, 7, 22, 27; trolleybus 1, 5, 7, 10, 22; tram 12, 28 🔄 🆒 🗝 All major cards

🏨 NEVSKY DVOR
🍴 $$
4 POVARSKOY PEREULOK
TEL 575 5687 OR 575 6023
FAX 713 3596
www.nevskydvor.ru
This cozy, delightful hotel offers a friendly, homey respite for busy tourists. Secure accommodation includes all the essentials for a comfortable stay, including courtyard parking.
🛈 17 🅿
🚇 Mayakovskaya; bus 3, 7, 22, 27; trolleybus 1, 5, 7, 10, 22; tram 12, 28 🆒 🗝 All major cards

RESTAURANTS

🍴 FEDOR DOSTOEVSKY
$$$$
HOTEL GOLDEN GARDEN
19 VLADIMIRSKY PROSPEKT
TEL 572-2229
A complimentary dill vodka with slightly salted cucumber awaits those who come here to delight their taste buds. The cuisine is a blend of traditional Russian dishes with a French twist. A small library showcases original editions, while the menu features relevant Dostoevskyian references and quotes.
🔲 100 🚇 Vladimirskaya or Dostoevskaya; trolleybus 3, 8, 15 🗝 All major cards

🍴 MARIUS PUB
$$$
11 MARATA ULITSA
TEL 571-9597
This place may herald the dawning of a new trend: gastro-pubs. Those who enjoy fine food in a round-the-clock pub atmosphere can sample Russian and European cuisine, with a special Swiss menu.
🔲 80 🚇 Mayakovskaya 🗝 All major cards

🍴 MACARONI
$$
23 RUBINSHTEYNA ULITSA
TEL 572 2849
Some claim this place serves the city's best carpaccio. Spend a cozy, quiet evening here and decide for yourself.
🚇 Mayakovskaya; bus 3, 7, 22, 27; trolleybus 3, 8, 15; tram 12, 28 🗝 All major cards

🍴 LE GOGA
$
6 RAZEZZHAYA ULITSA
TEL 314-7574
Although really a coffeehouse, this place also serves a full restaurant menu. The food isn't always up to standard, but the cakes (baked on-site) make up for it.
🚇 Vladimirskaya; trolleybus 3, 8, 15 🗝 AE, MC, V

🚭 Nonsmoking 🆒 Air-conditioning 🏊 Indoor/🏊 Outdoor swimming pool 🗝 Health club 🗝 Credit cards | **KEY**

SHOPPING

Resign yourself to the fact that shopping is not St. Petersburg's strong suit. This doesn't mean the city is short on shops. On the contrary, the rise of the local consumer culture has been quite relentless, and there seem to be more shops than reasonably necessary. Practical shoppers, however, soon realize that expensive labels glut the market. Indeed, the main streets are clogged with brand-name stores, especially in foreign fashion and design. Another quirk of shopping here is the excessive number of shoe shops selling most impractical footwear. Impracticality is a recurring aspect that strikes one most in clothing shops—it's often hard to imagine the local climate would ever allow comfortable use of certain garments on sale.

Despite the drawbacks of its shopping situation, St. Petersburg does boast a strong fashion-design tradition, and quite a few fashion houses offer innovative and flattering clothes to a discerning public. As in most big cities worldwide, however, such clothes come with a hefty price tag. Thus many shoppers, particularly those of more modest means, browse the city's ten markets for their clothes, shoes, and other items.

Many—not all—shops accept credit cards.

Opening hours are fairly uniform citywide. Nonfood stores traditionally open at 10 a.m. and close at 8 p.m., enabling women to shop after work—though some stores have moved to a 10 a.m. to 7 p.m. pattern. Smaller shops observe a lunch break between 2 and 3 p.m. Nearly all shops remain open on weekends and close on Monday. The exception is food stores, which open each day between 8 and 9 a.m. and close at 10 p.m. You'll also find a number of 24-hour food shops.

Service in all but the most upscale shops is adequate but by no means overly enthusiastic. It's not so much a case of "customer disservice"—it's simply that the staff is often swamped with customers and can't spare a smile for everyone. Don't take this personally—it's just different to what you might expect or be used to. In fact, foreign shoppers nearly always draw extra help and smiles.

ANTIQUES

Antique shopping can be a costly venture in St. Petersburg. Given the size and history of the city, there are surprisingly few antique shops and no streets or areas dedicated to them. Most antiques are available either in upscale salons such as **Nabokov** (35 Bolshaya Morskaya Ulitsa; tel 325-6975; metro: Nevsky Prospekt) or in less formal shops, where you're more likely to pick up a bargain. Most places offer a broad selection rather than specializing in specific periods or styles. One of the oldest of this type is **Panteleymonovsky** (13–15 Pestel Ulitsa; tel 579-7235; metro: Chernyshevskaya). Across the road is **Renessance**, which tends to be a bit pricier. You'll find a few other antique shops within walking distance.

ART GALLERIES

While St. Petersburg is rife with art galleries, as with antique shops, there are no areas or streets principally reserved for them. Your best bet is to browse the main streets and a few select smaller ones. The following are just a few options:

Blue Room, 38 Bolshaya Morskaya Ulitsa; tel 315-7414; metro: Nevsky Prospekt. This space showcases paintings and sculptures by members of the St. Petersburg Union of Artists. You'll find all modern styles, as well as copies of paintings by Old Masters. The dim chandeliers and slightly shabby walls lend a somewhat bohemian feel to the place, adding to its charm.

Russian Icon, 15 Bolshaya Konyushennaya Ulitsa; tel 314-7040; metro: Nevsky Prospekt. Closed Sun. This unusual gallery sells contemporary Orthodox icons of startling and captivating beauty. Icons can be made to order, or you can create your own from the materials on sale.

Sol Art, 15 Solyanoy Pereulok; tel 327-3082; metro: Chernyshevskaya. This wonderful gallery of leading St. Petersburg artists sits in the beautifully decorated vestibule of the Stieglitz Museum.

S.P.A.S., 93 reki Moiki Naberezhnaya; tel 117-4260; metro: Nevsky Prospekt. Although this gallery of contemporary local artists is small, the variety of styles and media on display is by no means restricted.

BOOKS

Bukvoed, 13 Nevsky Prospekt; tel 579-8264; metro: Nevsky Prospekt. With branches around the city, this store offers an extensive collection of books and stationery, with some literature in foreign languages.

DVK, 20 Nevsky Prospekt; tel 312-4936; metro: Nevsky Prospekt. Surprisingly, this abbreviation stands for Dom Voennoy Knigi (House of Military Books). Having survived the Soviet era, this bookstore has little to do with military books anymore but maintains its reputation for a well-balanced stock and reasonable prices. Bibliophiles will love DVK's unusual practice of 24-hour bookselling.

John Parsons Bookshop, Turgenev House, 38 reki Fontanka Naberezhnaya; tel 331-8828. An English-language bookshop on the ground floor of Turgenev House. Most genres of literature are represented, including travel books and children's fiction.

St. Petersburg House of Books, 62 Nevsky Prospekt, 570-6546. The city's principal bookstore is in a beautiful period building. Delightful original features remain, and it's a pleasure to browse the array of books stocked on two extensive floors. Fine art reproductions, stationery, foreign and specialized literature, and maps are all available.

CLOTHING

As is typical of major cities, St. Petersburg sells its fair share of international labels such as Hugo Boss, Armani, Versace, Escada, and so on. However, the creations of talented local designers are certainly worth exploring. The following fashion houses and designer boutiques all showcase local designers' diverse and admirable quality.

Defile, 27 Kanala Griboedova Naberezhnaya; tel 117-9010. This basement shop offers apparel from Russian, Ukrainian, and Lithuanian designers. Everything on display is flaunted in the city's biannual catwalk fashion shows.

Dress Fashion, 5 Gorokhovaya Ulitsa; tel 670 4899. Selling top Russian brands, with styles that vary from bright and vibrant to subdued and simple, this shop has an unpretentious feel often absent from other boutiques.

Elena Badmaeva, 4 Mokhovaya Ulitsa; tel 272-3630. Closed weekends. One of the few places offering cutting-edge design for men prepared to experiment with their clothing.

F.O.S.P., 79 reki Moiki Naberezhnaya; tel 571-2902. High-quality men's clothing, suits (also available for boys), and accessories at reasonable prices. All produced at St. Petersburg's oldest clothes factory.

Irina Tantsurina, 16 Bolshaya Morskaya Ulitsa; tel 325-9976. This bright, spacious store sells exclusive (and unique) pieces by the distinguished designer for both men and women. Although the emphasis is on fine fur of the highest pedigree, you'll also find collections of cocktail dresses and jackets. A sister store is at 25 Nevsky Prospekt.

Lilya Kisselenko, 47 Kirochnaya Ulitsa; tel 274-1876; closed weekends. This fashion house is the choice of city intellectuals and quite a few stars of Mariinsky Ballet. The clothes are characterized by natural fibers, design simplicity, and expert tailoring.

Sunduk, 11 Kolomenskaya Ulitsa; tel 712 2294. This cheerful little lair sells imaginative, pretty, and uninhibited items. Makes for fun browsing and is ideal for those with an exhibitionist streak. There's also a small line of men's clothing and accessories.

Tanya Kotegova, 44 Bolshoy Prospekt, Vasilevsky Island; tel 238-0137. Occupying a studio flat in a charming period building, this is one of the city's oldest fashion houses. The style is described as "ready-to-wear sophistication," and the materials used are mainly natural (e.g., silk and fur). The quality of the tailoring is impressive, and it's possible to commission pieces.

CRAFTS

Lakir, 2 Muchnoy Pereulok, 310-2895. Lacquer boxes are a popular Russian keepsake among savvy souvenir hunters. Here you can find boxes of all shapes and sizes decorated with portrait, landscape, and traditional themes, as well as scenes of St. Petersburg.

Larusse, 3 Stremyanaya Ulitsa; tel 340-2043; metro: Mayakovskaya. This is both a shop and a museum of traditional Russian culture. All objects are handmade and commissioned from craftspeople in Russian villages.

Russian Flax, 151 Nevsky Prospekt; tel 717-5164; metro: Aleksandra Nevskogo Ploshchad. This nationwide chain sells flax and linen goods such as clothing, bedding, kitchenware, and tableware decorated with traditional Russian embroidery and lace. A good place to pick up practical, high-quality presents for reasonable prices.

DEPARTMENT STORES & SHOPPING CENTERS

The biggest, oldest, and best-known department store is **Gostiny Dvor** (35 Nevsky Prospekt; tel 710-5408; metro: Gostiny Dvor). With more than 40,000 brands housed under one roof, this is certainly a shopper's mecca. Buyer beware, however, as this place doesn't always offer a good value for your money.

Passage department store, on Nevsky opposite Gostiny Dvor, was modeled on British shopping arcades. Recently restored and refurbished, it offers relaxed, almost quiet shopping. The staff, many of who are holdovers from the Soviet era, are very unassuming and helpful. Offers a better value than Gostiny Dvor on many goods.

Other shopping centers lean toward high-end boutiques. One such place is the **Grand Palace** (44 Nevsky Prospekt/ 15 Italyanskaya Ulitsa; tel 710-5504; metro: Nevsky Prospekt). **Stockmann** (25 Nevsky Prospekt; tel 326-2637; metro: Nevsky Prospekt) is a relatively small Finnish-owned store with a beautiful atrium that houses a popular café. Browse for clothing, jewelry, and household goods.

FURS

In Russia there is no aversion to fur. Indeed, in winter most locals don fur coats and hats to keep freezing temperatures in check. The result is you'll find plenty of places to buy fur, ranging from exclusive upscale boutiques to more everyday shops. Besides those listed below, Irina Tantsurina (see p. 259) also specializes in fur.

Natalie Kvasova, 51 Nevsky Prospekt; tel 713-1901; metro: Mayakovskaya. This three-store chain offers top-end furs for sale and made to order. Other branches are at 1 Vladimirsky Prospekt and 6/3 Blokhina Ulitsa. Browse for bargain smaller items (hats and scarves) in summer.

Paloma, 27 Bolshaya Konyushennaya Ulitsa; tel 314-7262; metro: Nevsky Prospekt. One of the city's top fur and leather emporiums, this shop sells pieces by Russian and Italian designers. Furs include astrakhan, marten, mink, and sable. Paloma is notable for its vast selection of fur hats (more than 3,000 at last count). Another branch is at 8 Malaya Morskaya Ulitsa; tel 315-7912.

HOUSEWARES & INTERIOR DESIGN

Argento, 22 Voznesensky Prospekt; tel 314-9336; metro: Sadovaya. This shop is the perfect destination for those with adventurous and perhaps slightly mischievous tastes in housewares and interior design. Classical furniture has been given a very funky twist to produce an eclectic collection of lively, creative objects guaranteed to brighten up any home. Cutting-edge modern furniture is also available for those who prefer a more sophisticated look.

JEWELRY

Ananov, 31 Nevsky Prospekt; tel 710-5592; metro: Gostiny Dvor Pricey Fabergé reproductions.

Juvelirtorg. This chain has 20 stores scattered around the city, each named after a different gemstone. Jewels are cut to a good standard, and the designs sparkle with innovation. One

outlet, **Yakhont,** occupies the old Fabergé building (24 Bolshaya Morskaya Ulitsa; tel 314-6415; metro: Nevsky Prospekt).

Kast, 41 Zhukovskogo Ulitsa; tel 272-8500; metro: Vosstaniya Ploshchad. This relatively new showroom features works by St. Petersburg designers, including exclusive pieces with contemporary motifs and more pedestrian neoclassic items.

Russkie Samotsvety, 8 Karl Faberge Ploshchad; tel 528-1091; metro: Ladozhskaya. This chain of shops offers a variety of styles and tastes to suit every budget.

Russian Jewelry House, 27 Nevsky Prospekt; tel 310-2883; metro: Nevsky Prospekt. This jeweler sells a dazzling array of high-quality precious and semiprecious stones in a range of cuts and styles.

MUSIC

505.RU, 72 Nevsky Prospekt; tel 272-9031. This chain operates eight shops throughout the city, all bearing its distinctive orange-and-white logo. While most genres are available, you'll find an especially good selection of Russian house music. You're encouraged to try before you buy at the listening station in this particular store.

Open World, 13 Malaya Morskaya Ulitsa; tel 715-8939. Stocking music from the Middle Ages to modern vanguards, this shop is a paradise for classical music lovers. The biggest of its kind in the city, it offers a plethora of CDs, DVDs, and SASDs. Particular emphasis is placed on Russian composers and performers, though jazz and literary audio recordings are available.

PORCELAIN

Lomonosov Porcelain, 160 Nevsky Prospekt; tel 577-4838. Offering a large selection of high-quality tableware and

decorative porcelain, this place is sure to have something to suit every taste, including some absolutely stunning (and pricey) collector's sets. Produced at the famous Lomonosov factory, all pieces are made using time-honored techniques and ecologically sound materials.

SOUVENIRS

Heritage, 37 reki Moiki Naberezhnaya; tel 312-6212. This chain sells contemporary paintings, amber, Fabergé-style objects, caviar, lacquer miniatures, and an array of other traditional souvenirs. This particular outlet is spacious and well lit, making for enjoyable browsing.

Vernissage Souvenir Fair, 1 kanala Griboedova Naberezhnaya; tel 572-1345. Adjacent to the Church of the Savior on Spilled Blood, this outdoor souvenir and memorabilia fair is a good place to browse for unusual objects. Haggling is a must, as most traders are on the lookout for gullible visitors and thus begin with unreasonably high prices.

TASTE TREATS

Sever, 44 Nevsky Prospekt; tel 571-2589; metro: Gostiny Dvor. The oldest patisserie in the city is a cult establishment in its own right. Exquisite cakes and tarts are the reason for its longevity and esteemed reputation.

Sladkoezhka, 88 Nevsky Prospekt; tel 579 6743; metro: Mayakovskaya. Aptly named, "Sweet Tooth" is a confectioner's paradise with enough treats to satiate the sweetest of teeth. Its vast cake menu is another sure temptation.

Yeliseev, 56 Nevsky Prospekt; metro: Gostiny Dvor. Besides purveying chocolate and other sweets, this fashionable art nouveau delicatessen vends all sorts of savories, including caviar and a range of alcoholic drinks.

ENTERTAINMENT

Petersburgers undoubtedly know how to enjoy themselves. This is a work hard, play hard city that comes to life in the evenings. It hosts a range of attractions that cater to all tastes, and its calendar of events is always full. Boasting a world-class reputation for classical music, St. Petersburg's concert venues host leading international stars, as well as supremely accomplished locals. Contemporary performance artists have also made the city a top tour destination. Perhaps not as wild or garish as Moscow, St. Petersburg nevertheless offers plenty for partying spirits. And for those so inclined, it's even possible to stay out all night.

Information about what's on tap is available from several sources. The monthly *Which* magazine publishes a comprehensive entertainment guide in English and Russian. Another good source is the *St. Petersburg Times,* published twice weekly in English. Most hotels, restaurants, cafés, and bars freely distribute these publications.

St. Petersburg's peak theater and concert season starts in September and runs through the end of May. Cultural offerings during this period are particularly intense, as both local and visiting companies offer performances. In summer most local companies go on tour as another wave of visiting theater, opera, dance, and music acts arrives on the ever-vibrant cultural scene.

Visitors can choose from a wide selection of live music and dance venues, while an increasing number of clubs offer nightlife not just for the young but for people of all ages and tastes.

Tickets (*bilety*) for most performances are available at centralized box offices (*teatralnye kassy*). Despite the name, tickets sold here are not just for theater but all kinds of performances. Some box offices stand amid rows of shops, while others operate from street kiosks or stalls in major museums and other tourist attractions. Call 380-8050 for reservations to most performances. To reserve tickets to the most popular shows, it's best to book well in advance. Major companies like the Mariinsky offer their own online booking services.

BARS

Bars are increasing in St. Petersburg, especially the trendy sort with live house or lounge DJs. The variety is truly impressive, and you're sure to find a drinking hole that suits your idea of a good time. Another trend is for bars to serve full menus, so they often double as a good place to grab a meal. Following is an overview of popular hangouts—but don't be afraid to find your own.

Barchat, 7 kanala Griboedova Naberezhnaya; tel 314-8250; metro: Nevsky Prospekt. A lounge bar spread out over two levels on the banks of the canal. Vaulted ceilings and large mirrors lend a trendy but sophisticated ambience.

Black & White, 25 6th Line, Vasilevsky Island; tel 328-3881; metro: Vasileostrovskaya. As the name suggests, the interior here is completely black and white. The service system of touch-screen computers on every table is pretty novel.

Lobby Bar, Grand Hotel Europe, 1/7 Mikhailovskaya; tel 329-6000; metro: Gostiny Dvor or Nevsky Prospekt. An extravagant venue for a drink before a concert in the nearby philharmonia.

Lyod, 2 Kazanskaya Ulitsa; tel 571-5065; metro: Gostiny Dvor or Nevsky Prospekt. Maintained at a temperature of 23°F (-5°C), this small ice bar is the first of its kind in Russia. Even the glasses are ice. Visitors are provided with capes and boots to keep warm.

Novus, 8 Bolshaya Morskaya, 2nd floor; tel 569-3818; metro: Nevsky Prospekt. A fashionably grungy bar, inspired by the Latvian billiard game *novuss.* Drinks are cheap, and the bar hosts regular poetry evenings and art discussions.

Probka, 5 Belinskogo Ulitsa; tel 273-4904; metro: Mayakovskaya. Offering a more relaxed venue, this wine bar is a favorite with trendy locals.

Sevensky Bar, 15 Italyanskaya Ulitsa; tel 449-9462; metro: Gostiny Dvor or Nevsky Prospekt. Despite its long onyx bar, this place is surprisingly affordable. Excellent views and live DJ music.

Shamrock Bar, 27 Dekabristov Ulitsa; tel 570-4625; metro: Sadovaya or Sennaya Ploshchad. One of the better-known Irish pubs in town, this lively place stands in stark contrast to the refined elegance of the Mariinsky across the street, yet still manages to pull in a large theater crowd. They come for the American steaks, Italian pastas, and Greek salads, as well as live Irish music.

Café Stirka 40°C, 26 Kazanskaya Ulitsa; tel 314-5371; metro: Nevsky Prospekt or Gostiny Dvor. A most unusual concept bar that doubles as a laundry. Relax with a cheap beer while you wait for the spin cycle. Offers occasional concerts and punk poetry recitals.

Von Witte, 22 reki Moiki Naberezhnaya; tel 335-9111; metro: Nevsky Prospekt. A lounge bar, yes, but with an open fireplace and a classy vibe.

CLUBS

Clubbing in St. Petersburg is a diverse experience. The choice of places to hit the dance floor ranges from the more grungy rock joints to überglamorous nightclubs. Be forewarned—

some of the more elitist places institute "face control" policies and strict dress codes. Following is a peek at possible options:

Decadence, 17A Shcherbakov Pereulok; tel 947-7070; metro: Vladimirskaya, Dostoevskaya. As its name suggests, this is where the local in crowd comes to splash its cash and flaunt its designer trappings. Patrons pass beneath a velvet curtained arch to a superbly decadent interior with gold-plated ceiling and crystal chandeliers. Restricted access includes a strict face control policy.

Fish Fabrique, 10 Pushkin-skaya Ulitsa (entrance through arch at 53 Ligovsky Prospekt); tel 764-4857; metro: Vosstaniya Ploshchad. A club popular with local rock musicians. Live gigs starting from 10:30 p.m. Under-ground films screened on Sunday nights.

Griboedov, 2A Voronezhskaya Ulitsa; tel 764-4355; metro: Ligovsky Prospekt. Rock and rap fans of modest finances frequent this former bomb shelter to hear aspiring musicians in a low-key atmosphere. A glass terrace serves as a chill-out spot.

Lvdovic, 4 Dumskaya Ulitsa; tel 702-6027; metro: Gostiny Dvor or Nevsky Prospekt. A glamorous nightclub full of beautiful young Russians. One room plays hip-hop and R&B, while the other spins house music.

Trizet, 30/7 Vosstaniya Ulitsa; tel 579-9315; metro: Vosstaniya Ploshchad, Chernyshevskaya. Stretch out and relax amid two rooms with soft silk walls and inviting sofas.

Tunnel, 2B Lyubansky Pereulok at Zverinskaya Ulitsa; tel 572-1551; metro: Sportivnaya. This military-themed club recently returned to its original bunker location. DJs turn out techno, house, and electro beats over two dance floors that boast state-of-the-art sound and laser light systems.

MOVIE THEATERS

The best place to try for recent films in original languages is **Dom Kino,** 12 Karavannaya Ulitsa; tel 314-0638; metro: Mayakovskaya). Center of the local movie scene, the House of Cinema screens a wide variety of mainstream and art house movies and regularly holds festivals. Houses a most stylish restaurant for post-movie eats.

If you know some Russian and feel like practicing it in the cinema, you should visit **Avrora** (60 Nevsky Prospekt, www.avro ra.spb.ru), one of St. Petersburg's earliest cinemas. The original interior and cozy halls have been fitted with the latest technical advances. Some Russian films are subtitled in English. Info on showings here and elsewhere are available by dialing 064, 050, or 089.

Alternatively, there are:

Cinema Mirazh, 35 Bolshoy Prospekt, Petrograd side; tel 498-0758; metro: Petrogradskaya or Chkalovskaya.

Jam Hall, 42 Kamennoostrov-skaya Prospekt; tel 346-4014; metro: Petrogradskaya.

Kolizey, 100 Nevsky Prospekt; tel 272-8775; metro: Mayakov-skaya. Ultramodern, with three bars and VIP seating.

Pik, 2 Sennaya Ploshchad; tel 449-2432; metro: Sennaya Ploshchad.

OPERA/DANCE/ CLASSICAL MUSIC

St. Petersburg is a mecca for lovers and connoisseurs of classical music, ballet, and opera. Many visitors come for the sole purpose of enjoying the Russian classical tradition in the city most associated with artistic brilliance, tradition, and innovation. In addition to the following venues, keep an eye out for posters advertising concerts and performances in smaller, less prominent spaces.

Ballet House of Rimsky-Korsakov Conservatory, 3 Teatralnaya Ploshchad; tel 571-8574; metro: Sadovaya. Affiliated with the world-famous music school, this company is rapidly gaining recognition for its ballet productions.

Beloselsky-Belozersky Palace, 41 Nevsky Prospekt; tel 315-5236; metro: Gostiny Dvor or Mayakovskaya. Once home to one of Russia's richest families, then a regional party headquarters, this striking red palace now serves as a multifunctional performance space and regularly features classical concerts performed by the St. Petersburg Concert Orchestra. Luxurious surroundings and top-notch performances make for memorable evenings. Watch for notices posted in front of the palace.

Glazunov Concert Hall, 3 Teatralnaya Ploshchad; tel 571-5108; metro: Sennaya Ploshchad. A magnificent interior and excellent acoustics make the conservatory chamber hall a must for every connoisseur.

Hermitage Theater, 34 Dvortsovaya Naberezhnaya; tel 571-9025; metro: Nevsky Pros-pekt. Former court theater of the Winter Palace, this small, romantic theater is particularly popular with foreign visitors. The repertoire includes gala concerts with famous ballet stars. Tickets can be pricey.

Mariinsky Theater, 1/2 Teatralnaya Ploshchad; tel 326-4141; metro: Sadovaya. Con-sidered by many to have the world's best dancers, the renowned ballet and opera house has been dazzling the world with its outstanding performances since 1859. Tickets sell out quickly, so book ahead to avoid disappointment. (See p. 94 for more on the Mariinsky.)

Mussorgsky Opera & Ballet House, 1 Iskusstv Ploshchad; tel 595-4284; metro: Nevsky Prospekt or Gostiny Dvor. Even though the Mussorgsky is not as renowned as the Mariinsky, the dancers and singers here perform high-caliber renditions of classic opera and ballet that are worth checking out.

Shostakovich Philharmonia, 2 Mikhailovskaya Ulitsa; tel 311-7333; metro: Nevsky Prospekt. Steeped in history, the city's principal classical music hall is associated with many stars of the genre. In addition to having two resident orchestras, it offers performances from national and international musicians. Marvelous acoustics and a world-famous organ.

St. Petersburg Capella, 20 Reki Moiki Naberezhnaya; tel 314-1058. Former concert space of the imperial court cappella, this extensive hall directly across from the Winter Palace showcases classical music of various eras, including many organ concerts. Particularly recommended is the Cappella Choir.

POP/ROCK/JAZZ

Top international and national musicians regularly perform at such venues as **Ledovy Dvorets** (metro: Bolshevikov Prospekt), **Oktyabrysky (October) Concert Hall** (6 Ligovsky Prospekt; metro: Vosstaniya Ploshchad), and the **Petersburg Sports & Concert Complex** (**SKK**, east of Victory Park; metro: Park Pobedy), as well as other large stadiums and halls.

The following list details more modest though lively venues across town:

ArcticA, 38 Beringa Ulitsa; tel 715-4838; metro: Primorskaya. Folk and heavy rock gigs start most evenings off, while weekend club nights keep 'em rocking till the crack of dawn.

Jambala, 80 Bolshoi Prospekt (Vasilyevsky Ostrov); tel 332-1077; metro: Vasileostrovskaya or Primorskaya. Following live reggae, ska, and Latin shows, DJs take center stage with reggae and dub music to keep you up and dancing into the early hours.

Jazz Philharmonia, 27 Zagorodny Prospekt; tel 764-8565, www.jazz-hall.spb.ru; metro: Vladimirskaya. This city boasts a solid jazz tradition, and this hall, founded by veteran jazz man David Goloshchekin, is a tribute. Often playing host to traditional jazz, the two cozy halls have a certain nostalgic feel to them. Food and drinks are served during performances.

JFC Jazz Club, 33 Shpalernaya Ulitsa; tel 272-9850; metro: Chernyshevskaya. One of the busiest and best jazz spots in town. All styles and influences performed. Also hosts classical, folk, and world music concerts.

Platforma, 40 Nekrasova Ulitsa; tel 314-1104; metro: Vosstaniya Ploshchad. St. Petersburg's foremost art music venue. Live jazz and rock, as well as literary events and film screenings.

Red Fox, 50 Mayakovskogo Ulitsa; tel 275-4214; metro: Chernyshevskaya. Live jazz, blues, and Latin music every night in a friendly, informal setting.

THEATER

The language barrier inhibits most visitors' appreciation for the wealth of Russian dramatic performances. Nevertheless, a theater visit is a must for devotees of the theatrical tradition.

Alexandrinsky Theater, 2 Ostrovskogo Ploshchad,

312-1545; metro: Gostiny Dvor. Founded in 1756 and recently restored to its former glory, this is Russia's oldest dramatic theater. The extensive repertoire includes classical and modern productions.

Bolshoy Drama Theater, 65 reki Fontanka Naberezhnaya; tel 310-9242. One of Russia's leading companies, the Bolshoy boasts an extensive repertoire from different genres. Home to countless stars of Russian theater and cinema.

Denmeni Marionette Theater, 52 Nevsky Prospekt; tel 117-1900; metro: Gostiny Dvor or Nevsky Prospekt. Russia's only professional marionette theater. The marionettes are as famous as the productions and have won many awards.

Komissarzhevskaya Theater, 19 Italyanskaya Ulitsa; tel 571-3102; metro: Gostiny Dvor. A stylish establishment with a bohemian touch. The company is famous for innovative productions.

Theater on Liteyny, 51 Liteyny Prospekt; tel 273-5335; metro: Mayakovskaya. A popular chamber theater acclaimed for its bold, interesting productions.

LANGUAGE GUIDE

Familiarizing oneself with the Russian (Cyrillic) alphabet before traveling overseas is well worth the effort. In spite of its distinctly different look, the alphabet is easily learned. Once you recognize individual letters, you'll have no trouble reading any word, as Russian is largely phonetic in nature.

А a	Ж zh	Л l	Р r	Х kh	Ы y
Б b	З z	М m	С s	Ц ts	Э e
Г g/'v'	И i	Н n	Т t	Ч ch	Я ya
Д d	Й y	О o	У u	Ш sh	
Е ye/'yo'	К k	П p	Ф f	Щ shch	

Ь – silent soft symbol, which softens the preceding consonant
Ъ – silent hard symbol, which hardens the preceding consonant

USEFUL WORDS & PHRASES

yes	da	да
no	net	нет
hello	zdravstvuyte	здравствуйте
hi	privet	привет
please	pozhaluysta	пожалуйста
thank you	spasibo	спасибо
you're welcome	pozhaluysta	пожалуйста
OK	khorosho/ladno	хорошо
goodbye	do svidaniya	до свидания
goodnight	spokoynoy nochi	спокойной ночи
sorry	izvinite	извините
here	zdes'	здесь
there	tam	там
today	segodnya	сегодня
yesterday	vchera	Вчера
tomorrow	zavtra	завтра
now	seychas	сейчас
later	potom	потом
this morning	segodnya utrom	сегодня утром
this afternoon	segodnya posle obeda	сегодня после обеда
this evening	segodnya vecherom	сегодня вечером
open	otkryto	открыто
closed	zakryto	закрыто
Do you have...?	U vas est'...?	У вас есть...?
Do you speak English?	Vy govorite po-angliyski?	Вы говорите по-английски?
I do not understand	Ya ne ponimayu	Я не понимю
Please speak more slowly	Pozhaluysta govorite medlennee	Пожалуйста, говорите медленнее.
Where is...?	Gde nakhoditsya...?	Где находится...?
I don't know	Ya ne znayu	Я не знаю
That's it	Da, tak	Да, так
What is your name?	Kak vas zovut?	Как вас зовут?
My name is...	Menya zovut...	Меня зовут...
At what time?	V kotorom chasu?	В котором часу?
When?	Kogda?	Когда?
What time is it?	Kotory chas?	Который час?
Can you help me?	Vy mozhete mne pomoch?	Вы можете мне помочь?
I'd like...	Ya by khotel...	Я бы хотел...
How much is it?	Skol'ko eto stoit?	Сколько это стоит?

MENU READER

I'd like to order	Mozhno zakazat'?	Можно заказать?
breakfast	zavtrak	завтрак
lunch	obed	обед
dinner	uzhin	ужин
appetizer	zakuska	закуска
first course	pervoe (blyudo)	первое
main course	vtoroe (blyudo)	второе
vegetables, side dish	ovoshchi, garnir	овощи. гарнир
dessert	dessert, sladkoe	дессерт, сладкое
menu	menyu	меню
wine list	karta vin	карта вин
the check	schyot	счет

DRINKS/ NAPITKI/напитки

water	voda	вода
orange juice	apel'sinovy sok	апельсиновый сок
beer	pivo	пиво
vodka	vodka	водка
white wine	beloe vino	белое вино
red wine	krasnoe vino	красное вино
champagne	shampanskoe	шампанское
coffee	kofe	кофе
short black	espresso	эспрессо
tea	chay	чай
with milk	s molokom	с молоком
with lemon	s limonom	с лимоном

CLASSICS/TRADITSIONNYE BLYUDA/традиционные блюда

cabbage and pork soup (very popular among Russians)	shchi	щи
carrot, beet, & potato salad	vinegret	винегрет
black caviar	chernaya ikra	черная икра
red caviar	krasnaya ikra	красная икра
fish broth	ukha	уха
fried meat (often with potatoes and onions)	zharkoe	жарко
kebab	shashlyk	шашлык
pancakes	bliny	блины
cheese pancakes	syrniki	сырники
silver dollar pancakes	oladi	оладьи
porridge	kasha	каша
ravioli	pel'meni	пельмени
red beet soup	borsch	борщ
soup spiced with gherkins	solyanka	солянка

MEAT/MYASO/мясо

beef	govyadina	говядина
chicken	kura	кура
ham	vetchina	ветчина
lamb	baranina	баранина
pork	svinina	свинина
sausage	kolbasa	колбаса
steak	bifshteks	бифштекс
veal	telyatina	телятина

SEAFOOD/MOREPRODUKTY/ морепродукты

lobster	kal'mar	кальмар
oyster	ustritsa	устрица
pike	shchuka	щука
prawn	krevetka	креветка
salmon	losos'	лосось
salmon	semga	семга
sturgeon	sevryuga	севрюга
trout	forel'	форель

VEGETABLES/OVOSHCHI/ овощи

beetroot	svekla	свекла
buckwheat	grecha	греча
cabbage	kapusta	капуста
carrots	morkov'	морковь
garlic	chesnok	чеснок
green peas	goroshek	горошек
mushrooms	griby	грибы
onions	luk	лук
potatoes	kartofel'	картофель
rice	ris	рис

FRUIT/FRUKTY/фрукты

apple	yabloko	яблоко
apricot	abrikos	абрикос
cherries	vishnya	вишня
grapes	vinograd	виноград
orange	apel'sin	апельсин
pear	grusha	груша
raspberries	malina	малина
sour cherries	chereshnya	черешня
strawberries	klubnika	клубника

SAUCES/ SOUSY/соусы

dill	s ukropom	с укропом
tomato	tomatny	томатный

ILLUSTRATIONS CREDITS

Abbreviations for terms appearing below: (t) top; (b) bottom; (l) left; (r) right; (c) center.

Cover, (l)Philip Gould/CORBIS; (c), Richard Nowitz/NGS Image Collection/Getty Images; (r), Sisse Brimberg.

All interior photographs by ITAR-TASS/Yuri Belinsky, unless otherwise noted:

19, ITAR-TASS/Sergei Guneyev/www.G8RUSSIA.ru); 20, Andriy Rovenko/Shutterstock; 23, The Art Archive/Corbis; 24, Courtesy of Historic Cities Research Project http://historic-cities.huji.ac.il The Hebrew University of Jerusalem The Jewish National and University Library; 29, Reproduced by permission of The State Hermitage Museum, St. Petersburg, Russia/CORBIS; 32, Bettmann/CORBIS; 34, Hulton-Deutsch Collection/CORBIS; 35, Bettmann/CORBIS; 45, The State Russian Museum/CORBIS; 48 (LE), Archivo Iconografico, S.A./CORBIS; 48 (RT), Bettmann/CORBIS; 49 (LE), Archivo Iconografico, S.A./CORBIS; 49 (RT), Reuters/CORBIS; 61, Jeremy Howard; 109, Steve Raymer; 112, Jeremy Howard; 122, The State Russian Museum/Corbis; 123, The State Russian Museum/Corbis; 140, Peter Y. Sobolev; 148, Jeremy Howard; 191, Jeremy Howard; 196, Jeremy Howard; 205, ITAR-TASS/Sergei Guneyev/www.G8RUSSIA.ru).

APPRECIATION

Special thanks go to The State Hermitage Museum for providing the museum floor plan on pages 66–71 and to The State Russian Museum for providing the floor plan on pages 120–121.

Founded in 1888, the National Geographic Society is one of the largest nonprofit scientific and educational organizations in the world. It reaches more than 285 million people worldwide each month through its official journal, NATIONAL GEOGRAPHIC, and its four other magazines; the National Geographic Channel; television documentaries; radio programs; films; books; videos and DVDs; maps; and interactive media. National Geographic has funded more than 8,000 scientific research projects and supports an education program combating geographic illiteracy.

For more information, please call 1-800-NGS LINE (647-5463) or write to the following address: National Geographic Society,1145 17th Street N.W.,Washington, D.C. 20036-4688 U.S.A.

Visit us online at: www.national geographic.com/books

For information about special discounts for bulk purchases, please contact National Geographic Books Special Sales: ngspecsales@ngs.org.

Order *Traveler* today, the magazine that travelers trust. In the U.S. and Canada call 1-800-NGS-LINE; 813-979-6845 for international. Or visit us online at www.national geographic.com/traveler and click on SUBSCRIBE.

Printed in Spain

National Geographic Traveler: St. Petersburg
by Jeremy Howard

Published by the National Geographic Society
John M. Fahey, Jr., *President and Chief Executive Officer*
Gilbert M. Grosvenor, *Chairman of the Board*
Nina D. Hoffman, *Executive Vice President; President, Book Publishing Group*

Prepared by the Book Division
Kevin Mulroy, *Senior Vice President and Publisher*
Leah Bendavid-Val, *Director of Photography Publishing and Illustrations*
Marianne R. Koszorus, *Director of Design*
Elizabeth Newhouse, *Director of Travel Publishing*
Carl Mehler, *Director of Maps*
Cinda Rose, *Art Director*
Barbara A. Noe, *Series Editor*

Staff for this book:
Caroline Hickey, *Project Editor*
Kay Kobor Hankins, *Designer & Illustrations Editor*
Jane Sunderland, *Text Editor*
Natalia Moroz, *Researcher*
Lise Sajewski, *Editorial Consultant*
Steven D. Gardner, Nicholas P. Rosenbach, Greg Ugiansky, and Mapping Specialists, *Map Research and Production*
Gary Colbert, *Director, Production & Managing Editorial*
Richard Wain, *Production Manager*
Rob Waymouth, *Illustrations Specialist*
Ken DellaPenta, *Indexer*
Fatima Eloeva, Sonia Harmon, Lynsey Jacob, Dave Lauderborn, Erica Rose, *Contributors*
Artwork by Maltings Partnership, Derby, England (pp. 168–169 & 208–209)

National Geographic Traveler: St. Petersburg (2007)

ISBN-10: 1-4262-0050-1
ISBN-13: 978-1-4262-0050-2

Printed and bound by Cayfosa Quebecor, Barcelona, Spain.
Color separations by Quad Graphics, Alexandria, VA.

The information in this book has been carefully checked and to the best of our knowledge is accurate. However, details are subject to change, and the National Geographic Society cannot be responsible for such changes, or for errors or omissions. Assessments of sites, hotels, and restaurants are based on the author's subjective opinions, which do not necessarily reflect the publisher's opinion. The publisher cannot be responsible for any consequences arising from the use of this book.

NATIONAL GEOGRAPHIC
TRAVELER

A Century of Travel Expertise in Every Guide

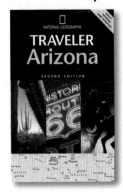

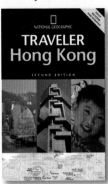

- **Alaska** ISBN: 978-0-7922-5371-6
- **Amsterdam** ISBN: 978-0-7922-7900-6
- **Arizona** (2nd Edition) ISBN: 978-0-7922-3888-1
- **Australia** (2nd Edition) ISBN: 978-0-7922-3893-5
- **Barcelona** (2nd Edition) ISBN: 978-0-7922-5365-5
- **Berlin** ISBN: 978-0-7922-6212-1
- **Boston & environs** ISBN: 978-0-7922-7926-6
- **California** (2nd Edition) ISBN: 978-0-7922-3885-0
- **Canada** (2nd Edition) ISBN: 978-0-7922-6201-5
- **The Caribbean** ISBN: 978-0-7922-7434-6
- **China** (2nd Edition) ISBN: 978-1-4262-0035-9
- **Costa Rica** (2nd Edition) ISBN: 978-0-7922-5368-6
- **Cuba** ISBN: 978-0-7922-6931-1
- **Egypt** ISBN: 978-0-7922-7896-2
- **Florence & Tuscany** (2nd Edition) ISBN: 978-0-7922-5318-1
- **Florida** ISBN: 978-0-7922-7432-2
- **France** (2nd Edition) ISBN: 978-1-4262-0027-4
- **Germany** (2nd Edition) ISBN: 978-1-4262-0028-1
- **Great Britain** (2nd Ed.) ISBN: 978-1-4262-0029-8
- **Greece** (2nd Edition) ISBN: 978-1-4262-0030-4
- **Hawaii** (2nd Edition) ISBN: 978-0-7922-5568-0
- **Hong Kong** (2nd Ed.) ISBN: 978-0-7922-5369-3
- **India** ISBN: 978-0-7922-7898-6
- **Ireland** (2nd Edition) ISBN: 978-1-4262-0022-9
- **Italy** (2nd Edition) ISBN: 978-0-7922-3889-8
- **Japan** (2nd Edition) ISBN: 978-0-7922-3894-2
- **London** (2nd Edition) ISBN: 978-1-4262-0023-6

- **Los Angeles** ISBN: 978-0-7922-7947-1
- **Madrid** ISBN: 978-0-7922-5372-3
- **Mexico** (2nd Edition) ISBN: 978-0-7922-5319-8
- **Miami & the Keys** (2nd Edition) ISBN: 978-0-7922-3886-7
- **New York** (2nd Edition) ISBN: 978-0-7922-5370-9
- **Naples & southern Italy** ISBN 978-1-4262-0040-3
- **Paris** (2nd Edition) ISBN: 978-1-4262-0024-3
- **Piedmont & Northwest Italy** ISBN: 978-0-7922-4198-0
- **Portugal** ISBN: 978-0-7922-4199-7
- **Prague & the Czech Republic** ISBN: 978-0-7922-4147-8
- **Provence & the Côte d'Azur** ISBN: 978-0-7922-9542-6
- **Rome** (2nd Edition) ISBN: 978-0-7922-5572-7
- **St. Petersburg** ISBN 978-1-4262-0050-2
- **San Diego** (2nd Edition) ISBN: 978-0-7922-6202-2
- **San Francisco** (2nd Ed.) ISBN: 978-0-7922-3883-6
- **Sicily** ISBN: 978-0-7922-9541-9
- **Spain** ISBN: 978-0-7922-3884-3
- **Sydney** ISBN: 978-0-7922-7435-3
- **Taiwan** ISBN: 978-0-7922-6555-9
- **Thailand** (2nd Edition) ISBN: 978-0-7922-5321-1
- **Venice** ISBN: 978-0-7922-7917-4
- **Vietnam** ISBN: 978-0-7922-6203-9
- **Washington, D.C.** (2nd Edition) ISBN: 978-0-7922-3887-4

AVAILABLE WHEREVER BOOKS ARE SOLD